Howard Newby is Senior Lecturer in Sociology at the University of Essex. Until recently he was director of an SSRC-financed study of farmers in East Anglia and has published several sociological studies of farming and farm workers.

International Perspectives
in
Rural Sociology

International Perspectives
in
Rural Sociology

Edited by

Howard Newby

Department of Sociology
University of Essex

JOHN WILEY & SONS

Chichester · New York · Brisbane · Toronto

Library of Congress Cataloging in Publication Data:

Main entry under title:
International perspectives in rural sociology.

  Includes index.
  1. Sociology, Rural—Addresses, essays, lectures.
I. Newby, Howard.
HT421.154   301.35   77-21274

ISBN 0471 99606 8

Typeset by Preface Ltd., Salisbury, Wiltshire, England.
Printed by Unwin Brothers Ltd., The Gresham Press,
Old Woking, Surrey

Contributors

SVEIN AASS   *Research Fellow, Agricultural University of Norway.*

EDUARDO P. ARCHETTI   *Research Fellow, Institute of Ethnography, University of Oslo.*

COLIN BELL   *Professor of Sociology, University of New South Wales, Sydney.*

THOMAS M. DAVIES   *formerly Research Officer, Planning Department, Polytechnic of Central London, now working in a local authority planning department.*

JOSEPH W. FOWERAKER   *Lecturer in Government, University of Essex.*

HOWARD NEWBY   *Senior Lecturer in Sociology, University of Essex.*

ANDREW PEARSE   *St. Antony's College, Oxford*

DAVID ROSE   *Lecturer in Sociology, Cambridge College of Arts and Technology.*

PETER SAUNDERS   *Lecturer in Sociology, University of Sussex.*

WILLIAM C. THIESENHUSEN   *Professor of Agricultural Economics and Agricultural Journalism. Land Tenure Centre, University of Wisconsin.*

GRAHAM WILSON   *Lecturer in Government, University of Essex.*

Contents

Editor's Preface

In the journey from original conception to final product this book has undergone a number of changes. The idea for a collection of essays on various aspects of rural sociology emerged from the conference of the European Society of Rural Sociology held in Rome in 1973. A number of participants at that conference expressed some impatience at what they, rightly or wrongly, considered to be the moribund state of the discipline. This led, among other things, to the establishment within the Society of a Scientific Committee which was to examine this and other related issues and to stimulate a broader debate on rural sociology within the Society. A particular source of concern was the tendency of much rural sociological research to verge upon what C. Wright Mills termed 'abstracted empiricism', and also to be largely untouched by, and unconnected to, sociological theory *tout court* (the latter being a familiar, if not traditional, complaint against rural sociology). There was also some concern that certain researchers were often institutionally excluded from what is customarily regarded as rural sociology, including social anthropologists and those interested in peasant studies.

Textbooks on rural sociology have, with a very few honourable exceptions, exacerbated these trends. There is therefore little to which the sociology student can be directed if he or she is interested in rural affairs and wishes to be stimulated in the direction of sociological theory in order to explain what is happening. An original conception was thus to investigate the possibility of producing a series of monographs which would incorporate recent research on various aspects of rural life in both the developed and the underdeveloped world. Unfortunately, double-digit inflation and the retrenchment in academic publishing has, for the foreseeable future, crushed these hopes. Nevertheless, this book of essays is an attempt to offer the student of rural sociology (among which can be included those who teach and research the subject) what rural sociology can offer, both in the way of research findings and theoretical insight — indeed the two should not be sharply differentiated.

The essays fall, somewhat uneasily, into two parts. Part I concerns the rural sociology of the advanced industrial world. While Part II also investigates the linkages between the developed and the underdeveloped world, it is primarily concerned with the latter, and particularly with the role of the peasantry within it. If the collection as a whole concentrates upon the issue of power and rural social stratification, then this merely reflects the editor's own interests. It is certainly not suggested that these essays represent a comprehensive coverage of rural sociology.

I would particularly like to thank the publishers for their help in making this book possible. The nature of the book has evolved from many lengthy, but enjoyable, conversations with Arch Haller of the University of Wisconsin, Benno Galjart, of the University of Leiden and Bruno Benvenuti of the University of Wageningen, whose help and support I gratefully acknowledge. Linda Peachey and Gilly Burrell at the University of Essex and Nadia Massoud at the University of New South Wales typed the final manuscript and their efficiency made my task considerably easier. Finally, my thanks to all the contributors.

Howard Newby,
Colchester, Essex,
August, 1977

PART I

Rural Sociology in Advanced Societies

1
The Rural Sociology of Advanced Capitalist Societies

Howard Newby

Much of the writing on agriculture and rural life in advanced capitalist societies seems to be influenced by two broad approaches. One is a brisk dismissal of the significance of the rural sector as an archaic and backward area which the more advanced urban, industrial sector somehow tows along in its wake as it marches inexorably onwards in its evolutionary progression. Economic and social innovation is alleged to emanate from the towns and from industry and the role of agriculture is supposed to be the passive receiver of these processes, to be in turn moulded and adapted by them. Such a view seems to underlie Marx's exasperated comment on the peasantry as 'non-existent, historically speaking', as well as more recent theories of industrial, or post-industrial, society which equally regard the rural as residual (Kerr *et al.*, 1960; Bell, 1974). The second approach has to some extent arisen in reaction to the first. Fuelled in part by the prevailing Romanticism of Anglo-Saxon cultural interpretations of rural life (Williams, 1973), this approach has sought to uphold the integrity of its distinctive qualities, a pattern discerned in much of the empirical rural sociology of the United States (Schmitt, 1968). Because of the empiricism with which it has been historically allied it is an approach which has impressed upon its practitioners the intractability of many rural phenomena to easy generalization. Hence a good deal of rural sociology in both Europe and the United States has exemplified a desire to catalogue the social attributes of the rural population and to compare them with the urbanized majority (see Sorokin and Zimmerman, 1929 and any subsequent American textbook on rural sociology). On the basis of such comparisons it has then become possible to produce guarded generalizations of the kind associated with the 'rural–urban continuum' (Redfield, 1947).

In recent years, however, both the of these approaches have come to be increasingly questioned. The peasant-based revolutions of the postwar era have led to a searching reappraisal of Marx's dictum by Marxist scholars and have produced an extraordinary growth in peasant studies, both Marxist and non-Marxist (Shanin, 1973). Similarly political events in the industrialized world have recently provided some sharp reminders to evolutionary theorists of industrial society that agriculture continues to be of great importance to the economies of even the most advanced, industrial nations. The soaring commodity prices associated with the chaos of the world's grain market in 1973 and the problems wrought by the EEC's Common Agricultural Policy are but two of the most recent examples of this. Such events have in turn prompted recent critics of theories of 'industrial society' (for example, Giddens, 1976; Kumar, 1976) to question the conventional assumptions of the relationship between agriculture and industry. For example, the assumption that capitalism is a process initiated by industrialization — that capitalist production develops first in the towns in manufacturing industry and is transmitted from there to the countryside — is at least questionable (Braudel, 1972; 1973), if not mistaken (Moore, 1966; Merrington, 1976). In Britain, for example, the commercialization of agriculture not only preceded the process of industrialization but was a precondition of it (Hobsbawm, 1969; Merrington, 1976). In the light of this, many of the conventional dichotomies around which theories of industrial society are based may, as Giddens (1976) has pointed out, be misleading.

Not only have these assumptions about agriculture and industry been challenged by recent critiques of theories of macrosocial change, however; they have also been criticized on empirical grounds as part of the gradual dismantling of the rural–urban continuum. Many empirical studies, beginning with Lewis's critique of Redfield (Lewis, 1949), have argued that the conceptual utility of the terms 'rural' and 'urban' in sociology is dubious. Moreover there has been a widespread recognition of the fact that, in advanced capitalist societies, rural—urban differences (however these may be defined) are declining. In this respect at least, the diligence of those who based their conceptions of rural society upon a cataloguing of social attributes proved to be their own undoing. By the late 1960s the convergence of 'rural' and 'urban' social patterns was such that first Gans (1968) and then Pahl (1968) were able to conclude that, in Pahl's words, 'Any attempt to tie patterns of social relationships to specific geographical milieux is a singularly fruitless exercise'. Such a statement threatened the extinction of rural sociology as a branch of the discipline in its own right — although Pahl was later (1971) to make a number of insightful suggestions as to how rural sociology might reorient itself, mainly based on the Chicago ecologists' notions of a locality as a social laboratory. Generally, however, it is probably fair to say that while peasant studies have become reinvigorated by challenges to the conventional wisdom, the intellectual morale of the rural sociology of advanced capitalist societies has never quite recovered from the blow delivered by Pahl (see Benvenuti et al., 1974). As one commentator has put it, it was as though 'the basic insufficiency of the sociological concepts with which rural phenomena have been apprehended has finally caught up with their users' (Galjart, 1973, p. 254).

As a result of this, rural sociology — as it institutionally defines itself — has recently experienced a certain crisis of confidence. There is, indeed, no shortage of diagnoses, most of which point to the organizational context within which much rural sociological research is carried out (see, for example, Anderson, 1959; Olson, 1965; Galjart, 1973; Nolan and Galliher, 1973; Benvenuti et al., 1974). Nevertheless there are as yet few signs that the 'arid contemporaneity and parochial cast' (Haller, 1973) of much of the research which such a context produces has been swept aside. The rural—urban continuum now lies generally discredited (although, for a contrary view, see Jones, 1973) but it has not been replaced by a new conceptual apparatus and set of theoretical problems which would give rural sociology a new impetus. On the contrary, rural sociology seems rather to have lost its way, a situation not aided by the tendency to institutionally separate it from peasant studies and the sociology of development, nor by the lack of a sociologically relevant political economy of agriculture furnished by contemporary agricultural economics (despite some insightful suggestions in Whitby *et al.*, 1974). Rural sociology still shows little sign of overcoming its basic definitional problem — namely, what constitutes the 'rural' — which the debate surrounding the rural—urban continuum manifested. Moreover it seems unlikely that rural sociology can recover until this problem is resolved.

At this point it is worthwhile referring to the contrast with *urban* sociology whose demise was equally presaged by that of the rural—urban continuum. For urban sociology has recently been confronted with exactly the same definitional problem and urban sociologists, like their rural counterparts, have been forced to come to terms with a topic area whose scope is defined by geographical not sociological categories (urban, urbanism). Indeed urban sociology has been revived, both in Europe and the United States, by a radical reappraisal of its purpose and possibilities and a considerable paradigm shift in the definition of what constitutes the field of 'urban' itself. Both Harvey (1973) and Castells (1976) have sought to regard the 'urban' as merely one manifestation of the overall development of (capitalist) society. An understanding of the dynamics of 'urbanism' and 'urbanization' must therefore, they argue, be sought in the general processes of capitalist society and how capitalism distributes its resources — primarily economic, but also spatial — around the population. Arguing from similar, though by no means coincidental perspectives, each has reasserted the linkages between the 'societal' and the 'urban' and to regard the *spatial* distribution of the population (into 'rural' and 'urban' areas) as part of this overall societal process, rooted in the economic order. On this basis urban sociology has set itself a new research agenda which both incorporates and transcends much of the previous work in this area (Pickvance, 1976).

There is undoubtedly much that rural sociologists can learn from this development. This is not to argue that the debate within urban sociology can be simplistically transferred to a rural context, for this would imply that agriculture develops according to the same process as industry, and this. as we shall see, is not necessarily the case. Nor, for that matter, does it imply that rural sociology must slavishly follow all the unresolved, and perhaps irresolvable, problems which the 'new' urban sociology has manifested (Pahl, 1977). However, rural sociology can usefully learn from the example of adopting a more holistic approach which addresses itself explicitly to the question of rural change under the conditions of a predominantly capitalist society. Moreover, as if to underline the parallel between the two sub-disciplines, whereas the 'new' urban sociology clearly has 'old' antecedents in the work of Engels on *The Housing Question* (see Bell, 1976), then so would a 'new' rural sociology have much to learn from a reading of Karl Kautsky's *The Agrarian Question* (Banaji, 1976). Kautsky's plea that 'we should look for all the changes which agriculture experiences under the domination of capitalist production' (Banaji, 1976, p. 3) rather than become immersed in studying agriculture in isolation is one which echoes the approach of Engels and of contemporary urban sociology. The organization of the material which follows reflects Kautsky's scheme, although some of Kautsky's detailed conclusions must perforce be questioned in the light of events since *The Agrarian Question* was first published.

Landholding and the Social Structure

'When we look at modern agriculture', wrote Kautsky (Banaji, 1976, p. 11), 'two basic characteristics immediately strike us: individual ownership of land and the commodity character of the products'. Each of these characteristics is decisive in shaping the nature of the rural social structure, but in this section consideration will be given to the nature of landholding.

In subsistence or near-subsistence economies access to and control over land is, almost by definition, a crucial resource; the structure of landholding is therefore both a cause of and closely follows the structure of power in such societies. Moreover, even in those societies which can no longer be described as underdeveloped, the obvious importance of land as a factor of production in agriculture compared with other industries ensures that the structure of land-holding remains decisive in shaping the rural class structure. Hence, as Stinchcombe (1961–62) has pointed out, property rather than occupation tends to be the defining principle of rural societies, and, rather than the division of labour *per se*, it is the organization of property relationships which shapes the nature of the class structure. For this reason agriculture has always sat uneasily beside most attempts to produce occupational rankings derived largely from an urban industrial standpoint. Hence studies of social mobility like those of Lipset and Bendix (1964) and Blau and Duncan (1967) have tended to 'classify all farmers together and regard them as an unstratified source of urban workers' (Stinchcombe, 1961–62, p. 183). This tendency to relegate the rural population to an amorphous mass — something which Lenski (1966) calls the 'farming class' — without distinguishing the various configurations of rural property relationships (and without even distinguishing between landowners and propertyless agricultural workers) has largely resulted from misguided attempts to apply urban-based occupational classifications to a rural context. Land is often insignificant as a factor of production in most urban, manufacturing employment; but its significance in agriculture means that any analysis must begin from how land is owned and controlled.

Land, however, is a factor of production which has very special qualities that introduce a number of peculiarities into the rural social structure. It is, for example, (relatively) fixed in quantity; certainly its quantity cannot be increased in the short term and neither can it be transferred from one physical location to another. Moreover, even though the quality of land can, in some instances, be improved quite quickly — by the addition of fertilizers, for example — even the limits of this can be quite strictly defined by the nature of topography and climate. Therefore land, unlike machinery or other forms of working capital, cannot become mobile according to the dictates of market conditions. The major decision which landowners must face is therefore one of utilization; in certain specific instances this may mean considering alternative uses to agriculture, but for the majority it will mean a decision whether or not to withdraw a portion of land from agricultural cultivation. Hence land cannot, for example, be moved to take advantage of market opportunities — and in general such are the topographical constraints that many cultivators and/or landowners are relatively insensitive to changes in market patterns: most landowners will have little choice other than to use their land for agricultural purposes and most cultivators have little choice other than to pursue their husbandry patterns. The main choices are quantitative rather than qualitative and hence in times of economic depression land tends to be simply withdrawn from cultivation rather than switched to an alternative use, agricultural or otherwise.

These generalizations need not always apply, but this relatively fixed quality of land — both geographically and qualitatively — renders land ownership a specific and peculiar category of the ownership of the means of production in general. These peculiar qualities were first recognised by Ricardo, who constructed his theory of economic rent around them. Ricardo noted that not only is land incapable of being increased in quantity in the short term, but the quality of a particular piece of land is not transferable. Land of above-average fertility produces above-average profits, but this inequality is determined by natural conditions and thus is a fixed quantity. This also applies to the opportunity-cost of the land, since this, too, is determined by its geographical location. By its very character, then, land may furnish its owner with continuous above-average profits or *ground rent*. Kautsky (following Ricardo and, indeed, Marx) recognized that it is the phenomenon of ground rent which enables the function of land ownership to remain separated from that of agricultural commodity production under capitalism. The immobility of land and the exclusivity of property rights together ensure that the increased competition, which in an analogous industrial situation would reduce super-profits, are circumscribed. Rack-renting — which means no more than charging what the market will bear for the rent of a particular piece of land — ensures also that the whole of the surplus profit which results from this accrues to the landowner, leaving the tenant cultivator the average profits accruing from commodity production. As long as the landowner charges the full market rent, there is also a strong incentive for the tenant to maximize the efficiency of his enterprise (usually by maximizing output). Indeed this may be a necessity if the tenant is to remain in business, for while the landowner may possess a local monopoly over land, there is no hindrance to competition over tenancies which may force the rent up to the market level.

For Kautsky, then, the commercialization of agriculture was marked not only by the growing market-orientation of agricultural production, but by the emergence of a fully-fledged commercial landlord–tenant system — and, as a further corollary, proletarianization of the agricultural labour force. A subsistence, landlord/peasant-based agriculture is replaced by the familiar tripartite structure of landlord, tenant farmer and landless farm labourer, which characterized British agriculture from the eighteenth century onwards. Wherever capitalism penetrates agriculture the peasantry is destroyed — polarized between a landless proletariat and a petty-bourgeois tenantry — and the division between landownership and the cultivation of the land is relatively clear-cut. As one participant in the anti-Corn Law debate in 1846 is reported to have stated, 'A landowner is no more a farmer than a shipowner is a sailor'. And as *The Economist* in a succinct summary of these differences remarked in 1857. (cited by Guttsman, 1969, pp. 104–105):

The business of a landowner — the management of land as property in the best manner — is something quite distinct from farming. It consists in rendering the land attractive to the best class of farmers, the men of skill and capital, by means of permanent outlays combined with conditions of letting which are consistent with profitable farming.

It was along these principles that English agriculture was organized following enclosure until the end of the nineteenth century.

Kautsky's analysis seems to stand up to most of the known facts concerning agricultural landownership under capitalist conditions up until the time of his writing. In Britain, for example, where the capitalist character of agriculture was the most extensive and longstanding of any in the world, the 'New Domesday' survey of landownership in 1873 revealed that 7000 men owned 80 per cent of the land and that farmers were six times as numerous as the landowners. As Caird (1878) put it, 'When we come more closely to analyse the purely landowning class, the aggregation of land among small numbers becomes very conspicuous'. Families like the Norfolks, the Derbys and the Bedfords, who owned the land on which the cities of Sheffield, Liverpool and London developed and expanded, had become enormously wealthy *rentier* capitalists on account of the fortunate geographical location of their property. The tenant farmers, whose business it was to cultivate the land, were quite separate and while they possessed (limited) capital, it was quite independent of that of the owner. By 1908, 90 per cent of farm land in the United Kingdom was tenanted and with landless farm workers five times as numerous as their tenant–farming employers, rural Britain appeared to correspond to the 'natural' pyramidal system of landed social stratification as Kautsky outlined it.

Unfortunately developments in the agricultural landownership of advanced capitalist societies since the time that Kautsky was writing have not always followed his prognostications. If we look at the character of agriculture in the most advanced capitalist societies today — Western Europe, the United States and Canada, Japan, Australasia — we find that this tripartite system of stratification is the exception rather than the rule. Now undoubtedly some of these exceptions, particularly in Europe and, possibly, Japan, relate to the continued resistance of the agrarian sector to penetration by capitalist organization. On the other hand we have the anomalous case of Britain: allegedly possessing the most thoroughgoing capitalist agriculture but evincing during the twentieth century a movement towards increasing owner-occupation. We must also take account of the rise of overseas competition from the former colonial satellites of metropolitan European countries, particularly Britain, for the relationship between the metropolitan countries and their (former) colonies has affected both the organization of agriculture in these colonies *and* agriculture in the metropolis (a factor which Kautsky himself recognized). Significantly, in both cases this has prompted the intervention of the state. Finally the implications of the tendency towards a falling rate of profit in agriculture must be examined more closely than Kautsky was prepared to consider.

The worry that the European peasantry was not quite so 'non-existent, historically speaking' as Marxist analysis had hitherto allowed was what first prompted Kautsky to examine the 'agrarian question'. The peasantry has, indeed, remained a stubbornly present feature of the organization of agriculture in Western Europe where even the most advanced industrial economies (France, Germany) have retained a sizeable peasant agricultural sector. The European peasantry has resisted blandishments to enter its 'final phase' (Franklin, 1969) to the extent that recent comment has referred to a 'new peasantry' being constantly created by advances in technology and the effects of the Common Agricultural Policy. Much of this, of course, depends upon how the peasantry is defined (Shanin, 1971; Mintz, 1973) but there can be little doubt that technological innovations in agriculture not only continually advance the margin of economically viable cultivation but, by diminishing the need for hired labour, continually create productive units in which the family is newly self-sufficient. The peasantry has survived therefore in even the most advanced capitalist societies in Europe partly because its nature has been transformed. In some respects this has involved production, not so much for subsistence but with the express purpose of participation in the market, with small plots continuing to exist in the interstices of the larger capitalist enterprises, often avoiding direct competition with them. The basis of their survival as commodity producers will, however, be considered more fully in the next section.

At this point we can merely note the effects which the survival of the peasantry has upon the structure of landholding. Its most demonstrable effect is to place a brake on the two broad movements which distinguish agrarian capitalism — accumulation and centralization (Banaji, 1976, pp. 30–31). In agriculture both of these tendencies occur, but the process is, as Kautsky pointed out (in Banaji, 1976, p. 30) more complicated:

To begin with, industrial means of production can be multiplied, whereas in agriculture land is, within the given conditions, a fixed resource . . . In agriculture the big landowner cannot generally increase his wealth except through centralisation, reuniting several holdings into one. In industry accumulation proceeds independently of centralisation: a big capital can farm without suppressing the autonomy of the lesser enterprises. When this suppression occurs, it is the *effect* of the formation of big industrial capital. Accumulation is here the starting point. On the contrary, where the land is fragmented into different properties and where small ownership prevails, large holdings can only acquire land by centralizing several smaller ones. The disappearance of the smaller holdings is thus the precondition for the formation of a larger enterprise. But this is not enough; it is also necessary that the holdings that are expropriated should form a continuous surface.

Unless the small landowner is to be removed by coercive force, therefore, his ambitious neighbour must wait for him either to become bankrupt or run out of heirs. In the meantime such small properties present stubborn obstacles to the growth of big landed conglomerations. Expansion can proceed only slowly, often through the purchase of detached holdings or by a process akin to spiralism (Watson, 1964) with accumulation by geographical mobility (Williams, 1964; Nalson, 1968).

The pace at which such accumulation proceeds depends largely upon the needs of the small landowner and the economies of scale which can be derived from an increased size of unit. The tenacity of small farmers and landowners, compared even with other sections of the agricultural population, is now a well-established fact (Gasson, 1974). This is because movement off the land is for them, unlike hired farm labour, frequently a downward move in terms of both class and status; for this reason, even part-time employment elsewhere is to be preferred to a complete break with the land (Franklin, 1969). Even where alternative part-time employment is unavailable, for the sake of his independence the smallholder may be prepared to suffer a standard of living below even that of a hired agricultural worker. In addition the economies of scale in certain types of agricultural production may not be very great, and may even be negative. Arable production seems to be the most conducive to capitalization since it is the most suitable for mechanization and requires little individual attention to the crop; similarly certain types of intensive livestock and poultry production have proved beneficial to automation — the so-called 'factory farming' techniques. Elsewhere, however, in horticulture, dairying, and sheep-farming, for example, the benefits of scale are by no means so apparent beyond a level still within the scope of the family proprietor. For these reasons agricultural accumulation can proceed very slowly indeed — it has taken more than ten years to increase the average size of farm in the EEC by one single hectare, for example (Clout, 1972, chapter 7; also Chisholm, 1962). And this slow pace has occurred despite the promotion by the state of consolidation schemes, not only in the EEC but in almost all Western European countries. Moreover, on the whole far less accumulation has been achieved in areas with small, owner-occupied farms than in areas with large, tenant-operated holdings (Clout, 1972, p. 109).

All this suggests that Kautsky's predictions concerning the rate of centralization and accumulation under a capitalist agriculture have been not so much falsified as only limited in their extent. Many of the accoutrements which Kautsky identified — the growth of landlordism, increases in scale and size of enterprise, the centralization of production — have only occurred in Europe in those sectors of agriculture which are highly capital-intensive — and this means mainly arable, especially cereals, production. Elsewhere, while similar changes are discernible, these tendencies have proceeded only very slowly indeed, even under the auspicies of the state. Hence a familiar spectacle in many European societies is the coexistence of a highly advanced industrial sector with an apparently 'backward' agriculture. However this is a division which is often present within the agricultural sector itself with a highly capitalized commercial agriculture, often associated with cereal production (East Anglia, the Paris Basin, for example) juxtaposed with a subsistence or quasi-subsistence agriculture of a peasant-like nature. This is not to suggest some kind of mechanistic ecological determinism, for the links between topographical and climatic features, the system of cultivation, the organization of landholding and the rural social structure do not run quite as deterministically as these airy generalizations might suggest, as even the most ecologically minded rural geographer would recognize.

It is precisely at this point that the contribution of rural sociology has proved to be so lacking. There remains a great need for sociological studies of how, under similar technological and ecological conditions, the property relationships which underpin the processes of agricultural production have been shaped and moulded by the historical development of the societies within which they are located. Indeed rural sociology's meagre contribution in this area has been limited to countless studies of the influences of customs, traditions, or more generally 'values' in hindering the spread of technological innovation (for summaries see Jones, 1967; Rogers and Shoemaker, 1971). It is as though, from rural sociology's standpoint, the only barrier to modern agricultural development were the failure to communicate new techniques of production; otherwise it is sufficient to rely for macrotheories of rural society upon naïve theories of technological or ecological determinism. There have been few attempts, then, to develop either a systematic, political economy of modern, capitalist agriculture or a comparative theory of rural social structures under modern economic conditions. However, while Kautsky offers a basis for constructing a political economy, it is apparent that we have not seen the universal growth of the kind of landholding structure and rural class relationships which Kautsky took to be the hallmark of capitalist agriculture. Indeed, if we take as an illustrative case the example of cereals production we can see a rather different historical development in the major cereals-producing countries like the United States, Canada, Australia and, to a lesser extent, Argentina, than in those European nations upon which Kautsky's analysis was largely based.

As far as their landholding structure is concerned the one factor which stands out about these countries is that they have not developed a classic landlord and tenant system, despite developing an agriculture which is undoubtedly thoroughly capitalist in its nature. The major reason for this was that the major cereal-producing regions — the midwestern prairies of North America, the pampas of Argentina and the plains and downland belts of south-eastern and south-western Australia — were all the product of European colonization, and, indeed, only made possible by the growth of the urban market for food-stuffs in Europe. In all these regions agriculture developed largely under the regulation of the state, insofar as landowning (and, indeed, commodity production at a later stage) was concerned. The most characteristic structure of landholding was therefore not the private estate but the family smallholding, either owned outright or leased from the state (see, particularly, Graham, 1966, chapter 1; also Lipset, 1950; Sower and Miller, 1964).

Such a pattern of landownership has clearly affected the social structure of these areas and rendered the political activity of these farmers very different to that of their Western European counterparts. Far from encountering the traditional aristocratic ambience of Britain and the northern plains of Europe, or the managerialism of large-scale modern, business-farming enterprises, the more obvious points of comparison seem to be with the urban petty dourgeoisie. Macpherson, for example, has emphasized the fierce individualism and assertion of independence manifested by these farmers. For unlike many of their European counterparts they employ little or no permanent hired labour and tend to be continually involved in the manual labour of their holdings.

Cut off . . . by the scale of his operations and by his independence of employed labour from the ranks of other entrepreneurs, yet not generally seeing how wide the gulf is between him and them, the farmer is apt to class himself with them, or at least to feel that he has an independent position in the economy akin to theirs. He is confirmed in this belief by his clear perception of his difference from the wage-earner. The wage-earner gives up the direction of his labour; the farmer retains the direction of his, making his own decisions as to how to use his land and capital, his skill and energy. His real independence in comparison with the employee thus confirms him in an illusion that he has or can have an independent place in the economy . . . It is an agrarian consciousness, not a class consciousness; it emphasises the common interests of agrarian producers, and their differences from all other producers, and in so doing it fails to comprehend the essential class position of the independent producers, that is, their ambiguous position in an economy increasingly dominated by capital. (Macpherson, 1952, pp. 22–23, 227; cited by Graham, 1966, pp. 14, 15).

Within the political philosophies evolved by such agrarian social structures, Lipset (1950) has detected the presence of socialist principles; however, as Graham points out, such agrarian political movements usually present two aspects: 'from one point of view it appears as a class demand for socio-economic concessions and for privilege; from another it represents the protest of a colonial region against metropolitan dominance, economic and political' (Graham, 1966, p. 15). Overlapping these demands there was also the desire to combat the acute insecurity deriving from often violent fluctuations in the market for cereals. The agricultural communities of these cereals-producing areas thus tended to have a relatively homogeneous class character but to exhibit a populist political activity aimed at the exploitative role of credit agencies, the banks, railways and merchants.

Despite often owning the land on which they farm, such a situation is distinctly different to the situation in Europe. Indeed the scale of their enterprises and the nature of their political demands often serve to emphasize the similarities with the farming *tenant* in Britain and elsewhere. In many Western European countries, however, we are dealing with what is often a rigid and very hierarchical class structure in the grain-growing areas and a coherent and readily identifiable rural ruling class of landowners (Bell and Newby, 1973; 1974). The differing historical development of Western Europe — both internally and between it as a whole and its former colonial satellites — has conferred a very different character onto the politics of landownership. In all cases while the state was once largely in the hands of a landowning class, such a situation has become more attenuated with the rise of industrialism. The precise way in which landowners have become involved in, or reacted to, such changes has, as Moore (1966) demonstrated, fundamentally affected the modernization process. In the case of Germany, for example, the promotion of both industrialism and the commercialization of agriculture by landowners produced a corporate state in which they could fully participate (Gerth and Mills, 1948, chapter 14; Moore, 1966, chapter 8). In England the commercialization of agriculture preceded the process of industrialization by a century or more and while the landowning class promoted the former it largely (though not entirely) reacted to the latter (Thompson, 1963), and subsequently lost control of the functions of the state. Much of the politics of landownership in Britain, particularly since 1910, has therefore been to adapt, on the whole successfully, to these changed political circumstances (Self and Storing, 1962).

These unavoidably perfunctory indications show the caution with which ecological theories of rural society must be handled. Undoubtedly ecological factors place limits on the type of agriculture that can be conducted in any particular area, but the patterns of landownership and the nature of the rural social structure can vary widely between these limits. Unfortunately, however, there are no systematic cross-national studies of landownership in advanced capitalist societies, so we have little information on which to base a comparative analysis of recent trends. Nevertheless, from the limited evidence available it is possible to draw some tentative conclusions concerning landownership which do not always conform to Kautsky's analysis. While the impact of overseas competition has indeed, as Kautsky himself recognized, fundamentally altered the character of European agriculture, it has not always done so in the manner in which Kautsky had foreseen. For example, while overseas competition, particularly over cereals production, certainly precipitated a crisis in European agriculture which eventually produced massive state intervention in commodity production (see below) in the sphere of landownership it precipitated, though not necessarily *caused*, a flight from the landlord–tenant system in Britain, so that Britain today possesses an agriculture which has the most thoroughgoing capitalist character of any in Europe, but which also has the highest rate of agricultural owner-occupation.

These changes have been brought about by certain aspects of the political economy of landownership which Kautsky overlooked. Because the amount of food which can be consumed is limited, then as a country develops the pro-portion of marginal income spent on food progressively declines, an increasing proportion being spent instead upon manufactured goods and services. Gross returns to agriculture therefore tend to decline in relation to gross returns to other sectors of the economy and in a predominantly market economy this in turn means that capital invested in agricultural land (where there is no other alternative use) will, other things being equal, produce a lower return than a similar amount of capital invested elsewhere. (Metcalf, 1969; Capstick, 1970). Long before the economic crisis in British agriculture of the final quarter of the nineteenth century it was possible to perceive an underlying structural weakness in the position of private landownership brought about by this long-term trend. Landowners who did not have at least part of their capital invested elsewhere were seeing their situation undermined (Thompson, 1963, chapter 10). The growth of tenant rights in the 1880s was partly in response to such weaknesses (Perkin, 1973), but, by increasing the political and economic power of the tenantry, it also precipitated the decision of landowners to remove their capital (that is sell the land) and invest elsewhere. Undoubtedly they were also encouraged to do so by the imposition of fiscal penalties on unearned income and inherited wealth (Sturmey, 1955). Around the period of the First World War the land was purchased mostly by former tenants; but since 1945, aided by state support of agricultural prices, the continuing increase in owner-occupation has been wrought instead by the tendency of landowners to foreclose on tenancies and farm the land themselves. By 1973, official statistics showed that only 46 per cent of land was tenanted — and this was almost certainly an over-estimate (Rose *et al.*, 1977). Rural England, in a celebrated phrase first used in *The Times*, has 'changed hands'. There is no doubt that owner-occupiers are now the single most important group of private owners of agricultural land in Britain.

Given that the problem of relatively declining returns to agricultural land is a function of all developing economies the question must arise as to why a similar domination of owner-occupation cannot be observed in other advanced capitalist societies. Only some tentative and wholly speculative answers can be offered here since again there is little systematic information upon which to base an analysis. It seems, for example, that while the agricultural sector of other societies have experienced similar problems it has been met in different ways. For example, in Europe, North America and Australia there has been a much deeper penetration into both landownership and commodity production by large, often multinational food-processing firms which have bought up land as a form of vertical integration in order to guarantee supplies. In areas like North America and Australia this has also been aided by the historically cheap price of land compared with England and much of northern Europe (Larson and Rogers, 1964; Encel, 1970, chapter 16). The British firm of Vesteys, for example, has expanded from a base in Norfolk to purchase extensive pastoral properties in Australia, Argentina and North America and thence to a multinational enterprise involved in slaughterhouses, meatpacking, cold storage, wholesale and retail meat trading (the latter through the Dewhurst chain), icecream manufacture, frozen foods and so on (Encel, 1970, pp. 308—310). Many more examples could be cited, but it is noticeable how meagre this vertical integration is in Britain: the long-term crisis in capital returns on land has been met in other ways.

There is also a view that the decline of the landlord–tenant system in Britain is merely a passing phase brought about by state intervention through fiscal policies and that the 'natural' state of affairs will soon reassert itself. Basically two sets of reasons are adduced for this. One is that the kind of fiscal policies which precipitated the demise of the private estate landowner in the first place will also destroy the private owner-occupier. Squeezed between Capital Gains and Capital Transfer Tax the owner-occupier will eventually be driven into the arms of some corporate landowning institution — either the state or financial institutions such as banks, pension funds and insurance companies (Gibbs and Harrison, 1973). The second set of reasons relate to these institutions themselves. Land offers them a secure investment in terms of long-term capital growth, releasing working capital to provide a higher yield (and therefore higher rents) for the tenant farmer. Since 1970 there has been a large increase in corporate ownership of land in the form of purchases by financial institutions — though in absolute terms, the amount remains small. If such trends continue, however, this will bring British landownership more into line with the situation in other advanced capitalist societies and ally agriculture with other industries in reasserting the separation of ownership and control. The extent to which such developments will continue remains, however, uncertain.

Commodity Production

In all advanced capitalist societies the major trend in farming as an occupation can be summed up as a transition from, to use the familiar clichés, 'farming as a way of life' to 'farming as a business'. That is to say that agriculture has become increasingly rationalized in the face of market conditions. The farmer is not, however, a participant in a single market, but several — markets for different produce which may be local, national or international in their scope, markets for various factor inputs, and so on. Each of these markets, though they are clearly related, need to be considered separately (Bell and Newby, 1974). Nevertheless the prevailing trend in all cases is towards an increased rationality of economic production, 'from agriculture to agribusiness' (Davis, 1956).

The rise of agricultural capitalism (as opposed to subsistence agriculture) has stimulated the application of scientific and technological principles to the production of food. The most visible consequences of this are the changes from a predominantly horse-and-hand technology to the use of tractors and combine harvesters, but agriculture has also been well served by science beyond just the application of the internal combustion engine. The science of genetics has contributed no less fundamentally to startling increases in output from both plant and animal breeding, while a greater understanding of nutrition has resulted in a more scientific application of animal feed and fertilizers. All of these innovations have produced immense increases in both production and productivity (Edwards and Rogers, 1974; Larson and Rogers, 1964; Williams, 1969; OECD, 1970.) The implications of these changes are both complex and far-reaching and most analyses of changes in contemporary rural society begins from them. However, they must be seen in the context of the *prior* commercialization of agriculture which thereby offers incentives to increase production and adopt new forms of agricultural technology.

Because of these massive increases in production, allied to the low income elasticity of demand for food, agricultural production left to the vagaries of a free market is always threatened by crisis of overproduction and by violent fluctuations in both production and price — the so-called 'cobweb' and 'scissors' cycles (McCrone, 1962; Metcalf, 1969; Capstick, 1970). All governments in advanced capitalist societies have therefore felt it necessary to intervene in order to save farmers from the full consequences of their own increases in productivity (Dexter, 1969). Such intervention has taken a number of forms — deficiency payments, intervention prices, direct subsidies, the formation of marketing cartels, the regulation of land allowed to be cultivated — but the overall effect upon the individual farmer has been basically similar. It has provided him with incentives to maximize production, for, rather than producing a violent drop in income, state support enables increases in production to go more or less hand-in-hand with higher returns. Tinkering with the precise way in which these schemes have operated has also enabled other desired policy objectives to be achieved — for example, increasing specialization, scale of production, centralization, and so on (for a review of these policies see Johnson, 1973). Although fluctuations have not by any means been entirely eliminated — the nature of the weather does, after all, remain a significant factor — they have been reduced in extent. The main regulator of agricultural returns in most product markets has thus become the state, so that farmers and their representatives find themselves bargaining with the government of the day in order to maintain or enhance their economic situation. This direct politicization of agriculture in all advanced industrial societies is an emergent feature of world agriculture in the twentieth century,[1] and has in most cases accelerated the trend in advanced capitalist societies towards 'agribusiness'.

The growth of 'agribusiness' has wrought associated problems of 'farm adjustment' — that is, the adjustment of the correct factor 'mix' to produce the optimum level of farm productivity and/or returns on capital investment (Ashton and Rogers, 1967; Throsby, 1972). The most apparent adjustment has been the wholesale substitution of capital for labour. As a consequence in countries like the United States and Britain productivity per man in agriculture now exceeds that in the other sectors of the economy. The demand for full-time agricultural labour has fallen considerably in all advanced capitalist countries (OECD, 1969) and will undoubtedly continue to do so. The drastic reductions in the agricultural labour force has also changed its composition. Farmers, who are the least mobile, constitute an increasing proportion of farm labour but male full-time hired workers have also been replaced by casual and part-time female labour. The pattern, now reasonably well-established in the United States, seems likely to become more universal: a predominance of family farms with casual or contract labour hired to cover the peaks of labour demand (Heath and Whitby, 1969; Gasson, 1974). The permanent hired labour that has remained on the land has become, and is likely to become in the future, more highly skilled, in either veterinary science or machine operation, and more highly trained and educated. Furthermore, the skills of the farmer must perforce change from an aptitude for crop and animal husbandry to an ability to employ the full range of entrepreneurial skills in management, finance, accountancy, marketing and investment. All this will render the farmer's skills less distinctive and less particular to agriculture; his outlook on agriculture and the nature of his work are thus likely to bring about a closer resemblance to his counterparts in industry.

The substitution of capital for labour, while it has dramatically improved productivity, has, however, brought persistent problems of accumulation. Often only the larger units can afford the latest technological innovations or make optimum use of them by taking advantage of economies of scale. In part farmers have coped with this problem by becoming increasingly specialized (Gasson, 1966; Larson and Rogers, 1964), thus limiting the spread of capital investment and making the fullest use of the capital available. Such a trend has also been aided by improved transportation and marketing techniques. However, specialization also increases risk; consequently specialization has also been accomplished by an increasing concentration of production among the larger producers who can claim economies of scale and draw upon reserves which will tide them over the periods of adverse market conditions. Such specialization also increases the division of labour in agriculture and so draws the farmer into an increasingly widespread network of economic relationships. Farming becomes more and more involved in a complex of food producing, processing and marketing industries both in the supply of farm inputs and in the forward marketing of farm produce. Indeed, as Larson and Rogers comment (1964, p. 49), 'the increasing dependence of farmers upon agribusinessmen is one index of the trend from subsistence farming to modern agriculture'.

On the supply side farmers purchase machinery, fertilizers, feedstuffs, seed, pesticides, petroleum products, and, not least, credit from national, or even multinational organizations against whom they are in a very weak bargaining position. Their suppliers are often free to raise prices to them without hindrance, while the individual farmer is in turn frequently uncertain as to whether he can recoup his costs. For farmers are so numerous and individually have such little influence on the market that they are price-takers rather than price-makers for their products. They are not always able to pass on their increased costs of production in full, partly because of the low income-elasticity of demand for food or because the government of the day feels unable or unwilling to bear the burden of support. Farmers, then, in most advanced capitalist societies have found themselves in a cost-price squeeze (Glau, 1972; Metcalf, 1969, chapter 5) whose severity may vary from time to time and from product to product, but which most governments have used as a lever to stimulate an even further growth of productivity and efficiency. And so the spiral of increased capitalization, specialization and concentration of production is given an extra twist.

Farmers have typically attempted to circumvent this squeeze and its consequences in a number of ways. First, although it is dealt with in more detail elsewhere in this book, they have attempted to apply political pressure in order to allow the effects of increased costs to be mitigated by increased prices for farm produce (Self and Storing, 1962). Secondly, there have been attempts to form co-operatives — often sponsored by governments — that will improve the bargaining power of farmers through collective means. However, given that the whole economic reationality of capitalism is based upon competition (albeit less apparent in agriculture) it is not surprising that co-operative schemes have met with only limited success (Hunt, 1974, pp. 54–55). Marketing boards — a form of producer-controlled cartel — have, however, been more successful in providing farmers with the necessary countervailing power (Warley, 1963). Thirdly, some form of vertical integration may be attempted. Complete vertical integration usually results in the loss of the farmers' independence and identity to a particular food-processing firm. Hence more common is some variation of contract farming whereby farmers bypass the state apparatus for determining the price of farm produce and negotiate contracts directly with processed-food manufacturers. These have certain advantages for the farmer by providing a guaranteed market, shifting the burden of risk and providing easier access to credit, technical advice and marketing expertise, while the manufacturer is assured of continuity and quality of supply. However, the farmer usually cedes some of his autonomy over husbandry and once more is brought into close contact with large industrial corporations with all the attendent risks of dependence and a weak negotiating position. Overall it is not perhaps surprising that farmers have been receiving a declining share of the final retail price of food as they have become sucked into this large-scale agroindustrial complex (Metcalf, 1969, chapter 6).

Thus attempts to circumvent the cost-price squeeze by contract farming merely increases the problems of agricultural adjustment even further. As Metcalf (1969, p. 104) sums it up:

These contractual arrangements . . . accentuate the problems of agriculture adjustment. For example, the adoption of new technology is hastened, accentuating the pressure on supplies; this is especially likely if contracts are accompanied by significant credit extension, which facilitates the adoption of the most technically efficient production methods. The resulting increases in supply lead to downward pressure on prices and possibly lower incomes for non-contracting farmers. These arrangements also lead to fundamental changes in farm structure. They encourage both fewer, larger holdings and increased specialisation so that the size of individual enterprises can be enlarged to fully achieve the prevailing scale economies. This trend . . . is likely to lead to both a reduction in the numbers employed in agriculture, and a decline in the managerial role of those farmers remaining . . . leaving them with caretaker functions.

Kautsky (Banaji, 1976, pp. 44–45), in rather more colourful language, makes much the same point:

Agroindustries are subject to the law of concentration and centralisation, to scale economies and the law on increasing firm size (cf. the example of Nestlé), like other industries. Where this industrialisation of agriculture does not entirely eliminate the smallholder, it binds him to the monopsonist power of the factory and converts him into a serf of industrial capital, working to its requirements. The domination of agriculture by industry which these examples signify is carried further, finally, by the more and more efficient utilisation of raw materials, including the recycling of waste products, and by the production of synthetic substitutes (margarine, artificial cheese) which compete directly with the natural products ...

We cannot say that agriculture has been ruined under these pressures. But its conservative character has gone forever wherever the modern mode of production has taken root. The entire economic life of the countryside which revolved eternally in the same orbits has today fallen into a state of perpetual revolution which is a necessary feature of capitalism.

Most of these trends are by now well documented by agricultural economists, but their sociological consequences remain largely underexamined. It is true that sociologists have noted the increased rural–urban interaction that has resulted from this growing incorporation of agriculture, but the consequences in terms of the consciousness of the farmers themselves, their political mobilization, the 'industrial relations' of agriculture and the changing configuration of property relationships all require further investigation. Instead we must rely upon a number of sensitive community studies which have traced the 'eclipse' of community (Stein, 1964) consequent upon the centralization of decision-making in rural areas and in agribusiness firms; what Gallaher calls the 'ever-widening circles of awareness of, participation in, and dependency upon the surrounding urban world' (Gallaher, 1961, p. 226). It should be noted, however, that this process of rationalization in economic terms has nevertheless produced, on the farm, an increased tendency towards particularism owing to the declining size of the labour force (to be discussed below). In other words, we need to be somewhat cautious in assuming that, within the rural locality, such centralizing tendencies have wrought a change from primary to secondary relationships to the extent that it is often assumed, particularly by community studies embedded within the rural–urban continuum tradition.[2]

How, then, has the small farm survived in the face of all these trends? In part, as was indicated earlier in this paper, the tenacity of the small farmer is a product of his willingness to accept lower economic rewards than his capital could earn elsewhere, and often he is prepared to do so in order to retain his 'independence' (Gasson, 1969). In part, too, the small farmer is increasingly a part-time farmer obtaining a second income, often from urban employment (Gasson, 1966). However, by no means all types of farming benefit from increases in scale to the same extent — for example, dairying — so that concentrations of small farms can remain over long periods and the tendencies towards larger units may proceed only very slowly. Elsewhere, however, small farms have continued to coexist with the larger enterprises and have done so by withdrawing from direct competition with them, concerning themselves instead with highly specialized types of production (for example horticulture, market gardening, nurseries, etc.) or by taking advantage of local market opportunities and/or soil conditions. Nevertheless in terms of their contribution to gross agricultural output, proportion of the land surface cultivated and employment of labour, such holdings are much less significant in the agriculture of advanced capitalist societies than their numbers might suggest. In Britain, for example, the top 30 per cent of holdings account for 75 per cent of agricultural output, 75 per cent of the acreage farmed and 85 per cent of all hired workers.

Social Relations

Given the general movement towards a more economically rational organization of agricultural production it would be tempting to assume that relationships between employers and employees in agriculture are following a similar course to those in other industries. Only in the broadest possible terms is this the case, however. Undoubtedly the 'industrialization' of agriculture in all advanced capitalist societies has converted the agricultural worker into a wage labourer whose market situation is not too dissimilar to that of workers in manufacturing industry. As elsewhere there has been a tendency in agriculture to strip the nexus between employer and employee down to a contractual one involving a wage payment. However, the social relations which overlay this market situation have by no means exhibited the tendencies apparent in industry, owing to the peculiarities of the conditions of agricultural production. Hence the precise nature of these changes must be examined in some detail.

There seems little doubt that the widespread changes in the relationships between farmers and farm workers in modern agriculture have been wrought by the revolution in the techniques of production already outlined in the previous section. Mechanization, for example, has not only drastically reduced the number of workers required in absolute terms, it has also affected the nature of the work itself and both the relations among workers and between workers and their employers in the work situation (Newby, 1972). Indeed the impact of mechanization on agricultural work has been, with a few exceptions to be discussed below, almost the reverse of that in industry. Mechanization has, for example, decreased rather than increased the division of labour among agricultural workers and has done so without reducing the autonomy, discretion or variety which the modern agricultural worker experiences in his job. In part, this is once again because of the different factor mix in agriculture compared with industry. Whilst land remains important as a factor of production, it remains impossible to control the environment in a way which will fundamentally revolutionize the productive process. In industry the change from handicraft to machine production enabled the productive process to be broken down into a number of stages which were carried out *concurrently*; in agriculture, however, the continuing importance of land and seasonal conditions means that production, even after mechanization, must be carried out sequentially. Thus mechanization has fundamentally changed the *pace* of work on the land, but left its *rhythm* largely unaltered (Brewster, 1970). Moreover it enabled the machine to remain the servant of the worker rather than vice versa and in so doing removed most of the routine drudgery and physically arduous labour.

The exceptions to this concern those branches of agriculture where land is of less importance and/or have proved amenable to the artificial control of the environment in such a way as to remove the importance of seasonal factors. Principally these are certain types of intensive horticultural and livestock production, particularly poultry. These are the so-called 'factory farms' where the production processes have been altered in such a way as to render them almost identical to those in manufacturing industry, including extensive automation and assembly-line production in some cases. On these 'farms' the work situation thus resembles that in many factories. Some types of livestock — most notably sheep — have proved resistant to such farming methods, however, while the majority of arable production continues on conventional, albeit larger and more specialized, farms. Nevertheless the situation of workers in factory farms — many of whom are female — has received little or no sociological attention.

How, then, have the technological changes that have taken place in agriculture affected the relationships between employers and employees? One important effect has been to increasingly isolate the agricultural worker from his workmates. They no longer work together in groups as much as they used to, except where plantation agriculture prevails and even here mechanization has made substantial inroads into the demand for gang labour. Most farm workers today work in considerable isolation on board a piece of agricultural machinery. Any collectivist impulse which may have emerged from the frequent and pervasive contact between workers on the land has therefore become attenuated. Furthermore the continuing outflow of labour from agriculture, often accompanied by rural depopulation, has undermined the solidarities of whatever rural working-class sub-culture existed in rural communities in an era when labour was more numerous on the land (Newby, 1974). Thus, while in the past agricultural workers often developed a strong, if covert, sense of group identity based upon their shared experience with neighbours and workmates, it seems likely that this has declined — although it has not yet entirely disappeared — and will continue to do so in the future (Newby, 1977; Rushing, 1972).

Relationships with farmers and landowners — that is, the rural employing class — have also been affected by these changes. Perhaps the most important concerns the debureaucratization of farms that has been a consequence of the diminution of the labour force. In the past the employer was a remote and authoritarian figure to most agricultural workers, particularly on those farms specializing in relatively labour-intensive crop production. The nature of arable farming, in particular, with the need for a careful and protracted tending of the crop under a horse-and-hand technology, together with the necessity of organizing a large labour force for often complex and arduous tasks like harvest, made the social structure of such farms very rigid and hierarchical. The labour force was regimented by a strict discipline of control in order to ensure that, almost like a military operation, the productive process was brought to a successful conclusion. Control of the labour force was mediated through a series of foremen and managers so that the degree of interaction between farmer and worker was perfunctory and usually highly formal. Almost by definition in a rural area farmers and landowners possessed a near monopoly over employment opportunities — and often education, housing and the administration of justice, too. Therefore farmers and landowners, whatever their internal differences of opinion, formed from the point of view of the agricultural worker a rural ruling class, often to be counterposed to the equally coherent group solidarity of the workers themselves. However the power of this rural ruling class was usually such that opposition could only be expressed covertly and sporadically (see the comparative material presented by Jayawardena, 1968; and in Landsberger, 1973). For the most part there was little *visible* conflict although the extent to which this was merely the 'necessary pose of the powerless' (Lemisch, 1970), rather than a harmonious arcadian consensus, has often been overlooked.

With the enormous decline in the farm labour force, however, the organization of the farm has become debureaucratized. Farms which twenty years ago may have employed 30 to 40 workers today employ less than ten. Many of the intermediaries between employer and employee have been removed and increasingly they interact on a personal and diffuse basis, so that rather than control being exerted in a formal and impersonal way through a code of rules and regulations it is increasingly exerted through informal, face-to-face contact. Under these circumstances it is often far easier for the employer to obtain the identification of his employees than it was under the old conditions. Moreover the former communal solidarities of the village have been disrupted by the arrival in many rural areas of a new, non-agricultural and usually ex-urban population. Such an influx has had a profound effect on undermining the 'closed' aspect of many rural villages and has been a widespread phenomenon in Western Europe (Connell, 1974). One consequence has been that new social divisions have been created which have tended to cut across class lines, between on the one hand the close-knit 'locals', who will include both farmers and farm workers, and on the other the ex-urbanite, often middle-class newcomers (Pahl, 1965; Bell and Newby, 1973). Taken together such changes have tended to decrease the *social* distance between farmers and farm workers, whatever the wide divergencies in wealth, income and lifestyle that undoubtedly remain in many cases.

The general trend of labour relations in agriculture has therefore been the reverse of that in industry. Capitalist development in agriculture has not in general, produced larger concentrations of labour, a growth of bureaucracy or a more distant and authoritarian managerial style — on the contrary. Neither have the potentialities of collective action through agricultural trade unions markedly improved. Although the farm worker has become less isolated in a cultural sense — less limited in his access to knowledge about the world beyond the farm gate and with expectations no longer noticeably dissimilar to those of the rest of the working population — there are fewer opportunities to sustain the animosities of rural class conflict that operated under the old conditions. Farm workers today tend to be more isolated from each other, brought into a greater degree of face-to-face contact with their employers and less inclined to regard their relationships with farmers as a conflictual one in consequence. Even where large concentrations of workers remain in order to provide a basis for organization and collective action they are more likely to be migrant or casual workers and hence less easy to organize on that account (Friedland and Thomas, 1974). In general, then, recent changes in the structure of rural societies in which capitalist agriculture predominates have not been of a kind which might allow agricultural workers to dramatically alter their generally exploited situation through their own collective action.

In terms of structure, then, it appears that rural class relationships are becoming, in Weberian terms, more 'traditional' — that is, more particularistic and more diffuse. But what of their *content* — are they becoming more 'traditional' in content, too? Again the absence of any systematic comparative research hinders safe generalization. Frequently the backwardness of the rural sector of industrial societies has been inferred from the observation of their more traditional social relationships, although this need not mean that they are 'feudal' or 'neo-feudal' (Carter, 1976) in the precise meaning of these terms, for such relationships are firmly located within a capitalist economic context. On the other hand there is a good deal of comparative evidence to show that where a hierarchical and largely ascriptive system of rural stratification is combined with a highly particularistic structure of relationships then a system of traditional authority tends to ensue no matter how rational or 'modern' the economic activity of the dominant class (see, for example, Genovese, 1971, 1974; Newby, 1977; Scott and Kerkvliet, 1974; Jayawardena, 1968) Patriarchalism or paternalist capitalism would perhaps be more accurate descriptions of these systems of authority than 'feudalism' (Newby, 1975, 1976). Nevertheless it is noticeable how much rural protest has resulted from a failure by those possessing such authority to conform to the canons of traditional behaviour (Landsberger, 1973) even under capitalist conditions (Hobsbawm and Rudé, 1971). The particularism of rural society has enabled paternalism to remain a viable means of stabilizing the rural social hierarchy and maintain the identification of the rural poor, should those in power wish to avail themselves of the opportunity (Newby, 1975).[3]

Undoubtedly the more particularistic social structure prevalent on most modern farms has enabled the social influence and judgements of employers to prevail more than was generally the case in the past, when it was doubtful whether the values associated with paternalist capitalism were transmitted across the class boundary with the efficacy that has sometimes been assumed. However it is doubtful whether any generalized notion of patriarchal traditional authority is anything like so ingrained among farmers and landowners in advanced capitalist societies as it once was. Partly this is because there has been a decline in the importance of traditional authority in general in these societies. Their growing industrialization with ever-increasing technological innovation has led to a much greater complexity that has permeated all spheres of activity. This growth in complexity has perforce placed an increasing premium on the possession of specialized knowledge and technical expertise. Tradition, the cult of the gentlemanly amateur, has been overtaken by efficiency and the professional. In agriculture such changes have been imported via the growing commercialization of commodity production, referred to in the previous section of this chapter. Hence it is possible to observe, in terms of values, the change to a more professional entrepreneurial agriculture, to farming as a 'business' (Beresford, 1975).

This points to a possible irony in the social structure of modern agriculture. In the past when, if we are to believe the literature, farmers and landowners preferred to legitimate their authority by traditional means, the organizational structure of the farm and the nature of the village community together rendered it only partially effective. Such was the social distance between employer and employee that the identification with the farmer's authority was (probably) only partial and spasmodic. Wholesale mechanization and the consequent outflow of labour have, however, produced conditions more favourable for the maintenance of traditional authority — in most cases it is now easier for the farmer to obtain the identification of his workers than it was in the past. Such, however, have been the changes in the economic organization of agriculture that farmers are increasingly inclined to adopt an ethic of professionalism and abjure the traditional obligations of the rural gentleman. Indeed they may regard such notions as anachronistic and faintly embarrassing. Caught up in these general changes — possibly more so than their workers — farmers may be inclined to treat their workers in ways that are little different to the majority of contemporary employers.

Such changes will be particularly pronounced on those farms which have reversed the trend towards a diminishing labour force, often by amalgamation with other holdings, including cases of vertical integration. Farm amalgamation, which has been one response by farmers to changing market factors, has in some cases created extremely large holdings, both in terms of acreage and labour force. These farms have continued to operate through a bureaucratic organizational structure similar to that of any large manufacturing business. Indeed a growing trend, as already noted, is for farms to become associated with manufacturing, or at least food-processing, companies. Such a structure involves the separation of ownership and control in many cases, and often entails a degree of impersonality in the running of the enterprise that may lead workers to respond more readily to market factors than workers on smaller farms. In other words, cash nexus may replace personal loyalty, as the disciplines which are exerted on the farm worker are those long familiar to his urban, industrial counterpart.

In most advanced capitalist societies the trend towards a smaller labour force per unit has sufficiently outpaced that towards farm amalgamation to continue the overall tendency towards more personal, informal relationships between farmers and farm workers. What is perhaps less clear is the extent of the trend towards farm amalgamation in the future. Perhaps the situation already apparent in North America and Australia will become more widespread in Europe, namely a *slow* concentration of hired labour on the large units that have resulted from amalgamation while on those farms which do not amalgamate family labour will predominate with contractors and casual labour covering the busy periods. Much will depend, however, on the rate at which future farm amalgamation and vertical integration will take place; in any event, the process will be a slow one and labour will remain thinly spread across the industry for many years to come. But should hired labour become concentrated on fewer, larger units in the future than the distinctiveness of farm workers compared with those in other industries is likely to decline still further. As Kautsky put it, 'the modern mode of production thus returns, at the end of its dialectical process to the original point of departure, *to a suppression of the separation of industry and agriculture*' (Banaji, 1976, p. 47; emphasis is in the original.)

Conclusions

The peculiarities of capitalist development in agriculture, a number of which have been outlined in this chapter, suggest at least a basis on which rural sociology might proceed in the future. The 'rural' need not, of course, be regarded as coterminous with the 'agricultural' but all meaningful definitions of 'rural' have at least a basis in agriculture and so a consideration of the development of agriculture remains at the heart of any rural sociology. Unfortunately the close affinity which exists between rural sociology and agricultural economics (Gasson, 1971) has not proved to be particularly beneficial for either discipline. While, as this chapter has sought to indicate, a consideration of the economics of agriculture is likely to be crucial for a renewed theoretical impetus in rural sociology, the past history of both disciplines seems rather to have served to emphasize the divisions between them than to have led to fruitful areas of joint enquiry. Sociological variables have largely been relegated to residual factors by many agricultural economists, while much rural sociology has been carried out in almost total isolation from a consideration of the economic context of modern agriculture.

Where rural sociology can establish itself as a viable sub-discipline is by basing its enquiries upon a recognition that agriculture does *not* develop in advanced capitalist societies in a manner which merely mirrors other industries. Much of the distinctiveness of agriculture, as this chapter has sought to demonstrate, derives from the importance of land as a factor of production. If for no other reason, agriculture therefore throws into sharp relief the nature of property relationships in capitalist societies and much rural sociology could be profitably reoriented to a consideration of property, which continues to remain an underexamined aspect of modern societies generally (Rose *et al.*, 1976). In addition, the importance of land as a factor of production increases the spatial constraints upon the social and economic organization of agriculture, so that if rural sociology has much to gain from agricultural economics on the one hand it can also learn from the recent work of rural geographers on the other. An example of such multidisciplinary co-operation already exists in the field of peasant studies where expertise from a wide variety of disciplines has been brought to bear upon the 'problem' of the peasantry, sometimes with considerable success.

If such reorientation is to be successful, however, rural sociology must, like the recent trend in peasant studies, adopt a more holistic approach. This is not a simple repetition of that oft-repeated cry in rural sociology for 'more theory', for an overdose of 'grand theory' could prove as stultifying as the current surfeit of 'abstracted empiricism' (Mills, 1964). Perhaps what is required is a recognition that the construction of theory and empirical research are not necessarily, or even preferably, separate exercises. Then the closeness to the 'object of study' which is characteristic of rural sociology as a sub-discipline, could become one of its greatest strengths.

Notes

1. The nature of the politicization is discussed in more detail in the chapter by Wilson, below.
2. See the chapter by Saunders *et al.* in this book for further discussion.
3. For an example of this see the chapter by Saunders *et al.* in this book.

References

Anderson, C. A. (1959), 'Trends in rural sociology', in R. K. Merton, L. Broom and L. S. Cottrell (eds.), *Sociology Today* (New York: Basic Books).

Ashton, J., and Rogers, S. J. (eds.) (1967), *Economic Change and Agriculture* (Edinburgh: Oliver and Boyd).

Banaji, J. (1976), 'Summary of selected parts of Kautsky's "The Agrarian Question"', *Economy and Society*, 5, 1, 2–49. (There is no complete English translation of Kautsky's book; a French edition was published by Maspero (Paris) in 1970 and an Italian edition by Feltrinelli (Milan) in 1971.)

Bell, Colin (1976), 'Towards a political economy of housing', in E. L. Wheelright and K. Buckley (eds.), *Essays in the Political Economy of Australian Capitalism*, Vol. 2 (Sydney: A.N.Z.).

Bell, Colin, and Newby, Howard (1973), 'The sources of variation in agricultural workers' images of society', *Sociological Review*, 21, 2, 229—253.

Bell, Colin and Newby, Howard (1974), 'Capitalist farmers in the British class structure', *Sociologia Ruralis*, 14, 1 / 2, 86—107.

Bell, Daniel (1974), *The Coming of Post-Industrial Society* (London: Heinemann).

Benvenuti, Bruno, Galjart, Benno, and Newby, Howard (1974), 'The current status of rural sociology', *Sociologia Ruralis*, 15, 1/2, 3–21.

Beresford, Tristram (1975), *We Plough the Fields* (Harmondsworth: Penguin).

Blau, P., and Duncan, O. D. (1967), *The American Occupational Structure* (London: Wiley).

Braudel, Fernand (1972), *Capitalism and Material Life, 1400–1800* (London: Weidenfeld and Nicolson).

Braudel, Fernand (1973), *The Mediterranean*, Vols. 1 and 2 (London: Collins).

Brewster, J. (1970), 'The machine process in agriculture and industry', in K. A. Fox and G. D. Johnson (eds.), *Readings in the Economics of Agriculture* (London: Allen and Unwin), pp. 3–13.

Caird, James (1878), *The Landed Interest and the Supply of Food* (London: Cass).

Capstick, Margaret (1970), *The Economics of Agriculture* (London: Allen and Unwin).

Carter, Ian (1976), 'The peasantry of Northern Scotland', *Journal of Peasant Studies*, **3**, 2, 151–191.

Castells, Manuel (1976), *The Urban Question: A Marxist Approach* (London: Edward Arnold).

Chisholm, M. (1962), *Rural Settlement and Land Use* (London: Hutchinson).

Clout, Hugh D. (1972), *Rural Geography* (Oxford: Pergamon).

Connell, J. (1974), 'The metropolitan village: spatial and social processes in discontinuous suburbs' in J. H. Johnson (ed.), *The Geography of Suburban Growth* (London: Wiley).

Davis, John H. (1956), 'From agriculture to agribusiness', *Harvard Business Reviews* **34**, 107–115.

Dexter, J. (1969), 'Some economic influences on agricultural policy' in the symposium, *A Discussion of Current Policies and the Future Structure of Agriculture* (University of Newcastle, Agricultural Adjustment Unit, Bulletin No. 8), pp. 16–26.

Edwards, Angela, and Rogers, Alan (eds.) (1974), *Agricultural Resources* (London: Faber).

Encel, S. (1970), *Equality and Authority* (Melbourne: Cheshire).

Franklin, S. H. (1969), *The European Peasantry: The Final Phase* (London: Methuen).

Friedland, William H., and Thomas, Robert J. (1974), 'Paradoxes of agricultural unionism in California', *Society* **May/June**, 54–62.

Galjart, B. (1973), 'The Future of Rural Sociology', *Sociologia Ruralis*, **13**, 3 / 4, 254–262.

Gallaher, Art, Jnr. (1961), *Plainsville Fifteen Years Later* (New York: Columbia University Press).

Gans, Herbert (1968), 'Urbanism and suburbanism as ways of life' in R. E. Pahl (ed.) *Readings in Urban Sociology* (Oxford: Pergamon), pp. 95–118.

Gasson, R. (1966), 'Part-time farmers in south-east England', *Farm Economist*, **XI**, 3, 135–139.

Gasson, R. (1969), 'The Occupational Immobility of Small Farmers' (Cambridge: University of Cambridge, Department of Land Economy).

Gasson, R. (1971), 'Use of sociology in agricultural economics', *Journal of Agricultural Economics*, **XXII**, 1, 28—38.

Gasson, R. (1974), 'Resources in agriculture: labour' in Angela Edwards and Alan Rogers (eds.), *Agricultural Resources* (London: Faber).

Genovese, E. D. (1971), *In Red and Black* (London: Allen Lane).

Genovese, E. D. (1974), *Roll Jordan Roll* (New York: Pantheon).

Gerth, H. H., and Mills, C. W. (eds.) (1948), *From Max Weber* (London: Routledge and Kegan Paul).

Gibbs, Richard, and Harrison, Alan (1973), 'Landownership by public and semi-public bodies in Great Britain' (Reading: University of Reading, Department of Agricultural Economics and Management, Miscellaneous Study No. 56).

Giddens, Anthony (1976),'Class, social theory and modern sociology', *American Journal of Sociology*, **81**, 4, 703–729.

Glau, T. E. (1972), 'The cost-price squeeze on Australian farm income' in C. D. Throsby (ed.), *Agricultural Policy* (Ringwood, Victoria: Penguin Books Australia).

28

Graham, B. D. (1966), *The Formation of the Australian Country Parties* (Canberra: A.N.U. Press).

Guttsman, W. L. (1963), *The English Political Élite* (London: MacGibbon and Knee), pp. 104–105.

Haller, A. O. (1973), Review of 'Seventy years of rural sociology in the United States' (ed. A. Bertrand), *Contemporary Sociology*, 3, 2, 138.

Harvey, David (1973), *Social Justice and the City* (London: Edward Arnold).

Heath, C. E., and Whitby, M. (1969), *The Changing Agricultural Labour Force* (Newcastle: University of Newcastle, Agricultural Adjustment Unit).

Hobsbawm, E. J. (1969), *Industry and Empire* (Harmondsworth: Penguin).

Hobsbawm, E. J., and Rudé, G. (1971), *Captain Swing* (London: Lawrence and Wishart).

Hunt, Alan (1974), 'Agriculture and the market', in Angela Edwards and Alan Rogers (eds.), *Agricultural Resources* (London: Faber), pp. 39–60.

Jayawardena, Chandra (1968), 'Idealogy and conflict in lower class communities', in *Comparative Studies in Society and History*, 10, 3, 413–446.

Johnson, D. G. (1973), *World Agriculture in Disarray* (London: Fontana).

Jones, G. E. (1967), 'Adoption and diffusion of agricultural practices', *World Agricultural Economics and Rural Sociology Abstracts*, 9, 3, 1–34.

Jones, G. E. (1973), *Rural Life* (London: Longmans).

Kerr, Clark, *et al.* (1960), *Industrialism and Industrial Man* (Cambridge, Mass.: Harvard University Press).

Kumar, K. (1976), 'Industrialism and Post-Industrialism: Reflection on a Putative Transition', *Sociological Review*, 24, 3, 439–478.

Landsberger, Henry A. (ed.) (1973), *Rural Protest: Peasant Movements and Social Change* (London: Macmillan).

Larson, Olaf F., and Rogers, Everett M. (1964), 'Rural society in transition: the American setting' in James H. Copp (ed.), *Our Changing Rural Society: Perspectives and Trends* (Ames, Iowa: Iowa University Press), pp. 39–67.

Lemisch J. (1970), 'The American Revolution seen from the bottom up' in B. J. Bernstein (ed.), *Towards a New Past* (London: Chatto and Windus).

Lenski, G. (1966), *Power and Privilege* (New York: McGraw-Hill), pp. 382–386.

Lewis, Oscar (1949), *Life in a Mexican Village* (Urbana, Ill.: University of Illinois Press).

Lipset, S. M. (1950), *Agrarian Socialism* (Berkeley, Cal.: University of California Press).

Lipset, S. M., and Bendix, R. (1964), *Social Mobility in Industrial Society* (Berkeley, Cal.: University of California Press).

Macpherson, C. B. (1952), *Democracy in Alberta: The Theory and Practice of a Quasi-Party System* (Cambridge: Cambridge University Press).

McCrone, Gavin (1962), *The Economics of Subsidizing Agriculture* (London: Allen and Unwin).

Merrington, John (1976), 'Town and country in the transition of capitalism' in Paul Sweezy *et al.* (eds.) *The Transition from Feudalism to Capitalism* (London: New Left Books). pp. 170–175.

Metcalf, D. (1969), *The Economics of Agriculture* (Harmondsworth: Penguin).

Mills, C. Wright (1964), *The Sociological Imagination* (New York: Oxford University Press).

Mintz, S. (1973), 'A note on the definition of peasantries', *Journal of Peasant Studies*, 1, 1, 91–106.

Moore, Barrington, Jnr. (1966), *The Social Origins of Dictatorship and Democracy* (London: Allen Lane).

Nalson, J. S. (1968), *Mobility of Farm Families* (Manchester: Manchester University Press).

Newby, Howard (1972), 'Agricultural workers in the class structure', *Sociological Review*, 20, 3, 413–438.

Newby, Howard (1974), 'The changing sociological environment of the farm', *Journal of Farm Management*, **2**, 9, 474–487.

Newby, Howard (1975), 'The Deferential Dialectic', *Comparative Studies in Society and History*, **17**, 2, 139–164.

Newby, Howard (1976), 'Paternalism and Capitalism' in R. Scase (ed.), *Industrial Society: Class, Cleavage and Control* (London: Allen and Unwin).

Newby, Howard (1977), *The Deferential Worker* (London: Allen Lane).

Nolan, M. F., and Galliher, J. F. (1973), 'Rural sociological research and social policy: hard times, hard data', *Rural Sociology*, **38**, 4, 491–499.

OECD (1969), OECD *Agricultural Review* (Paris: OECD).

OECD (1970), *The Growth of Output, 1960–1980* (Paris: OECD).

Olson, P. (1965), 'Rural American community studies: the survival of public ideology', *Human Organization*, **10**, 3, 342–350.

Pahl, R. E. (1965), *Urbs in Rure* (London: Weidenfeld and Nicolson).

Pahl, R. E. (1968), 'The rural–urban continuum' in R. E. Pahl (ed.), *Readings in Urban Sociology* (Oxford: Pergamon), pp. 263–305.

Pahl, R. E. (1971), *Whose City?* (London: Longmans).

Pahl, R. E. (1977), 'The state and collective consumption in capitalist and socialist societies' in R. Scase (ed.), *Industrial Society: Class, Cleavage and Control* (London: Allen and Unwin).

Perkins, H. (1973), 'Land reform and class conflict in Victorian Britain' in J. Butt and I. F. Clark (eds.), *The Victorians and Social Protest* (Newton Abbott: David and Charles), pp. 177–217.

Pickvance, C. G. (ed.) (1976), *Urban Sociology: Critical Essays* (London: Tavistock).

Redfield, Robert (1947), 'The folk society', *American Journal of Sociology*, **52**, 293–308.

Rogers, E., and Shoemaker, F. (1971), *Communication of Innovations: A Cross-Cultural Approach* (Glencoe, Ill.: Free Press).

Rose, David, Saunders, Peter, Newby, Howard, and Bell, Colin (1976), 'Ideologies of property: a case study', *Sociological Review*, **24**, 4, 699–731.

Rose, David, Newby, Howard, Saunders, Peter, and Bell, Colin (1977), 'Land tenure and official statistics', *Journal of Agricultural Economics*, **28**, 1.

Rushing, William A. (1972), *Class, Culture and Alienation* (Lexington, Mass.: D. C. Heath).

Schmitt, P. J. (1968), *Back to Nature: The American Myth in Urban America*, (New York: Oxford University Press).

Scott, James C., and Kerkvliet, Benedict K. (1974), 'How traditional patrons lose legitimacy', *Cultures et developpement*, **Summer**, 501–540.

Self, P., and Storing, H. (1962), *The State and the Farmer* (London: Allen and Unwin).

Shanin, Teodor (1971), *Peasants and Peasant Societies* (Harmondsworth: Penguin).

Shanin, Teodor (1973), 'The nature and logic of the peasant economy', *Journal of Peasant Studies*, **1**, 1/2, 63–80, 186–206.

Sorokin, P. A., and Zimmerman, C. C. (1929), *Principles of Rural–Urban Sociology* (New York: Henry Holt).

Sower, Christopher, and Miller, Paul A (1964), 'The changing power structure in agriculture: an analysis of negative versus positive organization power' in James H. Copp (ed.), *Our Changing Rural Society: Perspectives and Trends* (Ames, Iowa: Iowa State University Press), pp. 127–158.

Stein, M. (1964), *The Eclipse of Community* (New York: Harper).

Stinchcombe, A. (1961–62), 'Agricultural enterprise and rural class relations', *American Journal of Sociology*, **67**, 2, 169–176.

Sturmey, S. G. (1955), 'Owner-farming in England and Wales, 1900–1950', *Manchester School*, **23**, 246–268.

Thompson, F. M. L. (1963), *English Landed Society in the Nineteenth Century* (London: Routledge and Kegan Paul).

Throsby, C. D. (ed.) (1972), *Agricultural Policy*, part two (Ringwood, Victoria: Penguin Books Australia).

Warley, T. K. (1963), 'The future role of marketing organizations', *Journal of Agricultural Economics*, **14**, 4, 550–571.

Watson, W. (1964), 'Social mobility and social class in industrial communities' in M. Gluckman (ed.), *Closed Systems and Open Minds* (Edinburgh: Oliver and Boyd).

Whitby, M. C., Robins, D. L. J., Tansey, A. W., and Willis, K. G. (1974), *Rural Resource Development* (London: Methuen).

Williams, H. T. (1969), 'The place of agriculture in the national economy' in the symposium, *A Discussion of Current Policies and the Future Structure of Agriculture* (Newcastle: University of Newcastle, Agricultural Adjustment Unit, Bulletin No. 8), pp. 7–15.

Williams, Raymond (1973), *The Country and the City* (London: Chatto and Windus).

Williams, W. M. (1964), *A West Country Village: Ashworthy* (London: Routledge and Kegan Paul).

2
Farmers' Organizations in Advanced Societies

Graham Wilson

Farmers, throughout the western, world, have become scarcer since the last war. Though agricultural production has increased sharply in both Western Europe and North America, technical change and market forces have driven many farmers and farmworkers from the land. Yet this trend has not weakened farmers' organizations (Rogers, 1970). Indeed, it can be argued that the reverse is true, that a reduction in their numbers encourages farmers to form organizations. In spite of the fact that Great Britain has long been one of the world's most urbanized countries, its National Farmers Union is arguably the best and organizationally strongest of western agricultural interest groups. The American Farm Bureau Federation (AFBF) has claimed a steady rise in its membership while the number of farmers in the USA has fallen sharply.

Social scientists have reason to be grateful for the continued strength of farm organizations. Research on interest, or 'pressure' groups would be the poorer had it not been for the study of farmers.

Apart from studies which specifically focus on farmers' organizations, scarcely a study of politics in any individual country, much less of interest groups in general, is complete without some mention of them. The reasons why farmers' organizations have proved so interesting for social scientists are almost obvious. Farmers' interest groups are usually long established, yet their very existence seems puzzling in an industry characterized by family ownership of farms, physical isolation or dispersal and individualistic ethics. The variety in the allegiance and character of rural interest groups, too, is impressive ranging from the Communist peasant organizations of Italy or France through the liberalism of the American National Farmers' Union, its technocratic apolitical British namesake to the conservatism of the Coltivatori Diretti in Italy or Farm Bureau Federation in the USA. The very fact that these contrasts so often occur in one country (the American Farm Bureau Federation versus the National Farmers Union in the USA; the Coltivatori Diretti versus the Peasants Alliance in Italy) itself suggests obvious questions for research. Finally, the condemnation of agricultural protectionism, which has increased steadily since the last war, by classical trade economics has provided political scientists with an apparently ideal testing ground for the power of a sectional interest — farmers — against the common good of freer trade. The political success of farmers has become a major testing ground for generalizations about the power of organized interests within a political-system.

Membership and Structure

Nothing illustrates better the use of farming organizations to illustrate general problems in the study of pressure groups than arguments about why people join, or do not join pressure groups. Though the 'density' of an interest group's membership (the degree to which it succeeds in recruiting potential members) has been seen as a major determinant of its influence, social scientists have differed widely on the reasons why people join. Olson (1968) of course has argued that joining a voluntary organization is irrational for people be they selfish or idealistic, unless membership produces benefits not otherwise available. A farmer receives, let us say, agricultural subsidies, whether or not he belongs to the appropriate pressure group. He would, therefore, be foolish to take out membership, and pay the subscription, for he can enjoy whatever subsidies the pressure group achieves without incurring the costs of membership. Indeed, as but one farmer among many, he has no valid reason to suppose the fact that he joins will either make a significant difference to the strength of the pressure group or influence many others to join. The joiner of a pressure group, *ceteris paribus*, benefits neither himself nor others.

Olson is faced with a problem in explaining the fact that people do, in fact, join pressure groups. His explanation rests on the fact that many interest groups, American farming organizations being one of his examples, do, in fact, provide benefits restricted to members. Access to grain elevators and concessionary insurance rates provided by pressure groups is restricted to members, thus providing an incentive to join. The American Farm Bureau Federation (AFBF) has used cheap insurance extensively as an inducement for membership. Indeed, its critics contend that the Farm Bureau has been more concerned to sell its insurance services than to represent farmers' interests.

Olson's arguments are so well known to social scientists that general criticism of them need not be rehearsed at great length. Two, however, seem particularly apposite. Barry (1970, p. 29) has pointed to the poor performance of Olson's theories in comparative politics. For example, one might expect that the incentive to join a farm organization in order to obtain the use of grain elevators, discounts on medical or farm insurance and other such benefits would be particularly strong in societies such as the USA where the government does comparatively little for its citizens. Yet membership of farm organizations is much higher — possibly twice as high — in Britain's welfare state than in the USA (Beer, 1956). Secondly, Olson at best provides an explanation for joining *an* organization, when there is a variety to choose from, all of which provide equally valuable 'selective benefits'. Yet such an omission is important as it is more common to find competing, or even conflicting, farm organizations than one united group.

Postwar agrarian politics in France, for example, has involved a sharp conflict for control of the Fédération Nationale des Syndicats d'Exploitants Agricoles (FNSEA). Traditionalist leaders who sought to preserve the existing pattern of rural life were ultimately supplanted by a distinct group growing out of a Church organization, the Jeunes Agriculteurs. Both groups were opposed by a Communist Party grouping, the Comité General d'Action Paysanne aimed at saving a peasant agriculture doomed to extinction by the realities of agricultural economics. Similarly, in Italy, the dominant Coltivatori Diretti have been opposed by the Communist Party's National Peasants Alliance whose stated goal is the 'renewal of Italian agriculture based upon the small peasant farm' (Tarrow, 1967).

Nor can the occurrence of divisions among the farming community always be explained by the presence of the deep division between Catholics and Communists that affects all aspects of French and Italian politics. For example, in Denmark farmers' organizations are split three ways into a farmers' union, a grouping of smallholders and an alliance of co-operative societies reflecting basically a division between small and large-scale farmers. Perhaps the best example of divisions between farmers' organizations occurs in the USA which has literally dozens of commodity organizations representing producers of only one crop. In addition, there are fiercely antagonistic farm organizations. On the 'left' the National Farmers Union (NFU) and National Farmers Organization (NFO) have advocated major government intervention to stabilize prices and raise farm incomes. The Farm Bureau Federation has, equally energetically, worked to 'get the government out of agriculture' advocating the repeal of farm subsidy laws which have probably doubled its members' incomes. The NFU and NFO have been drawn into an almost formal alliance with the liberal wing of the Democrat party; the Farm Bureau Federation has forged equally strong links with the right wing of the Republican Party. The National Grange has followed a cause closer to the NFU than to the AFBF but has been more of a social than a political organization. The united front presented to the British government by farmers through their Farmers' Unions is decidedly unusual.

Beyond Olson

Olson's theory seems to explain neither the differences in the proportion of potential farmers recruited by pressure groups nor the number of such organizations which compete for his favours. Is it possible that the two weaknesses in his theory are related?

Olson's theory has attracted so much attention because of its apparently perverse conclusion that people do not join pressure groups because they wish to have an organization to advance their common group interests. Though Olson can bolster his deductive argument with some empirical examples, there is no reason to suppose it is universally applicable. It is quite possible that in some countries interest groups have attracted members specifically by their promise to defend group interests. Self and Storing (1962, p. 41), for example illustrate how conscious were the founders of the English National Farmers Union of the need for English agriculture to have more formal representation in an age when other interests were organizing, too.

The question we propose to ask you is whether you think you are safe at a time when every trade is combining AGAINST EVERY OTHER in remaining outside your own Farmers' Union. Against every other, mind you. Every trade in the world is combined against yours. Dare you risk isolation?

To this day, the Union's publications emphasize not the benefits which accrue to the individual through membership such as arguably cheaper insurance from the NFU Mutual, but the Union's role in representing farmers' collective interests to the government and commercial concerns. It is tempting to take on Olson by seeking a general refutation of his arguments. It is, however, quite possible that no general theory is convincing. The differences in the unity and cohesion of farmers' organizations may reflect the strength of a variety of factors in a society. Amongst these factors not only the individual benefits described by Olson, but many others spring to mind. In particular, we shall examine the impact of farm structure, other organizations, and the political system.

The Impact of Structure

The most obvious influence on the number of farmers' organizations is the structure of the industry itself. It seems reasonable to suppose that farmers are more likely to form one united organization if they live in a country where agriculture is relatively homogeneous. Thus, it might be argued, farmers are more united in Britain than in the United States because the regional or class differences between them are slight. Nearly all British farmers are entrepreneurs employing very little labour but working themselves; mixed farming is something of a tradition. The sheer diversity of American agriculture, in contrast, is striking. All too often, statistics simply describe as 'farmers' people as diverse as the small-scale subsistence, sharecropper in the South and the 1200 ha (3000 acre) wheat farmer in the Dakotas. Yet the contrasts between the dairy farmer of New England, the Southern cotton producer, the California grape producers and the Colorado rancher pose obvious problems for those who would create a single united farm organization. It is not surprising that the United States has so many organizations which represent the interests of producers of a single commodity. Similarly, the contrasts between fully commercial agriculture and peasant farming in France and Italy have obviously complicated rural politics in those countries.

Yet any simple relationship between the diversity of agriculture and the number of farmers' organizations is not easy to establish. British agriculture, in spite of the unity of the NFU, is more diverse than it appears at first sight. The culture, income and problems of a dairy farmer in Devon with 24 ha (60 acres) or a Welsh hill farmer with a similarly sized holding of rough land are very different to those of an East Anglian 'grain baron', with a large holding, a high income and perhaps ten employees. All, however, are very likely to join the

National Farmers Union of England and Wales, (NFU). Though there have been challenges to the NFU's hegemony by splinter groups in Wales and the West of England, they have been contained. Moreover, the United States, in spite of the diversity of its agriculture has three organizations, the National Farmers Union, (NFU), the National Grange and the American Farm Bureau Federation which claim nationwide membership. Though the Grange and the NFU have most of their members in one region (the East and the northern Midwest respectively) the AFBF does have a legitimate claim to be a national organization, containing wheat farmers, Midwestern corn-hog farmers and Southern cotton, tobacco or rice producers. Even at the local level, studies in the Midwest have failed to establish a clear relationship between the crop a farmer grows and the organization he joins (Crampton, 1965). As the NFU is liberal (that is, interventionist) in farm and non-farm politics while the Farm Bureau Federation is extremely conservative (or *laissez-faire*) in both, such findings constitute a problem for those who, like Lipset, link liberal or social democratic voting to the instability of income of, for example, wheat farmers.

The contrast between the American's NFU commitment to the 'family farm', its opposition to 'agribusiness' and support for general liberal causes and the Farm Bureau Federations conservatism, *laissez-faire* economic or agricultural policies and belief that farming is a business not a way of life causes many to believe that the organizations have a different class base. Differences in their policies lead us to suppose that the NFU recruits poorer farmers and the AFBF larger-scale producers who neither need nor want government assistance.

There are, in fact, two liberal national farmers' organizations in the USA, the NFU whose strategy has always been political, and the National Farmers Organization (NFO) which has put more stress on collective action by farmers, including 'strikes' or withholding produce to raise prices. Yet surveys show that neither organization recruits farmers who are poorer than the members of the AFBF; they may, indeed, have a more affluent membership. The members of both liberal and conservative farm organizations are, however, readily identifiable from farmers who do not join any organization; they are richer. American farm organizations illustrate perfectly Schattschneider's comment that the pluralist choir sings with an upper-class accent (Rohwer, 1952; Crampton, 1965; Des Moines Register 1972; Schattschneider, 1960).

Income predicts equally poorly agrarian politics in France. The PCF (Partie Communiste Française) has long had a strong base in rural areas, but the rural *departements* which have elected Communists are not the poorest. Thus the PCF has been stronger in the Dordogne than the poorer Auvergne. Gordon Wright (1964), in valuable descriptions of life in six villages at the end of his study, describes almost inexplicable differences between villages where the farmers have similar holdings and incomes, with some supporting bourgeois parties, and others supporting the PCF. Indeed, Wright describes one village which, without any apparent change in social structure or attitudes, moved from supporting the radicals to voting for the PCF.

Perhaps both the American and French examples should encourage further work on a problem which Lipset's study of Saskatchewan raises (Lipset, 1950, Bartell, 1971), namely the conditions under which rural discontent spreads beyond the apolitical sectionalism of the English NFU or even the incoherent populism of much of rural America into a general critique of the existing order and capitalism. Such studies have to step far outside the confines of farmers' organizations and into the political history and sociology of the regions in which the movement occurs. Thus Crampton (1965) links the American NFU to the 'sense of rural deprivation' which made many farmers in the northern midwest, as Rogin (1967) and Sundquist (1973) demonstrate, supporters of liberal heroes such as La Follette and opponents of such conservatives as Joseph McCarthy.

Support for the Communist and Socialist parties in the French countryside provides an even more dramatic example of rural radicalism. It is, like American rural radicalism, poorly correlated with income. Though the Communist Party does enjoy the support of some poor farmers in central France, it makes little headway in the heart of the Auvergne or Brittany. It is usually argued that French rural radicalism can be understood only as a product of French history rather than current income, land ownership or similar variables (Dogan, 1967). The leading British writer on French politics notes that

In rural areas, its [the Communist Party's] influence derived less from its championship of the proletariat than its annexation of the tradition of 1789 . . . Its influence on the peasantry was not confined to the poor sharecroppers but extended to southern farmers and sharecroppers who voted to express a political rather than a social choice.

In particular, rural anticlericalism favours Communist voting; 'in Gard, most Protestant peasants (who own their own land) probably voted Communist' (Williams, 1964).

Examples from Canada, the United States and France all suggest, therefore, the complexity of explaining rural radicalism. Convincing accounts of the political allegiance of farmers or their organizations in different regions will certainly have to progress beyond crude correlations with income, size of holding or types of crops produced.

Yet if the crude material factors predict the political allegiance of farmers and their organizations poorly, it will still be surprising if farm structure has no effect, particularly on the solidarity of farmers. In particular, the success of the American Farm Bureau Federation or the FNSEA in France in forging truly national organizations may lead to an overestimate of agrarian solidarity amongst different types of farmers. In the case of the Farm Bureau Federation in the USA, the cost of organizational unity has been political inconsistency between the state Farm Bureaus which comprise the Federation. The AFBF's constitution recognizes the inability of the national leadership to control individual states by providing a formal procedure for 'dissents', through which a State Farm Bureau can declare its refusal to follow national policy. Such procedures are rarely used because the State Federations more commonly merely quietly ignore national policy, sometimes lobbying local Congressmen or Senators against it without even recording their opposition at the AFBF conventions. Such hidden disagreements on farm subsidies have pitted the interventionist South against the *laissez-faire* Midwest, and remind us that in a diverse country national organizations may look more united on paper than they are in practice. We shall see, however, that unity is determined not merely by the characteristics of farming in a country but by broader features of its society and politics.

The Strength of Other Groups

We may recall that the recruiting leaflet issued by the British NFU in its early days called upon farmers to unite to defend their collective interests because 'Every trade in the world is combined against yours'. This immediately suggests that farmers organize to the degree that other interests do. Indeed, it is a common observation that strong employers' associations, farmers' organizations and unions occur in the same country simultaneously. This has led many authorities into arguments resting on the concept of political culture. Thus Samuel Beer would explain the unity and organization of British farmers by reference to the 'widespread acceptance of functional representation in British political culture' (Beer, 1965, p. 329). Similarly, Eckstein emphasizes the 'persistent corporatism' in British attitudes (Eckstein, 1960, p. 24). Both Barrington Moore (1967) and, with some glee, Brian Barry (1970) however, have, rightly, pointed to the circularity of such explanations. People in Britain because of their 'corporatist' attitudes join pressure groups; we know they have corporatist attitudes because they join pressure groups. Values are deduced from the very behaviour they are used to explain. Yet explanations based on political culture do at least remind us that the success of an interest group may well be explained more by features of the society or policy within which it operates than by its own characteristics.

If we return to our example of the British NFU, it was, according to their recruiting leaflet, *because* other interests were organized that farmers needed a union. In short we may hypothesize that interest groups feed off each other. To the degree that one sector of society is organized and united, so every other comes under pressure to follow suit. Prompted by concern that one interest may achieve an advantage through organizations, others seek to neutralize that advantage by also organizing. Such a process, it may be objected, requires a trigger. Something or somebody has to start the competition, just as one power starts an arms race. Such a trigger might be found in the degree of success of the labour movement in different countries. To the degree that labour is unionized, so, it might be argued, are other interests organized. Why might this be?

It has been argued by specialists in industrial relations that employers' associations are formed in response to the existence of trade unions (Gespal *et al.*, 1972). Some farmers' organizations, including the British NFU, actually fulfil the functions of employers' associations, taking part, for example, in national negotiations over the pay of farm workers. Indeed, the early growth of the British NFU parallels the development of the National Union of

Agricultural and Allied Workers and periods of unusual militancy in the English countryside. Even where farm workers are unorganized themselves, however, the growth of trade unions and consequently employers' associations creates a climate of organization in which non-industrial groups such as farmers feel both the urge to organize and are receptive to appeals for unity. This explains the paradox that farmers become more organized as they become a smaller proportion of the population. Thus it is the strength of industrial organizations, first of unions, then of employers which explains the strength and unity of the British National Farmers Union or the German 'Green Front'. Conversely, the low percentage of farmers organized in the USA and the disunity of its agricultural interest groups may reflect the absence of an impetus towards organization and unity from the industrial sector.

Even in Sweden, where farmers were the first economic interest to organize, agrarian politics and organizations took on their modern form only in the 1920s after industrialization was well under way (Särlvik, 1974). Conversely, farmers' organizations were slower to develop in societies where the 'threat' from other organized interests seemed less. Thus in the United States, where until recently the proportion of farmers in the population was much higher than in Britain while unions (and consequently employers' associations) were not only disunited, but between them recruited considerably less than half the proportion of British farmers organized by the NFU Farmers' organizations need some impetus from the city.

The Impact of the Political System

The very term 'pressure group', coupled with such misleading simple accounts of policy-making as 'input–output' models, may lead us to forget that not only do pressure groups affect the political system, but the political system affects pressure groups. Though regrettably little has been done to examine such influences systematically, the structure, style and strategies of pressure groups are all affected by the rules, conventions and understandings which characterize a political system.

It is commonly thought that the number and unity of pressure groups is a mirror of the policy process. When a policy-making process is characterized by unity, interests are represented by a few large and prestigious organizations. Little has been done to explain this methodically. It might be that interests feel a particular need to present a united front to a strong state. Alternatively, or additionally, policy-makers may require or secure, through the regulation of access to them, that factions sink their differences and produce one united organization.

The predominantly two-party parliamentary régimes such as Germany and Britain are the most obvious cases. In both countries, the general characteristics of the political system reinforce the tendency towards organization and one implicit in the structural factors described above. In Germany as in Britain, the strong state encourages 'exceptional unity and qualitative strength amongst agricultural interests' (Edinger, 1968, p. 217). Britain supplies a particularly clear example. The British Ministry of Agriculture, Fisheries and Food (MAFF) has consciously helped to maintain the monopoly position of the NFU by refusing to negotiate with, or even consult, splinter groups from the Union such as the Farmers Union of Wales. The usual explanation given for the Ministry's behaviour is its desire to force farmers to 'aggregate' their demands so that the Ministry is not forced to choose between conflicting or competing claims. It is also probable that the Ministry has been anxious to preserve the position of what had been a moderate and reasonable pressure group, the NFU which shared many of the Ministry's attitudes and ways of doing business. Whatever its motives, the Ministry, because of the unified policy-making process in Britain, was able to regulate 'access' to decision-makers in a way which left only the NFU with conspicuous, privileged and influential contacts with government. Though the relationship between the Union and the Ministry followed rather than caused the Union's early growth and hegemony it was a decided advantage. A clearly visible increase in the Union's role in policy-making during the Second World War produced a surge in the Union's own membership and discouraged splinter groups. For once the Ministry granted the NFU a monopoly on representing farmers, there was no effective way for any rival rural interest group to operate. Appeals beyond the Ministry to Members of Parliament would be futile. A unitary policy process not only encouraged but almost required farmers to have but one united interest group.

In the United States, in contrast, the policy process encouraged no such unity. The American policy-making process in agriculture is itself almost the epitome of disunity. Sharp partisan differences on the role that government should play in the industry, regional and commodity rivalries find expression in institutional conflict between Congress's Agriculture Committees, House, Senate and the Executive. This fragmentation, combined with the openness of the system, means that an agricultural interest group representing almost any conceivable view held amongst a segment of America's commercial farmers can find a friendly hearing with the policy process. (Unfortunately for them, subsistence farmers have not been so lucky.) The incentive to create one united organization and arrive at a common viewpoint has, therefore, been minimal.

One apparent exception to the pattern of a unified policy process producing strong pressure groups is Italy. There the Coltivatori Diretti have carved out a position of undoubted strength and virtual hegemony in spite of the weakness of Italy's governments. The CD's success is very probably connected with its penetration of the machinery government. It is not merely that the CD has an important influence over many Christian Democratic deputies they have helped elect, but that the organization has come to control the administration of many government programmes. Under the leadership of Paolo Bonomi, the CD was quite willing to use this power to punish farmers whose districts voted the 'wrong' way in national elections. The CD was even more prepared to punish farmers who did not join it by discriminating against them. La Polambara (1964, p. 149) tells us that 'when [in Italy] an association such as Coltivatori Diretti establishes close links with the government and is directly involved in the administration of certain social welfare activities, the individual farmer refuses to join the organisation at his great peril'.

It is interesting to ask why none of the American agricultural interest groups could capture, and similarly exploit, the administration of the American farm subsidy programmes which were controlled by committees elected by farmers. The answer probably lies in the fact that the interest group best placed to do so, the Farm Bureau Federation, was deeply distrusted not only by rural interest groups but also by politicians, especially Democrats, who did not share its extreme *laissez-faire* views. Instead, the participatory policy process weakened all pressure groups, for the Department of Agriculture developed a tendency to use the committees elected by farmers to administer agricultural subsidy laws as a pressure group, directed at Congressmen and Senators as well as farmers to advance its own policies. If pressure groups cannot capture participatory administrative structures, such structures may become rivals and undermine their authority.

Intragroup Politics

The claim that farmers are influenced more by a desire for collective representation when they join pressure groups than Olson concedes, is not to argue that members of farmers' organizations have a clear conception of what constitutes their interests, or how their pressure group should advance them. Perhaps because Olson's theory is unusually applicable to the American Farm Bureau Federation it provides a clear example. Opinion polls have shown that members of the Farm Bureau Federation often disagree with the leadership's policies (Morrison and Warner, 1971; *Wallace's Farmer*, 1957). In spite of the AFBF's longstanding opposition to farm subsidies, for example, most of its members, like the members of the other agricultural interest groups, support them. Eisenhower's Secretary of Agriculture tried to reduce farm subsidies, a policy which the AFBF favoured. However, an opinion poll found that only 12 per cent of the Federation's members approved of the Secretary's performance. Such polls support the publicly and privately stated beliefs of American politicians that the agricultural interest groups are an imperfect guide to what their farmer-constituents are thinking.

One obvious explanation for disjunction between the thinking of a pressure group's leaders and followers is poor participation by members in the formally democratic machinery of their organizations. Examples of voluntary organizations which do not conform to Michels's 'Iron Law of Oligarchy' are few, and farmers' organizations are rarely among them. The difficulties for the farmer who wishes to play a major role in his organization are obvious. Even a comparatively minor post may involve lengthy spells away from the farm attending meetings at the group's headquarters, absences which the farmer can afford only if he employs several workers or a manager. The 'class' bias which this induces is obvious. A report on its structure commissioned by the British NFU argued that only wealthier farmers could afford to participate extensively in its affairs, while one of the standard complaints about the FNSEA in France during Blondelle's rule was the dominance of wealthier farmers in the Fédération du Nord et du Bassin Parisien (Wright, 1964).

Perhaps partly because of the poor participation rates which characterize farmers' organizations (like other voluntary associations), politics within farm organizations are veiled. Élites tend to remain in office for years, apparently enjoying enormous discretion over policy. American farm organizations again provide a clear example.

Throughout the New Deal era, the Farm Bureau Federation had steadfastly supported interventionist farm subsidy laws, which, indeed, it had helped draft. This had brought the Federation into a close working relationship with liberals on a variety of issues. The AFBF's President, Ed O'Neil, worked with New York's Fiorello La Guardia to find Congressional votes for urban relief, while La Guardia made impassioned pleas for liberals to support farm subsidies. After the Presidency passed from O'Neil to Charles Shuman, the Federation adopted a sharply critical attitude to farm subsidies and government involvement in the industry. This brought the Federation into a right-wing coalition of interest groups including business groups and the American Medical Association. The Farm Bureau speedily took a right-wing position on almost every conceivable issue in domestic or foreign politics. Yet it is almost impossible to find any trace of opposition to these radically different policies in the minutes of the Federation's conventions.

Similarly, the National Farmers Union took many positions on diverse political issues which closely reflected the personal views of James Patton, who, on his retirement in 1967, had led the Union for over a quarter of a century. The National Farmers Organization has been led by Orin Lee Staley since its formation, and it caused great surprise when, in 1972, he was faced with a serious challenge to re-election. Staley won by the unprecedently low margin of three to two.

The British NFU is a less perfect example of the security of tenure for leaders. In the postwar era, the Union became almost synonymous with its President, Lord Netherthorpe, who, as if determined to prove Michels right singlehanded, was regularly re-elected until his retirement in 1963 in spite of a constitutional requirement that a President seeking re-election obtain 85 per cent of the votes cast at the electing Council. However, Netherthorpe's two successors, Lord Woolley and Sir Gwilym Williams, were unsuccessful in attempts to retain office. Indeed, the present incumbent, Sir Henry Plumb, seems to have arrested a trend towards short-term Presidencies. The effectiveness of the constraint on leaders provided by elections should not, however, be overestimated; both Woolley and Williams were succeeded by their vice presidents, men associated with formation and implementation of all their major policies.

Wright's account suggests that perhaps because it was a Federation consisting of different power bases, politics within the FNSEA were, though still veiled, more observable than in most farm organizations. The attempts by small farmers to weaken the influence of the Fédération du Nord et du Bassin Parisien came to little because of regional divisions. However, the Centre National de Jeunesse Agricoles (CNJA) proved to be a stronger faction. In 1961 one of the CNJA's leaders, Marcel Bruel, was elected Secretary General of the FNSEA and, seizing the opportunities presented by a sympathetic Minister of Agriculture, Pisani and the new constitution of the Fifth Republic led the FNSEA in a different style towards new objectives.

Contrasts between the visibility of politics within groups can be over-drawn, however. In all cases where dissent does occur, the internal politics of farmers' organizations involve rival élites, and the battles between them pass unnoticed by the membership. Differences between the visibility of intragroup politics in the USA, Britain and France may be explained in Hirschman's terminology. Hirschman (1970) suggests the actively dissatisfied member of an organization has two options, 'voice' (complaining, campaigning and voting to change his leaders) to 'exit' (transferring to a rival organization). The plethora of farmers' organizations in the USA makes 'voice' not worthwhile. The dissatisfied farmer can, unlike his British or French counterpart, find an equally prestigious organization to transfer to. In brief it may well be that as Hirschman would predict, intragroup politics are more important and visible when there is only one established interest group. Dissatisfied members have no rival to join, and are therefore more likely to work within a group to change its policies.

The Definition of Self-interest

The absence of clearly visible and readily comprehensible intragroup politics has led social scientists to neglect, as King (1974) notes, the study of the way in which groups define what constitutes their interest. Most political philosophers regard it as a difficult, or impossible task, to specify an individual's *interests* without any knowledge of his *preferences*. Yet political scientists have often assumed that it is so obvious what constitutes the group interest, that the way in which an interest group defines it is of little interest.

Farmers' organizations provide a clear warning of just how varied a content specific statements of 'the farmers' interest' may have. The United States is a very obvious example. There the Farm Bureau Federation, which, in spite of the criticisms of its rivals, has always been led to former 'family farmers', has argued that the farmers' main interest is in freedom from government interference. To achieve this freedom, the Federation has advocated the gradual reduction of farm subsidies which, according to economists, more than doubled its members' incomes during the 1960s. The NFU has taken the opposite view. Farmers, the Union argues, need government assistance, and should be prepared to accept extensive regulation in return. The contrast may well rest on a difference between whether farming is seen as a way of life, or just another business.

The same issue has appeared in French farming politics. Under Blondelle, the FNSEA worked to preserve the existing character of the French countryside at the cost of large subsidies to keep the peasant's head above water and the larger farmer prosperous. The Jeunes Agricolteurs, which, as we have seen, was ultimately to capture leadership roles within the FNSEA, had a radically different conception of the farmers' interest (Wright, 1964). Without going so far as the American Farm Bureau Federation in coolly accepting the demise of the small farmer, the CNJA has emphasized structural reform, rather than price supports. The CNJA's leaders have seen the French farmers' hope in ending the fragmentation of French farms, four-fifths of which were, even in the late 1960s, under 20 hectares (50 acres).

Even were we prepared to follow Barry (1965), who argues that it is possible to specify somebody's interests without knowing his preferences, important practical problems remain. Though farmers' organizations like to claim that there are no conflicts of interest in representing farmers, it is easy to see how some might arise. It is widely accepted that there are at least short-term conflicts of interest between the producers of certain commodities, such as feed grains on the one hand and livestock on the other. It is regrettably less frequently noticed that there are also potential divergences of class interest in the countryside. Stinchcombe (1966) rightly deplores the tendency for social scientists to treat farmers as a residual homogeneous group left after the bulk of the population have been accommodated within class categories based on urban society. As Stinchcombe goes on to argue, the countryside has supported a variety of classes with differing, sometimes conflicting, interests. The social scientist who is prepared to specify what farmers' interests are will find that different farmers have different interests; farmers' organizations may serve all, or only some of these.

Unfortunately, it is very difficult to establish whose interests a farmers' organization is furthering. Certainly few inferences can be drawn safely from the class composition of its leaders or members. In spite of its reputation for furthering 'agribusiness', the American Farm Bureau Federation's members and leaders are no richer than those of the National Farmers Union, which, as we have seen, defends the 'family farm' and can be seen easily but mistakenly as an organization for poorer rural groups. Similarly, Ardagh (1968) suggests that the leaders of the CNJA who advocate structural reform are not rich farmers from the north but are from the 'desolate smallholdings' of the south and west.

There are also dangers in drawing immediate conclusions from the effects of policies which farmers' organizations advocate. For example, the well-known tendency for subsidies paid on each unit of production to benefit disproportionately large-scale producers can scarcely be blamed on farmers' organizations; we cannot safely conclude that the tendency proves that farmers' organizations which work under such a system further only the interests of their wealthier members. However, it is certainly possible to make important inferences about a farmers' organization which knows about such effects of subsidy policy and is happy to live with them. The character of a pressure group may be revealed by issues it does not raise as well as those it does.

Once the social scientist has established which interests he thinks a particular organization furthers, the problem of explaining why remains. As has been noted several times already, class, and type of commodity produced by members or leaders of a farmers' organization are obvious but false explanations of its policies. The observer is also handicapped by the veiled politics of rural pressure groups discussed earlier. Yet perhaps this provides a warning against undue sophistication. I have argued that farmers' organizations, like other pressure groups, are characterized by low participation in their intragroup politics and the rule of élites enjoying significant freedom of action. No complex explanation may be required, therefore, for the way in which an interest group defines its members' interests; the policy of a group, like its wider political role may merely reflect the attitudes of who happens to be its leader. There are, after all, many well-known examples of non-agricultural organizations changing their policies drastically when a leader has retired and has been replaced by someone from within the organization's career structure. Thus the British Transport and General Workers Union shifted from the right of the Labour Party to the left with retirement of Arthur Deakin and accession of Frank Cousins. No fundamental change in the character of the membership had occurred, but the new leadership had a dramatically different conception of what was in the members' interests; the union's career structure had replaced a right-wing with a left-wing leader. As many farmers' organizations have been headed by long-established élites, men who may even have created the organization, the interest group's definition of its members' interests may merely reflect the sometimes idiosyncratic and unrepresentative attitudes of its leader. The tentativeness with which this argument can be advanced (or challenged), however, amply demonstrates the need for further research.

Pressure Groups in Politics: Varieties of Strategy

Pressure groups, Olson notwithstanding, exist to influence governments. Even the National Grange in the USA, which has been characterized as a rural Masonic movement, justifies its existence by political action. Yet farmers' organizations differ tremendously in the extent to which they participate in politics.

At one extreme lies the English National Farmers' Union which prides itself on an apolitical style. The Union tries to convince politicians and civil servants that though most of its members are loyal Conservatives, the NFU has nothing to do with party politics. So well has the Union succeeded in disassociating itself from the party loyalties of its members that in the mid-1960s it was convincingly accused of supporting Labour Party's agricultural policies and hence encouraging farmers to vote Labour in the 1964 and 1966 General Elections. The Union, however, has by and large succeeded in avoiding being identified with any of the major parties. Its strategy rests on a close and trusting partnership with the Ministry of Agriculture.

There are, in contrast, cases in which farmers' organizations are not merely *associated* with political parties but have actually formed one. Both the

Australian Country Party and the Swedish Centre (formerly Agrarian) Party started life as political parties formed to advance farmers' interests (Aitkin, 1966; Sarlvik, 1974). Both, while retaining a predominantly rural base, have been forced to broaden their appeal as the number and proportion of farmers in the electorate have declined.

Between the extremes of the British NFU's avoidance of party politics and the Swedish or Australian involvement lie many intermediate stages. In the United States, for example, the National Farmers Union, while preserving its formal independence, has forged steady ties with the liberal wing of the Democratic Party. The Union has played a major role in lobbying Congress for many measures not directly related to farmers such as the Full Employment Act of 1946, welfare and civil rights legislation, opposition to the Supersonic Transport and even repeal of legislation allowing states to outlaw union 'closed shops'). At the local level, the NFU played a crucial role in helping the Democratic Party become established in the Dakotas and other 'progressive' areas of the Midwest. The AFBF has been similarly involved in right-wing crusades, though less at the electoral level.

France and Italy also constitute intermediate cases. In both countries farmers have at times been drawn into party politics while still protesting their political innocence. During the French Fourth Republic, the FNSEA actively tried to influence the election of deputies. Its leader, Blondelle, did not favour forming a separate party but would endorse any candidate who backed the farmers' interest as defined by the syndicate. 'Blondelle wants to settle scores with the deputies who have betrayed us . . . he also wants hostages in parliament, men of our own who we can control and who will vote our way', commented one FNSEA official (Wright, 1964, p. 117). However, the FNSEA's apparently non-partisan electoral strategy actually took it into a more or less permanent alliance with liberal–conservative deputies. From 1951 to 1956, the FNSEA's 'peasant bloc', the Amicale Parlémentaire Agricole (APA) was of formidable strength.

Italian farmers have been even more closely associated with Party politics though without quite losing their identity as a separate group. The Coltivatori Diretti fully illustrates La Polambara's general dictum that 'practices . . . do not square with the pious — really ritualistic — claims of organisational institutions that the groups are non-political, non-party or both'. Indeed, La Polambara reports that all the 66 Deputies who belonged to the Coltivatori Diretti's Parliamentary group were Christian Democrats, and the organization functioned as an important arm of the Christian political movement. The Coltivatori Diretti's leader, Bonomi, had the capacity to influence the distribution of government subsidies. Bonomi was also said to use his control over the machinery of government to encourage farmers to vote the 'right', or Christian Democratic, way in national political contests. Districts which fell far short of their targets were punished through the CD's control of the *Federconsorzi* which distribute government grants (La Polambara, 1964; pp. 142, 242–243).

How are the variations in the political strategies used by political parties to be explained? Any simple constitutional explanation is inadequate. Thus the Parliamentary form of government, associated with the avoidance of party politics by the NFU in Britain, produced extensive involvement in electoral politics by farmers' organizations in the French Fourth Republic, Sweden and Italy. It is possible that part of the explanation lies in differences in the power of legislature and executive which occur even amongst Parliamentary régimes. Thus the broad involvement of farmers' organizations in Italy, Sweden and the USA may reflect the greater importance of the legislature in those systems than in Britain. The French example may make the case particularly clear; the legislature-oriented politics of the Fourth Republic encouraged the FNSEA to become involved in party politics, while the powerful Executive of the Fifth Republic encouraged the FNSEA's new leaders from the CNJA to adopt a more technocratic approach outside party politics very similar to that of the NFU in Britain.

Behind the institutional picture, however, lies a deeper factor. Pressure groups, including farmers' organizations, are drawn into party politics to the degree that coalition politics characterize the political system. That is to say, it is the fact that the outcome of legislation is indeterminate in some political systems that a dominant, stable majority will not blindly endorse the recommendations of a government which makes open involvement in politics necessary. The USA provides a clear example. The NFU is encouraged to enter Congressional politics because, in campaigning for interventionist government-spending policies, it must look to urban friends such as the labour unions to help find a majority. Similarly, the Farm Bureau Federation must enlist the support of conservative *laissez-faire* groups in campaigning for an end to government regulation.

Swedish politics provide an interesting variant of the impact of coalition strategies on interest groups. When modern Parliamentary democracy was established after the First World War, the party system produced no clear majority party. The long-established but divided Agrarian Party provided a perfect forum for the representation of farmers' interests. During the 1930s, the Agrarian Party formed a coalition with the Social Democrats, and the government they formed brought in many measure to help the farmer. (The coalition was repeated in 1951–57). Though Swedish politics since the 1940s have been dominated by the Social Democrats, the norms of coalition live on. Party loyalty in votes in the legislature is not as strong as in Britain, and indeed 'the chances are great that by the time this stage [of formal voting] is reached the differences between the parties will already have been resolved either in committee or by agreement between the leaders' (Board, 1970, p. 137) In such a setting, direct representation within the legislature is an attractive option for farmers' organizations.

Even in Britain, the confused multiparty politics of the interwar period made direct representation in Parliament attractive to the NFU. The Union experimented briefly both with promoting its own candidates and with endorsing Conservatives.

Yet though some political systems may have encouraged farmers' organizations to participate directly in electoral and party politics, the trends seem to be against such tactics. Thus, as noted above, both the Swedish Centre Party and Australian Country Party have tried to widen their base as the number of farmers has declined. The Parliamentary power of the FNSEA in France was on the wane before the advent of the Fifth Republic, and the continued fall in the proportion of the farmers in the French population makes the vigorous tactics of the Fourth Republic increasingly less viable.

No discussion of tactics would be complete without some mention of direct action. The problems of organizing militant action by farmers are obvious. Farmers are isolated, compete against each other in the market, and, as entrepreneurs rather than workers, own their produce and stocks. Any interruption of normal marketing hits farmers immediately, but also creates surplus stocks which have to be sold in the future. The American National Farmers Organization, not surprisingly, has been able to claim only limited success for 'withholding' operations designed to obtain higher prices for the farmer. Yet other forms of direct action have caused equally severe problems for established farmers' organizations. Any overt involvement in illegal activity may prompt not only prosecution but the destruction of links with politicians. Yet total disassociation may bring charges of disloyalty or treachery from militant members. Thus direct action places farmers' organizations in the dilemma of alienating the government or its members. The NFU of England and Wales has found itself in this position on several occasions. In 1975, Welsh farmers forcibly prevented imports of cattle from the Irish Republic at Holyhead; in the late 1960s, militants within the Union demanded a 'withholding' operation or market boycott. On each occasion, the NFU's leaders found a compromise acceptable to both the government and membership. The Union quietly dissociated itself from the action of the farmers at Holyhead, while in 1970 it ingeniously organized a market boycott at a time which it and, more importantly, the Ministry of Agriculture, knew would have no embarrassing effects on supplies or prices in the shops.

Yet it is equally obvious that in certain circumstances direct action can help established farmers' organizations, if only by reminding governments that there are worse people to deal with than they are. Thus though the FNSEA did not organize militant action by French farmers in 1961, it did benefit from a major change in policy which followed. The stern policy of reducing subsidies followed under Debré gave way in the face of militancy to conciliation and a more positive approach when Pisani became Minister of Agriculture (Williams and Harrison, 1971; p. 149). Not for the last time, de Gaulle was given a warning that distance and inflexibility could end in crisis and concession. To the limited degree that the lesson was absorbed, established groups such as the FNSEA were the beneficiaries.

The Effectiveness of Farmers' Organizations

An account of the variety of tactics used by farmers' organizations invites an assessment of their comparative effectiveness. As farmers' organizations throughout the West have been involved in a quest for agricultural subsidies and protection, the means for evaluating their success seems obvious. *Prima facie,* the organization which gains the largest subsidies is the most successful. Such a test would, however, be extremely misleading in principle and difficult in practice. There are, in fact, farmers' organizations such as the American Farm Bureau Federation which have opposed large government subsidies; the Danish farmers' organizations who, like the Farm Bureau are very conscious of the need to keep their exports competitive, have also been wary of extracting the largest possible amount from the government. Moreover, the dangers of attributing farm subsidies to the success of farmers' organizations rather than electoral competition, legislative or electoral politics are obvious. Allowance, too, would have to be made for the differing strengths of the opposition which had to be overcome.

Attempts by political scientists to compare agricultural subsidies, and hence the political power of farmers, in two or more countries are handicapped by the impression of economics and the variety of techniques used to subsidize agriculture. A prime example of the pitfalls which exist is J. Roland Pennock's (1962) argument that British farmers are more subsidized than American. Unfortunately, Pennock based his comparison on government expenditures. This was highly misleading. Whereas the British system was one of deficiency payments in which government payments constituted almost the total value of farm subsidies, the American subsidy programme was designed to raise the market price by support-buying so that the total value of subsidies would be several times (depending on elasticities of supply and demand) the value of government expenditure. Clearly Pennock's error weakens his general argument, based on the example of agriculture, that organized interests are more powerful in Britain than in the USA.

Indeed, attempts to measure precisely the value of subsidies in any one country have also failed. The reason is usually that systems resting on support-buying and import controls by their very nature prevent us being able to say what the 'natural' price would be. Since we can only guess at the natural price, we can only guess at the subsidy generated by the artificial price. Thus Howarth's [1971] praiseworthy attempts to estimate agricultural subsidies in Britain can be criticized because it relies heavily on a high estimate for the subsidy given to milk producers, an estimate open to question because there is no international market for liquid milk. Howarth was driven to use the price for dried milk as a substitute, an unsatisfactory substitute because it is a market often dominated by the 'dumping' of surplus products.

If it is difficult to compare the relatively tangible, quantifiable farm subsidies which farmers' organizations obtain, the problems in assessing their success from other legislation can be imagined. Perhaps it is safest to conclude merely by noting that farmers' organizations appear to have been successful in obtaining subsidies in a wide variety of political systems, and to assume that they will continue to adopt tactics which are the most apposite for each country. There are, however, natural fears amongst farmers that their declining members will lead governments elected by consumers to neglect their interests. What have been the implications of the almost universal trends towards fewer farmers working larger units?

The Future of Farmers' Organizations

There is no reason to suppose that a reduction in the proportion of farmers in the population will *ipso facto* damage their organizations. It is worth repeating that the strength of the British Farmers Unions rests to a considerable degree precisely on the fact that British farmers are so clearly a small, and potentially beleaguered minority of the population. The American Farm Bureau has grown steadily while the number of farmers in the USA has declined. Nevertheless, the assertion that, in western democracies, a decline in the number of farmers must reduce their political strength is made by many observers and has a certain *prima facie* plausibility.

Our willingness to accept that a reduction in the number of farmers must reduce their political strength must rest on an assumption that it is the number of farmers that gives their political organizations strength. Such an assumption is not necessarily true.

General studies of interest groups have distinguished a variety of reasons for their influence. Students of British pressure groups, for example, have long stressed the importance of their ability to persuade policy-makers. A close and trusting relationship with the Ministry of Agriculture, Fisheries and Food has been the brightest jewel in the NFU's crown since the Second World War. Such a relationship has rested more on the skills and technical competence of the Union's leaders or officials and on the high proportion of British farmers represented by the Union than on the numerical strength of its members. If the decline in the number of farmers in advanced societies makes a strategy based on an independent agrarian party less viable, it does nothing to undermine a strategy of persuasion.

Indeed, in many countries economic trends have at least temporarily turned in favour of the farmer. The era of surplus production or, as it was known in farming circles, 'cheap food' which stretched from the end of the Korean emergency to the early 1970s has been interrupted and, some argue, ended. Farmers, so long an embarrassment to their governments, have once again become a major economic asset. Even the United States, thought of as an industrial giant, now covers the cost of oil imports with agricultural exports which are themselves a foundation-stone for its diplomacy *vis-à-vis* the USSR. The 'confidence' of farmers, their willingness to invest and expand production has resumed the importance it had in Britain during the last war. Any farmers' organization which has the authority with its members and the government to affect this 'confidence' has gained a major new power to offset any decline in its political resources.

Yet the decline in the number of farmers might not even end their political influence as rapidly as is sometimes supposed. Particularly in two-party systems, minorities are still courted by politicians. The pursuit of 'the farm vote' in the USA continued long after farmers became a small proportion of the electorate. British political parties have shown an eagerness to seek the support of almost any identifiable minority, farmers included (Pennock, 1962). The eagerness of politicians to court a minority 'farm vote' is not new. Kautsky passionately criticized a policy proposed by the German Social Democratic Party: 'There is only one obvious reason for this serious political relapse, regard for the peasants. We have not yet captured them, but they have already captured us' (Tarrow, 1967). However, as the two-party system provides a particularly strong incentive for politicians to attract the support of minorities to push them past the magic 50 per cent it may well be that it is in the two-party systems, rather than multiparty systems that electoral competition will continue to aid the farmer. This could be ironical, as the predominantly two-party systems include many countries such as Britain, the United States and Germany which are among the world's most urbanized.

Yet if farmers' organizations are not as endangered with a decline in member-ship or influence as is often supposed, a more amorphous trend threatens. Farmers have long been the beneficiaries of popular support. Conservatives in many countries have seen the countryside as the location of attitudes which embody their ideals. In Britain, for example, rural society manages to be simul-taneously competitive and hierarchical, efficient and traditional, subsidized yet proudly independent. There can be few industries which could thus appeal to every wing of the contemporary Conservative Party. More puzzling has been the tendency of Socialist and radical parties to support farm subsidies. We have encountered Kautsky's criticisms of the German Social Democratic programme of 1894. Similarly, British farmers often argue that the best Minister of Agriculture they ever had was Tom Williams, Socialist Minister of Agriculture in Atlee's administration. Swedish farmers received great help from a prewar government in which the Agrarian Party played a role but which was supported primarily by Social Democrats. Farm subsidy legislation in the United States has frequently been adopted with the aid of urban liberals over the opposition of conservatives, including many Republicans representing rural districts. The independent liberal from New York city (later its Mayor) Fiorello La Guardia, was an eloquent advocate of farm subsidies. La Guardia told the House during a debate on New Deal agricultural legislation that 'It is the exploited masses that now require the attention of this Congress, and in this great army of exploited masses is to be included the farmer' (Zinn, 1966).

The reasons for the somewhat surprising tendency for social democrats and radicals to be amongst the truest friends of farmers whom we normally think, on balance correctly, to be comparatively wealthy and conservative, are varied. The tendency for any party, supporting Antony Downs's arguments (1957) to compete for votes by changing its policies and ideology is one important factor we have already noted which explains, for example, the French Communist Party's bidding for the support of the peasantry. Logrolling within legislatures is another influence, particularly in the United States. Yet everywhere Socialists and radicals have been influenced by a somewhat dated picture of the farmer. Centre-left politicians have not lumped farmers with shopkeepers, or self-employed businessmen, much less capitalist manufacturers. Farmers have been pictured as hard workers, often cheated by more purely capitalist sectors such as merchants and credit institutions.

Recent trends have decreased whatever plausibility this picture of the country-side ever had. The trends are not towards the 'industrialization' of the country-side with farmers becoming directors of joint stock companies, but they are towards fewer, larger farms owned by rather wealthy men. Farmers' organizations find themselves increasingly concerned with issues which set them against the centre-left. Wealth taxes, income tax concessions, opposition to strict government controls over pesticides and the design of farm buildings are all legitimate concerns for farmers' pressure groups. They are all, however, likely to pit them against their erstwhile friends.

At the same time, the governments of almost every advanced society, European and American, have shown a major interest in techniques of policy analysis during the last ten years. Though some techniques such as PPBS or cost benefit analysis have been extensively criticized, politicians are gradually acquiring a better knowledge of what their policies actually achieve. In both Britain and America, the distribution and impact of farm subsidies have been subjected to searching analysis by economists on the fringe of the policy process (Howarth, 1971; Josling, 1972; Johnson, 1973; Schultze, 1971). Even the European Economic Community is carrying out a major reappraisal of its woefully in-efficient Common Agricultural Policy. The days when farm subsidies could be justified by eloquent reference to the plight of the small farmer are fast disappearing as the tendency for subsidies to line the pockets of their richer colleagues becomes better known. If farmers' organizations face new opportunities to convince their governments that agricultural subsidies are in the public's as well as farmers' interest, they must do so in a world in which many of the illusions about the nature of modern agriculture and the effects of agricultural policies have been dispelled.

References

Aitkin, Don (1966), 'The Australian Country Party', in Henry Mayer (ed.) *Australian Politics* (Melbourne: F. W. Cheshire).

Ardagh, J. (1968), *The New French Revolution* (London: Secker and Warburg).

Barry, Brian (1970), *Sociologists, Economists and Democracy* (New York: Collier-Macmillan).

Barry, Brian (1965), *Political Argument* (London: Routledge and Kegan Paul).

Bartell, Fred (1971), *Farmers' Journal*, 18 February.

Beer, Samuel (1956), 'Pressure groups and parties in Britain', *American Political Science Review*, **50**.

Beer, Samuel (1965), *Modern British Politics* (London: Faber).

Board, Joseph B. (1970), *The Government and Politics of Sweden* (New York: Houghton Mifflin).

Crampton, A. J. (1965), *The National Farmers' Union: Ideology of a Pressure Group* (Lincoln Neb.: University of Nebraska Press).

Des Moines Register (1972) 14 January.

Dogan, Mattei (1967), 'Political cleavage and social stratification in France and Italy' in Seymour Martin Lipset and Stein Rokkan (eds.) *Party Systems* (Glencoe, Ill.: Free Press).

Downs, Antony (1957), *An Economic Theory of Democracy* (New York: Harper and Row).

Eckstein, Harry (1960), *Pressure Group Politics, the Case of the B.M.A.*, (London: Allen and Unwin).

Edinger, Lewis J. (1968) *Politics in Germany* (Boston, Mass.: Little Brown).

Gespal, H. (with I. Beardwell and F. Woodcock) (1972) *Employers' Organisations and Industrial Relations*, Royal Commission on Industrial Relations, Study No. 1, p. 7.

Hirschman, A. O. (1970), *Exit, Voice and Loyalty* (Cambridge, Mass.: Harvard University Press).

Howarth, Richard (1971), *Agricultural Support in Western Europe* (London: Institute of Economic Affairs Research Monograph 23).

Johnson, D. Gale (1973), *World Agriculture in Disarray*, Fontana World Economic Issues. (London: Fontana).

Josling, Timothy Edward *et al.*, (1972), *Burdens and Benefits of Farm Support Policies* (London: Trade Policy Research Centre).

King, Anthony (1974), 'Ideas, institutions and the policies of government', *British Journal of Political Science*, 3.

La Polambara, Joseph (1964), *Interest Groups in Italian Politics* (Princeton; N.J.: Princeton University Press).

Lipset, Seymour Martin (1950), *Agrarian Socialism*, the Co-operative Commonwealth Federation in Saskatchewan, A Study in Political Sociology (Berkeley, Cal.: University of California Press).

Moore, Barrington (Jr.) (1967) *Social Origins of Dictatorship and Democracy* (London: Allen Lane).

Morrison, D. E., and Warner, W. Keith (1971), 'Correlates of farmers' attitudes towards public and private aspects of agricultural Rural Sociology, 32.

Olson, Mancur (1968), *The Logic of Collective Action* (New York: Schoeken Books).

Pennock J. Roland (1962), 'Responsible government', separated powers and special interests: agricultural subsidies in Britain and America', *A.P.S.R.* 56, 3.

Rogers, S. D. (1970), 'Farmers as a pressure group', *New Society*, **February**.

Rohwer, Robert A. (1952) 'Organised farmers in Oklahoma', *Rural Sociology*. 17.

Rogin, Michael Paul (1967), *The Intellectuals and McCarthy, The Radical Specter* (especially chapter 3) (Cambridge and London: The MIT Press).

Särlvik, Bo (1974), 'Sweden: the social bases of the parties in a developmental perspective' in Richard Rose (ed.), *Electoral Behaviour* (London: Free Press).

Schattschneider, E. E. (1960), *The Semi-Sovereign People* (New York: Holt, Rinehart and Winston).

Schultze, Charles L. (1971), *The Distribution of Farm Subsidies, Who Gets the Benefits?* (Washington D.C.: The Brooking Institution).

Self, Peter and Storing, Herbert (1962), *The State and the Farmer* (London: Allen and Unwin).

Stinchcombe, Arthur L. (1966), 'Agricultural enterprise and rural class relations' in R. Bendix and S. Lipset (eds.), *Class, Status and Power* (London: Routledge and Kegan Paul).

Sundquist, James L. (1973), *Dynamics of the Party System, Alignment and Realignment of Political Parties in the United States* (especially chapter 2) (Washington, D.C.: The Brookings Institution).

Tarrow, Sidney G. (1967), *Peasant Communism in Southern Italy* (New Haven and London: Yale University Press).

Wallace's Farmer, (1957), 4 May.

Williams, P. M., and Harrison, Martin (1971), *Politics and Society in de Gaulle's Republic* (p. 149) (London: Longmans).

Williams, P. M. (1964), *Crisis and Compromise, Politics in the Fourth Republic,* (especially p. 78) (London: Longmans).

Wright, Gordon (1964), *Rural Revolution in France, The Peasantry in the Twentieth Century* (Stanford: Stanford University Press).

Zinn, Howard (ed.) (1966), *New Deal Thought* (Indianopolis, Ind.: Bobbs Merrill), p. 226.

3
Rural Community and Rural Community Power

Peter Saunders, Howard Newby, Colin Bell, and David Rose

In the person of Ferdinand Tonnies, both community studies and rural sociology may be said to have acquired a common 'founding father' (Tonnies, 1957), so it is not surprising that community studies have remained a central concern of rural sociologists. Certainly his twin concepts of *gemeinschaft* ('community') and *gesellschaft* (variously translated as 'society', 'organization' or 'association') have had an enormous influence on both aspects of the discipline. In purely formal terms *gemeinschaft* included any set of relationships characterized by emotional cohesion, depth, continuity and fulfilment; *gesellschaft*, on the other hand, referred to the impersonal, the contractual and the rational aspects of human association. Adopting the prevailing nineteenth-century idealized views of rural life, however, Tonnies believed that the rural village most fully embodied the characteristics of *gemeinschaft* — 'it is stronger there and more alive' (Tonnies, 1957, p. 35) — while *gesellschaft* predominated in the city. Hence a very common nineteenth-century cultural standpoint, namely that 'real' communities existed only in the countryside (Williams, 1973), was imported into one of the 'unit ideas' of sociology (Nisbet, 1966). Beginning with Galpin's pioneering *Social Anatomy of an Agricultural Community* literally thousands of community studies have now been carried out taking Tonnies' framework as their point of reference.

The mechanistic way in which Tonnies' typology has been applied has recently come under considerable attack, not only in rural sociology generally (Anderson, 1958; Pahl, 1966; Nolan and Galliher, 1973; Benvenuti, Galjart and Newby, 1975), but in the particular field of rural community studies (Olson, 1965; Bell and Newby, 1971). On empirical grounds, studies from Lewis (1951) onwards have questioned the validity of the easy elision between rural settlements and 'community' and have noted the presence of remarkably *gesellschaftlich* qualities in the social life of many rural areas. (The list is now a long one, but it includes Littlejohn, 1963; Williams, 1964; Pahl, 1965; Bailey, 1969, 1971; Brody, 1973.) Partly as a result of these empirically based criticisms, the very notion of 'community' has also come under attack both on the grounds of its ambiguity and because it is theoretically misleading (see for example, Stacey, 1969). Recently it has seemed that no article or book on community

© Peter Saunders, Howard Newby, Colin Bell, and David Rose. Based on research financed by the SSRC.

and/or a community study could begin without reference to the problems of definition. Indeed the analysis of various definitions still remains (as we have described elsewhere) a 'thriving sociological industry' (Bell and Newby, 1971, p. 27), although Hillery's well-known analysis of 94 such definitions remains the *pièce de resistance* (Hillery, 1955). Finally rural community studies have become bound up in a generalized attack on community studies as 'abstracted empiricism' (Mills, 1964), on account of their impressionistic methodology, their excessive descriptions of local ecology, social organizations and social participation, and their parochial and non-historical bias (Olson, 1965; Glass, 1966). It is little wonder, then, that during the late 1960s there was a weakening of confidence in the sociological value of rural community studies and a consequent reduction in their output.

Only very recently has there occurred something of a revival based upon a more realistic appraisal of the limits and possibilities of rural community studies. In part this revival has been due to the reassertion of a Romantic anti-urbanism and anti-industrialism in Western societies during the early 1970s. The increasing outcry against environmental pollution, the movement towards greater environmental conservation and protection, the awareness of the possible 'limits to growth' (Mishan, 1968) and the belief that 'small is beautiful' (Schumacher, 1973) have all contributed to a remarkable revival of Arcadian values, to which rural sociology has not been entirely immune. Quite suddenly there seems to be once more a social, as well as a sociological purpose in studying the dynamics of small rural communities and the threats to their existence which the centralizing and bureaucratizing trends of modern society are alleged to represent. The rural commune movement has, of course, been a manifestation of such feelings (see Kantor, 1972 and 1973; Abrams and McCulloch, 1976; Smith and Crossley, 1975). Within the narrower academic field of sociology, a revival of interest in community studies has also been accompanied by a far greater emphasis on the use of the community as a method of analysis rather than as an object of study (Arensberg, 1961; Bell and Newby, 1971, chapter 2). That is, communities have not been studied as self-contained objects in their own right, but for what they can elucidate about wider societal processes. Remote villages, because they are customarily considered to be the most backward, stable and unchanging areas of society, have therefore been investigated partly as microcosms, or even symbols, of wider social trends, but also for what they can illuminate about the effect of widespread and often revolutionary macrosocial changes at the 'grass roots' (see, for example, Hinton, 1973; Yglesias, 1972; Myrdal, 1975; Beteille, 1965; also the synthesis of American studies (some of them urban) by Stein, 1964). The recent spate of rural community studies of this kind shows few signs of abating, and should it continue this use of the community study as a method will take the sociological study of rural villages much closer to a more firmly established tradition of studies in social anthropology. Moreover, in so far as it involves a much greater emphasis upon change and process then this trend will overcome one of the traditional weaknesses of this area.

How far the revival of interest in rural communities will lead to a greater clarification of the concept of community is not yet discernible; certainly if past experience is anything to go by the renewal of Arcadian values will merely lead to 'community' continuing to be equated with a bucolic 'good life'. This vexed question of definition has arisen, as we have analysed in more detail elsewhere (Bell and Newby, 1976*b*), because of a largely unexamined assumption of coincidence between three analytically separable perspectives: community as a 'geographical expression', in other words a finite and bounded physical location; community as a 'sociological expression', that is, a local social system (cf. Stacey, 1969), and community as a particular kind of human association irrespective of its local focus. Tonnies, it should be noted, was concerned with the third of these in his concept of *gemeinschaft*. On the other hand much of the debate around the 'rural–urban continuum' (Pahl, 1965, and Wild, 1975) has arisen because it was that first assumed that all three aspects ran together (in other words a village was a *gemeinschaftlich* local social system) whilst later investigators failed to confirm this. Most current urban and rural sociologists have therefore concentrated on the second of these approaches, the community as a local social system, and this will be broadly what we have in mind in this chapter. It is worth emphasizing, however, that Tonnies himself understood the contingent nature of localism — for him *gemeinschaftlich* relationships were linked to the 'community of place' only in so far as those who affirmed a 'community of blood' (kinship) and a 'community of mind' (friendship) wished to live in reasonable proximity (Tonnies, 1957, p. 55). As Schmalenbach, in a seminal paper, has pointed out:

Tonnies (and everyone else) knows that rural neighbours may become mortal enemies when, for example a boundary is disputed, just as brothers may become enemies when an inheritance is challenged. Despite this, neighbours and brothers always remain neighbours and brothers. Neighbourliness and brotherhood persist psychically. There is probably no better example anywhere to demonstrate how minor a role 'feelings' play as a basis of community. (Schmalenbach, 1961, p. 335).

Likewise in our use of the term we are implying no affective prescriptions. While it is apparent that what most people mean when they articulate their desire for 'community' is precisely these 'feelings' of community (especially with regard to rural villages and in communes), we believe, following Schmalenbach, that the latter should be reserved for the term 'communion', which implies no specific form of territoriality such as localism.

Giddens (1972 and 1976) has recently provided a provocative critique of what he calls 'the theory of industrial society' that has emerged from classical sociological theory to which Tonnies is a key contributor. His characterization of this theory is so relevant to the themes of this paper that we will quote it in full. He writes that:

The fundamental contrast in the modern world, it is held, is between traditional, agrarian society, normally based upon the dominance of land-owning élites, sanctioned by religion, though in reality often deriving from military power and coordinated within an authoritarian state; and industrial, urban society, fluid and 'meritocratic' in its structure, characterized by a diffusion of power among competitive élites, in which social solidarity is based upon secular exchange transactions rather than upon religious ethics or coercive military power, and in which government is transformed into a mass democratic state, The theory of industrial society recognizes the phenomenon of class conflict but holds that is is characteristic of the *transitional* phase in the emergence of industrialism out of traditional society and that it becomes transcended (read 'regulated' or 'institutionalized') when the industrial order reaches maturity. In some versions — including the original Saint-Simonian one — it is held that the very concept of 'class' loses its relevance once the transition to industrialism has been achieved. Further, an end of class conflict in the contemporary era means an end of ideology, save in a few industrialized countries, such as France or Italy, where the continuing existence of an archaic, peasant sector means that the old class conflicts and ideological movements have not yet dropped away. Conceptually, the theory of industrial society involves a polar typology of forms of societal organization made familiar under a variety of names: 'status' versus 'contract', 'mechanical' versus 'organic' solidarity, *'Gemeinschaft'* versus *'Gesellschaft'*, and so forth. (Giddens, 1976, pp. 718–719)

We thoroughly concur when he tells us that this theory of industrial society 'must be *abandoned*, or at least *dismantled* and its assumptions and promises subjected to scrutiny'. In part we have attempted such a scrutiny above and elsewhere (Bell and Newby, 1976*b*). What follows provides a test of Giddens' claim that

some or most of these assumptions [as quoted above] are obsolete in an era when the main 'internal' divisions and strains in the advanced societies are no longer as in the nineteenth and early twentieth centuries, based upon the tensions between the urban-industrial centres and the still strong centrifugal pull of a rural hinterland. (Giddens, 1976, p. 719).

The Study of Community Power in Rural Areas

Since 1953, when Floyd Hunter published his famous study of Atlanta, *Community Power Structure*, the examination of the nature of power in local communities has become almost a sub-discipline in its own right. An exhaustive bibliography would now run into hundreds of titles, particularly in the United States where the study of community power has generated an acrimonious, though fascinating, debate from which general lessons are to be learned about the close relationship between ideology, theory and methodology (for a summary see Bell and Newby, 1971, chapter 7). Here the community has become a battlefield on which fundamental epistemological issues have been fought out, issues which go far beyond the scope of this paper. In the United States the study of community power has been concerned mainly with cities and small towns, while the examination of community power in rural areas has hardly been tackled. The concerns of urban sociologists from the time of Park and Wirth have found a common cause with the traditional concern of political scientists to study power to produce a prodigious output of work on the distribution of power at the local level. Rural sociology, however, has until very recently remained firmly in the grip of a *gemeinschaftlich* framework which has inhibited the analysis of similar issues — indeed this is a consequence of 'the theory of industrial society' outlined above.

Outside North America studies of community power remain few and far between. In Britain, for example, there is a dearth of studies so far, and these are concerned almost exclusively with urban areas. Only Madgwick's (1973) study of rural politics in Cardiganshire represents and exception. The reasons for this are not difficult to find. The methodological problems encountered merely by attempting to gain access to powerful influences in Britain can be considerable (see Stanworth and Giddens, 1974), for a pall of secrecy surrounds much of the dealings of even the smallest local council. Furthermore, the theoretical problems generated by the American community power debate are enough to intimidate any researcher inclined to reproduce similar work in different political cultures. In addition British political culture has traditionally lacked the distinctively Jeffersonian aspects of grass-roots democracy which have enabled American researchers to argue that the community is a suitable locus for the study of power. Consequently the view of Britain as consisting of a more centralized and homogeneous political system has been reflected in a predisposition to regard local power as not worth studying. Most localities have not been seen to contain within them much power over their own futures in comparison with higher authorities; moreover the alleged 'eclipse' of community in modern industrial societies (Stein, 1964), has symbolized a process whereby more and more power has become placed in the hands of extra-local agencies, whether they be Parliament, the Civil Service, the EEC Commission or the boards of multinational companies. Most of these points have been well-founded and it is therefore not surprising that the study of community power in Britain, in particular, has been somewhat moribund. Whether the movement towards increasing decentralization and the devolution of control from Westminster and Whitehall will be sufficient to stimulate a new interest in community power remains to be seen.

Nevertheless, the issue of whether community power is worthy of serious attention is an empirical matter and not something which can be legislated *a priori*. Whilst not denying the centripetal tendencies of modern societies, there is a good deal of evidence to show that the immediate locality remains the focus of many people's lives and that local political processes have retained an important significance in the determination of their life-chances — and this applies as much in Britain as in the United States. Nor, indeed, can the traditional assumption that local politics is a formal game played entirely by the rules be any longer taken for granted. Analysis of the formal political process — for example, of the bureaucratic structure of local government administration and of the formal and public activities of pressure groups in relation to that structure — cannot unproblematically be taken as synonymous with the analysis of the distribution of power in the community (Newton, 1975). Indeed, not only can community power research be justified on the grounds that the immediate locality remains a significant locus of power for many, particularly working-class individuals, but it can also advance our theoretical understanding of power *tout court*. This needs to be stressed for problems of 'the state' potentially loom so large in current sociological thinking as to obscure the problems of local power.

There are, moreover, good theoretical reasons for supposing that the study of community power may be more salient in rural areas than in large industrial centres. For notwithstanding the increasing state intervention in the everyday life of the citizens of all advanced industrial societies, in rural areas the local political process has retained a good deal of its influence. In the advanced capitalist economies of Western Europe, North America and Australasia, agriculture, despite varying degrees of vertical integration with the broader food-processing and manufacturing complex, remain predominately in the hands of family proprietorships, *de facto* even if not always *de jure*. The importance of land as a factor of production has inhibited the concentration of capital and the construction of national and multinational quasi-monopolies which has been a recent feature of capitalist industry. Thus employment in rural areas has remained largely in local hands, and rural areas in advanced capitalist societies have been less dominated by a handful of large-scale enterprises with head-quarters outside the locality than many cities and towns. Hence while the decisions of, say, Luton or Banbury Council might arguably affect the everyday lives of the citizens of Luton or Banbury less than those made by the board of General Motors in Detroit (see Goldthorpe *et al.*, 1969) or General Foods in Philadelphia (Stacey *et al.*, 1975), in many rural areas local political decisions remain important, especially for those who are employed locally in agriculture and the related service industries. The community may not therefore have been 'eclipsed' in these rural areas to the extent that might be apparent in other localities.

While these issues suggest reasons why community power may be worth studying in many rural areas these matters can only be settled empirically rather than on the basis of universalistic prescriptions and empty theoretical specu-lation. Much will depend upon the precise configuration of locally and extra-locally held resources. Absentee landlordism, vertical integration, state planning and the nature of the product market may all seriously reduce the extent of local control (see Walton, 1966a and 1966b). All this suggests that before a viable study of rural community power can be undertaken the parameters of local power need to be carefully specified and the relationship between the local social system and the wider societal context must be indicated (see for example, the comments on Banfield (1956), by Davis, 1970; Galtung, 1971; and Pizzorno, 1966). Neither of these problems have, however, been prominent among those dealt with in the community power literature (see Geertz, 1965; Pahl, 1966; and Wild, 1975). Only in the area of peasant studies has a systematic attempt been made to examine the relationship between the local and the national and to discuss what effect each has upon the other in terms of the peasantry's political consciousness and political mobilization. In part this has been due to the peculiar emphasis in peasant studies on the local orientation of peasant culture, which, following on from a predominantly American tradition of cultural anthropology, has been regarded as a defining characteristic of the peasant (Redfield, 1930: Kroeber, 1948, Shanin, 1970; Wolf, 1966 and 1970). Hence Landsberger, summarizing much of the literature on rural protest, has pointed to the 'critical' organizational obstacle which a peasant movement faces, namely that of 'creating a viable organizational structure — authority, communication, decision-making mechanisms, etc. — beyond the level of the community' (Landsberger, 1974, p. 46, also Galtung, 1971). Similarly Galeski (1972) has explained the tenacity of the peasant's community orientation by noting that while society needs the peasant (or some such agricultural cultivator) in order to produce food, the peasantry does not need society and can subsist without its interference with considerable equanimity. Thus while the study of rural community power in the areas dominated by the capitalist mechanized agriculture of the developed world are very few and far between (see, for example, Wild, 1974), there is quite an extensive literature with regard to peasant societies, albeit concerned very often with the uninstitutionalized, personal politics of patron–client relationships (summarized by Campbell, 1964) or the institutions of personal influence like the Mafia (Blok, 1974).

Landholding and Stratification

As Stinchcombe (1961–62) has pointed out, in agrarian social structures the institutions of stratification are based not so much upon occupation, as in an urban, industrial social context, but around the institution of property. This property is, moreover, expressed less in the tangible form of working capital as in the form of land. Access to land therefore constitutes the crucial power resource in all agricultural societies irrespective of the degree to which agriculture is based upon a subsistence or a commercial economy. Indeed, because of the necessity to perform the productive tasks sequentially rather than concurrently in agriculture, technological change has hardly disturbed the length of the production cycle nor the importance of the land itself as a factor of production (except in certain stock-rearing operations). The manner in which land is held and the property rights which surround its ownership therefore become virtually the defining characteristics of agrarian-based systems of stratification. Stinchcombe has developed this notion to produce a fivefold typology of landholding systems and rural class relations based upon: the manorial / hacienda system, family-sized tenancies, family smallholdings, plantations and capitalist extensive agriculture (Stinchcombe, 1961—62).

However satisfactory or otherwise this typology may be (and there are certain obvious *lacunae*), what Stinchcombe's paper forces us to confront is the importance of examining the precise nature of the landholding structure and the system of stratification erected upon it, rather than being satisfied with amorphous descriptive terms like 'peasant', or even 'peasant mode of production'. Similarly what constitutes the political interests of 'farmers' or 'peasants' cannot be taken for granted. As Stinchcombe demonstrates, the ideological character of the political movements which such systems of stratification throw up varies considerably across a wide spectrum from Poujadist populism to revolutionary communism (see also Moore, 1966). Thus, as far as the landowning upper class is concerned the different landowning structures imply different problems of maintaining stability and of exercizing power in a manner which will ensure the ongoing perpetuation of the system from which they continue to draw their privileges. Thus the delineation of 'objective' interests in agrarian societies is often fraught with difficulties (Lukes, 1975), as attempts to consider the class characteristics of the peasantry (Shanin, 1966; Chayanov, 1966) demonstrate only too clearly. We shall have reason to elaborate on this problem of definition of interests later in this chapter.

For the present, however, we may note that whatever the system of stratification, there seems to be a good deal of evidence to suggest that the methods which landowning élites employ in order to confer stability are very similar. That is, that the methods and strategies used to confer and reinforce legitimacy centre around those Weber (1964) referred to as traditional authority. Weber himself associated traditional authority primarily with feudalism in both its Asiatic and European versions, but more recently traditional authority in various forms has been identified as the prevailing method of legitimation not only under feudalism (Bloch, 1961), but under the slave plantation agriculture of the United States and Caribbean (Genovese, 1971 and 1974) and the capitalist extensive agriculture of lowland England (Bell and Newby, 1973; Newby, 1977). The persistence of traditional authority in rural society, whatever its economic basis, seems to relate more to the scattered nature of rural populations (which in turn depends once more on the importance of land as a factor of production). By urban, industrial standards both the size and density of settlement in most rural areas is of a kind which produces a highly particularistic social structure in which persistent face-to-face contact can be maintained. Where such particularism is accompanied by a rigidly hierarchical and ascriptive system of stratification then traditional forms of authority seem to ensue no matter how rational the economic activity of the dominant class (Genovese, 1974; Newby, 1975).

We have argued elsewhere that the landowning class in each case operates an elaborate web of paternalistic relationships because of the stability which this confers on an otherwise highly inegalitarian social system, and that the exercise of traditional authority essentially involves a handling of the contradictions that arise from, on the one hand, the social *differentiation* which a hierarchical structure engenders, and on the other, the *identification* which must be inculcated if stability is to be achieved (for further details, see Newby, 1975; Bell and Newby 1976*a*). Within most rural settings these contradictions are capable of being handled because paternalism is exercized through personal contact rather than on the basis of impersonal abstractions and rules. Hence the social influences and judgements of traditional élite members are experienced directly, whilst in many types of rural society the segmentary character of the social structure separates the subordinate groups — whether peasants, slaves, or landless rural proletariat — from their fellows. Thus, the rural villages become encompassing enough to be called total institutions (Goffman, 1968), or as Coser (1974) has preferred to describe such small-scale and total social structures, 'greedy institutions'.

Greedy institutions, though they may in some cases utilise the device of physical isolation, tend to rely mainly on non-physical mechanisms to separate the insider from the outsider and to erect symbolic boundaries between them ... Nor are greedy institutions marked by external coercion. On the contrary they tend to rely on voluntary compliance and to evolve means of activating loyalty and commitment. (Coser, 1974, p. 6).

The interclass relationships of many rural communities could profitably be investigated from the perspective of 'greedy institutions'. While attention has often been drawn to the docility of the underprivileged sections of the rural world (for example, see Genovese, 1971; Wylie, 1961), compared with the gross exploitation which they have been forced to suffer, the mechanisms whereby such stability is promoted remain underinvestigated (for some lines of enquiry see Newby, 1975). However, as we shall see, one of the ideological buttresses that has maintained the rural community as a greedy institution has been the very notion of 'community' itself. By elevating the principle of localism and endowing it with the almost sacred connotations that the word 'community' often seems to imply, landowners have often found it to be in their interests to retain the self-contained character of the rural village, both geographically and symbolically (for English examples, see Davidoff *et al.*, 1976). This is not to say that the local social structure may not have a real basis in the necessity of reciprocal co-operation, especially at the margin of subsistence. However, it is community in this sense that has often been promoted but an *affective* community (what earlier in this chapter we termed 'communion') which has attempted to redefine the class-like relationships of the locality as an organic partnership lacking any fundamental division of interest (Bell and Newby, 1976b).

Empirically, the rural community *as an ideology* has hardly been regarded as a problem worthy of study. This is because, until very recently, the study of rural communities has been dominated by an almost undiluted Romanticism, in which rural sociology has merely reflected the idyllic view of rural life predominant in Anglo-Saxon culture generally (Williams, 1973; Schmitt, 1969; Petersen, 1968; and Glass, 1966). According to this view the rural village has been regarded as the repository of all that is stable, immemorial, harmonious, pleasant and reasuring in modern society, but also constantly at risk against the encroaching influences of urban industrialism (see, for example, Sorokin and Zimmerman, 1929: Rees, 1951; Arensberg and Kimball, 1949; and the studies cited by Williams, 1964). This conception of the rural village views 'class' and 'community' as polar opposites (for a recent example, see Ambrose, 1974) and it has not been surprising, therefore, to see the 'phenomena of the distribution of power' examined not so much in terms of class and party as the more consensual notion of status (Weber, 1964). The plausibility of this approach to the study of stratification in rural communities has remained for so long, partly because of the strength of the cultural tradition of the rural idyll, but also because, until the peasant-based revolutions of the 1960s produced a radical reappraisal, there seemed few overt acts of conflict and rebellion on the part of the great majority of the rural population. The myth of the rural idyll was therefore able to feed upon itself. Where this perspective was not subscribed to, the effect on the sociological analysis which ensued could be startling, as the famous studies of Tepotzlan by Redfield (1930) and Lewis (1951) all too clearly demonstrated (see the discussion in Bell (1974) for the epistemological basis of this extraordinary controversy). However, in general, such has been the hegemony of this approach until quite recently that the issue of rural community power has hardly been addressed, let alone solved to anyone's satisfaction.

There seems little doubt that dominance of the *gemeinschaftlich* approach to rural community power was also helped by the absence of any strong Marxist tradition in the study of rural society until the peasant-based revolutions of the 1960s kindled an increased enthusiasm for peasant studies among Marxist scholars. Marx himself, however, offers only limited guidance, for he despaired of the revolutionary potential of the oppressed and underprivileged rural classes and devoted little attention to them — this is epitomized by Marx's famous comments about 'the idiocy of rural life' and the peasantry's similarity to 'sacks of potatoes'. Marx was quite explicit — if the revolution was to come, it would be from the industrial proletariat in large urban areas. Rural workers and peasants were, in contrast, an essentially conservative and reactionary force, falsely conscious of their objective class interests. Marx, too, took the harmonious and stable appearance of the countryside largely at its face value (references to an agricultural workers' strike in *Das Kapital* notwithstanding) and this has remained very common throughout the twentieth century. However, accompanying the idyllic view of the countryside there has always been a vague recognition of a rural underworld which reflects a rather more antagonistic basis of rural class relationships. During the nineteenth century this underworld occasionally broke through in the great explosions of rural unrest characteristic of what Hobsbawm (1968) has called 'primitive rebellion' (for example see Landsberger, 1974). This duality remains to confront the student of rural community power, at least as far as Britain is concerned. For most of the time it seems that rural politics operate relatively harmoniously, generating little hostility, few complaints and virtually no resolute opposition. We would wish to argue that it is precisely this lack of 'rancorous conflict' (Gamson, 1966) which poses a central problem in any attempt to study rural community power rather than being a taken-for-granted aspect of the 'rural way of life'.

We wish to elaborate this argument both at the theoretical level, with reference to recent contributions to the study of community power, and empirically, with reference to evidence collected during a recent study of rural community power conducted by us in the county of Suffolk, England.

Political Stability and Rural Community Power: An Illustrative Case

Suffolk is a primary agricultural county in the Eastern lowlands of England. Farming in the area is almost entirely arable and agricultural units are on average relatively large in scale by European and British standards. The county is one of what Frankenberg (1966, p. 252) has termed 'the capitalist-organized business farming areas of Britain'. As Frankenberg notes, such specialized and highly rationalized agricultural areas tend often to be characterized by very low population densities, and Suffolk is no exception with a density of 0.58 persons per acre. Nevertheless, it is an expanding county. The population has been increasing by some 10 000 per year in the early 1970s, and recent planning forecasts envisage a continuing expansion, making Suffolk one of England's fastest growing counties. At first sight, this is perhaps surprising given the agricultural base of the local economy, and the often-noted 'drift from the land' of rural workers. This net increase is, however, largely accounted for by a continuing influx of mainly urban and overwhelming middle-class immigrants from London and the South-east: business commuters, rural retreaters, weekend cottagers and retired professionals. As we shall see, the fissions and fusions which this middle-class immigration has created in the politics of the county have had considerable significance, for the horizontal local/newcomer cleavage has at times cross-cut (or appeared to cross-cut) any vertical economic cleavage of class interests among the locals themselves.

Like the other 'non-metropolitan' counties in England, Suffolk's local government structure is divided into three levels. At the lowest level are the *parish councils*, each with a membership of around ten or twelve local villagers. Elections for parish councils are often spasmodic and frequently uncontested, this reflecting the paucity of their powers and responsibilities. At the middle level are the *district councils* each with around fifty or so members. There are seven district councils in Suffolk, each representing some 80 000 people, and each responsible for the provision of public housing, development control aspects of planning, and various local services such as refuse collection, public parks, and other civic amenities. At the third level is the Suffolk County Council whose 82 members are responsible for strategic planning, education, highways, police, social services, and a range of minor functions.

This local government structure in Suffolk has been in existence in its present form only since 1974. Before that, the county functions were divided between two county councils (East and West Suffolk) and a county borough council (Ipswich), while in the middle range, a larger number of smaller district councils shared rather less power than do their successors. But although the 1974 reorganization significantly reshaped the structure and redefined the functions of the various local authorities in the area it has had little impact on the social and political composition of their memberships. The new county and district councils, like their predecessors, are dominated by politically conservative middle-class professionals, managers and, most significant, landowners and farmers. Of course, as Giddens (1974, p. xii) points out, 'Because a man emanates from a specific type of class background, it does not inevitably follow that he will later adopt policies which are designed to promote class interests corresponding to that background'. Thus, although farmers and landowners so dominate the county council that they control the chairmanship and vicechairmanship of the council in addition to the chairmanships of such major committees as Planning, Education, Finance and Policy, it does not follow that county politics in Suffolk are necessarily reflective of an agricultural or landed interest. The question, therefore, is the extent to which farming and landowning interests in the area are able to achieve their ends, even against the resistance of others (Weber, 1964).

It was in an attempt to consider this question that we began our researches in Suffolk by scanning local and regional newspapers dating back to 1960 with the intention of discovering a number of political issues which could usefully be analysed. Following Dahl's prescriptions we intended to assess the power of the farming and landowning interests in the county by analysing the course and outcome of those issues where these interests had been mobilized against opposition (Dahl, 1961; Polsby, 1963). Yet after some diligent searching, it became apparent that Suffolk's recent political history was remarkably devoid of issues, or indeed of any outward manifestations of political conflict. With only one or two exceptions (discussed later), Suffolk politics appeared notably non-contentious. So it was that our chief research objective shifted from the analysis of issues to the explanation of political tranquility. Why were there so few issues?

According to Dahl (1961), a situation of political stability such as this can only be explained in terms of a theoretical model of democratic pluralism. That is to say, although power may be unevenly distributed within a given political system among leaders and led, the latter nevertheless retain the crucial power to vote their leaders in and out of office, and to organize politically to defend or sponsor their interests. If they are dissatisfied with the way in which their leaders are using their power, therefore, they enjoy both the right and the capacity to do something about it. The corollary of this is that where people do not act in defence or pursuit of their interests, they must be reasonably satisfied with the way in which power has been exercized on their behalf. Mass political inaction, such as we found in Suffolk, is thus for Dahl indicative of a well-integrated and smoothly functioning system of local representative democracy.

Fundamental to this model are the twin concepts of legitimacy and community. Thus, power is seen to be exercized with the consent of those subject to it (in other words it is legitimated), and to the benefit of collective rather than narrow sectional interests (that is, it is communal in benefit). Thus, power relationships, according to this model, involve moral obligations of deference on the part of subordinates, and of altruism on the part of superordinates. As Parsons (1966, p. 85) has expressed it, power is 'a means of effectively mobilising obligations in the interests of collective goals'. Although such mutual obligations may at times have to be enforced (for example, by subordinates pressurizing their leaders, or by leaders invoking the law against recalcitrant subordinates), they are more generally *morally* binding. Thus, people accept the actions of their leaders because they recognize their legitimate right to take such actions on their behalf. It need hardly be added that such a theoretical formulation appears particularly apposite to rural politics where relations of domination may often be morally sanctioned according to tradition as much as to office (Weber, 1964). The norms of upper-class philanthropy (seen in the notion of *noblesse oblige*) have proved remarkably resilient, and provide an excellent example of Parson's emphasis on the moral character of power relations.

The problem with the pluralist explanatory model of Dahl and Parsons is that it can take no account of the possibility that power may be used amorally to prevent opposition from arising. There is another face of power (Bachrach and Baratz, 1970). The powerful may be in a position to mask, repress, or pre-empt the emergence of any issues which may threaten their material or political dominance, and thereby to avoid any visible manifestation of class antagonisms. In this sense, political stability may be as much the consequence of a prior exercise of manipulative power, as of the continuing exercise of truly authoritative power. Such manipulative power may successfully be exercized in at least three ways (Bachrach and Baratz, 1970). First, potential conflict may simply be side-stepped by powerful groups, perhaps by ignoring it, or by buying off the leaders of a protest movement, or whatever. Secondly, the power of a dominant local group may be such that potential opponents consider it wise not to raise complaints, perhaps because they fear the possible repercussions. Clearly, where (as is the case in may parts of Suffolk, for example), the same individuals dominate the local political system, the local employment market, the distribution of local housing, the local legal institutions, such as the magistracy, and the sources of local welfare and patronage, there is likely to be a strong disincentive for less powerful and more dependent groups to mount a challenge against them (see the discussion of the power of 'Jones' in 'Springdale' — Vidich and Bensman, 1958). Thirdly, inaction may be indicative of the power exercized by dominant groups over the political consciousness of their subordinates. The work situation of most manual employees in the countryside is relatively small-scale, and the management structure is often particularistic rather than bureaucratic (Newby, 1977). Furthermore, the spatial location of the different classes is likely to bring them into geographically (though not necessarily socially) close proximity. As a result, relationships between master and man, farmer and farm worker, squire and tenant, are often particularistic, with the result that vertical, rather than horizontal, identification may thereby be encouraged (Bell and Newby, 1973 and 1974). Social cohesion in other words, may be ensured through personal ties, and a spurious 'legitimacy' achieved by those with power through the transmission or imposition of their values, rationalizations, and ideologies on subordinate groups (see, for example, our discussion of the ideological justification of landownership by dominant groups in Suffolk — Rose *et al.*, 1976). Far from legitimacy springing spontaneously from below as the *source* of power for community leaders, it may therefore be the case that it is imposed from above as a *consequence* of their hegemony. As Gouldner has observed (1970, p. 297), the powerful can 'enforce their moral claims and conventionalise their moral defaults'.

How, then, are we to assess these two conflicting explanations of political inaction? Given the fact of political stability and tranquillity in Suffolk, is it to be explained in terms of the altruistic use of legitimate power, or the self-interested use of manipulative power? If the former, then it is necessary to demonstrate both the existence of attributed legitimacy and the generation of communal benefit; if the latter, then it is necessary to demonstrate the generation of sectional bias and the means whereby inaction has been maintained in the face of this bias (Lukes, 1975).

Such conditions, however, raise the fundamental problem of how benefit is to be assessed. According to Dahl (1961, p. 52 footnote), for example, if an individual *believes* that he has benefited from a given exercise of power, then he *has* so benefited, 'even though from the point of view of his observers his belief is false or ethically wrong'. Lukes (1975) on the other hand, suggests that interests may in many cases be inferred 'objectively', even where these conflict with the subjectively articulated and recognized preferences and political goals of those concerned. Taking an interesting case of inaction over the introduction of air pollution controls as his example (see Crenson, 1971), he seeks to show, through an implicit process of *verstehen*, how 'obvious'interests may be imputed to those affected. Thus: 'There is good reason to expect that other things being equal, people would rather not be poisoned (assuming in particular that pollution control does not necessarily mean unemployment) — *even where they may not even articulate this preference*' (p. 45, emphasis added). Now it may well be that, in other instances, the 'obvious' interests of the parties involved may be less clearly apparent. It may also be, that even in the example of air pollution controls, there is ultimately no philosophical justification for assuming that it is in people's interests not to be poisoned, Nevertheless, we find Lukes' arguments useful (if not entirely convincing at the philosophical level). It may reasonably be argued, for example, that in a capitalist economy, it is in people's interests to maximize their economic benefits and minimize their costs. This is not to deny the existence (or indeed the substantive rationality) of altruistic behaviour within a market system, but it is to recognize that the function of the market lies in allocating values, and that the functionally rational goal of actors in that market thus necessarily relates to profit maximization and the minimization of costs.

Therefore, we may argue, *Ceteris paribus*, that, for example, it is in the interests of employers to sponsor and support policies which, deliberately or otherwise, result in the maintenance of cheap labour supplies. Similarly, it is in the interests of property owners to support low property taxes, whereas it is in the interests of objectively and relatively deprived groups to support higher taxes, and thus higher levels of expenditure on social service provisions (that is, on additional sources of indirect income for poorer groups, such as subsidized public housing, increased welfare benefits, and so on). All such assertions are open to the retort, 'Says who?'. All, however, may be justified with reference to functionally rational modes of behaviour in a market economy.

Following this argument, we began our analysis of political inaction in Suffolk by considering the outcomes of the routine exercise of political power, and assessing their relative costs and benefits for different objectively defined sections of the county's population. The overall pattern soon became clear: a persistent and pervasive bias had been, and continued to be, generated through county and district policies, to the cumulative advantage of the relatively prosperous (and notably local landowners and farmers) and the distinct disadvantage of the already disadvantaged.

Take, for example, county and district expenditure and local taxation policies. Politicians in Suffolk have long been concerned, and at times obsessed, with maintaining a low level of public expenditure, and hence keeping the rates (a local property tax) down. In 1975, for example, drastic cuts in expenditure on education and social services were authorized by the county council's majority Conservative group in order to keep the rates down, and as a result, only six county councils in the whole of England and Wales succeeded in levying a lower rate than Suffolk. Council members themselves often deny any class bias in this policy. Indeed, one county councillor suggested to us that a low rate (and thus low levels of public expenditure) positively favoured the least privileged sections of the population: 'We have to be concerned about low rates because we're a low wage-earning community'. But such a comment not only ignores the very real material divisions within the 'community', and thus serves to present as unitary what objectively are totally divergent interests (see below), but it also ignores the effects of a low rate policy on the provision of indirect incomes for the least privileged sections of the population. Thus in the new county council's first year of operation, for example (1974—75), only four of the 37 counties in England and Wales on which information is available spent less *per capita* on education, only four spent less *per capita* on social services provisions, and Suffolk spent less than any other county authority per head of population on its library service (Return of Rates 1974—75). For some members of the population, of course, such low levels of public expenditure present no problems. Over half of all council members in the region themselves attended independent schools, for example, and at least as many may be expected in turn to use the independent sector for their offspring. The low level of expenditure on school books, materials, and equipment evidently only affects the less privileged sections of this 'low wage-earning community'. Similarly, the prosperous — the landowners, large farmers, immigrant middle-classes and so on — do not generally make use of council-aided social services. When, as happened in 1974—75, domestic help for the elderly and nursery provisions for the young are cut back, it is not *their* parents or children who are likely to suffer. When the level of expenditure on temporary accomodation stands as a fraction of the average for all countries, it is not they, in their fully-paid-for and modernized thatched and oaken-beamed homes who have cause for worry or complaint. On the contrary, the lower the rate, the less they stand to lose.

A similar pattern of sectional bias in council policy emerges when housing is considered. Between them, the county and district councils in the area have over the years relentlessly pursued a policy of encouraging high-priced, low-density, private housing development, while severely restricting public housing construction schemes. Over the years 1966–73, for example, East Suffolk County Council built an average of 1.3 local authority dwellings per 1000 population per year, compared with 5.6 private dwellings, and an East Anglian average of 2.7 and 6.6 respectively (figures computed from Local Housing Statistics, 1966–73). This lack of local authority building cannot be explained in terms of any lack of demand (we estimate that at least 10 000 families are waiting for houses in Suffolk, and these figures do not take account of those who have fatalistically not bothered to register, or those deemed 'unqualified' by the councils concerned). Nor is it due to any lack of suitable development land (sites have been found for private development with little problem). Rather it reflects both the low expenditure policy, and the county council planning policy which stipulates that housing development in rural areas should be of low density and very high quality (and hence price). So it is that only spacious private dwellings come to be built in such areas, while the rural working-class continued either to migrate in search of a house, or to be dependent upon local farmers for the hire of tied cottages.

Planning policies are significant beyond their effect on the provision of working-class housing, however. The point is that, at least in East Suffolk, any large-scale development scheme, whether it involves council housing estates, the construction of new factories, or the provision of public utilities such as reservoirs and arterial roads, has traditionally been strongly opposed. In 1960, for example, when other local authorities (including neighbouring West Suffolk) entered 'overspill' agreements with the Greater London Council in order to attract new industry and new centres of population, East Suffolk resolutely did nothing. In the mid-1960s, when the central government proposed that the town of Ipswich be expanded, the county council, in alliance with the National Farmers Union, the County Landowners Association, and a variety of local preservationist groups, persistently opposed the plans, and was adamant that if development had to come (and as a leading member put it, 'I do not particularly welcome the prospect'), then it should be on an area of poor agricultural land to the east, despite the plethora of other factors which all pointed to development to the west. And throughout this period, the trail of rejected planning applications has continued to grow. Despite the falling local demand for labour by the agricultural industry, there has been a marked reluctance to admit any new industries into the rural parts of the county. In the words of one district council chairman:

We all want the same thing — we want to preserve the countryside for ourselves, for the people who come to visit us, and for our children . . . Planning in this area is very strict compared with other areas. You cannot build . . . It's a place we want to hand on to our children and grandchildren as pleasant rural countryside . . . You don't want industrial development spoiling things.

It is this preservationist outlook which, perhaps even more than the parsimonious policies on public expenditure, has come to dominate local authority thinking in Suffolk. Many of our respondents echoed this deep concern with maintaining the rural environment, and preventing its 'desecration' by any large-scale housing or industrial development. But as a review of council expenditure on relevant items indicates, such a concern appears somewhat passive and negative, rather than active and positive. Expenditure on preservation of buildings and other rural amenities, for example, amounts to only £74.85 per 1000 population in Suffolk, compared with £104.64 average in England and Wales. Nor are outsiders encouraged to come and view the beauties of the environment which has been preserved 'on their behalf' — expenditure on promotion of tourism is £7.37 per 1000, compared with an England and Wales average of £10.35. Indeed, many council members and local organizations are positively hostile towards sponsorship of tourism. A leading county councillor, for example, observed: 'I suppose preservation isn't in everybody's interest, but it is terribly sad if places are ruined by bad development . . . I am also anti-tourist. We don't want more tourists — they spoil the places by coming to them. Perhaps I am being selfish'. Similarly, the chairman of a strong local amenity society explained:

One of my arguments is that we must leave something for the next generation to spoil — we can't spoil everything ourselves. Of course, if you're going to keep it beautiful, it means only a few people can enjoy it, because the moment you introduce more people with their cars and ignorance of the countryside, you get them leaving gates open, going into the middle of corn fields, filling ditches with refrigerators and cookers . . . You've got to be selfish about it.

We are reminded here of Lowe's perceptive comments (1975, pp. 19–20) on the environmental movement:

Environment groups [he argues] like other lobbies, legitimate their activities by couching their aims in terms of the national good . . . The Romantic movement, in which much pre-servationist sentiment is rooted, asserted nature against industry: the countryside, and especially wilderness, offered the possibility of escape and refuge from industrial mass society: an escape which must be protected both from the ravages of industrialization and from the whims of popular taste. Thus we see built into much preservationist thought an ambivalence: preservation for the nation, but not necessarily for the public.

Furthermore, in this anti-urban ideology, preservationist sentiment serves to reinforce vertical identity within rural areas — as we shall see, 'community solidarity' may be an effective ideology in maintaining rural political stability.

It is possible to explain the traditional county council concern (shared by representatives of the farming/landowning and residential middle-class interests) with environmental preservation on two levels. At the level of *verstehen*, we may assume that those with a vested interest in the countryside quite rationally seek to preserve it. The middle-class newcomers in their converted cottages seek to maintain their 'village in the mind' (Pahl, 1965), while traditional local landowners are similarly intent on preserving what they see as their heritage (on the significance of notions of 'heritage' and 'stewardship', see Rose *et al.*, 1976). Clearly, we see here an obvious bias in council policies, for the more of the environment which one owns and controls, the greater is one's interest in its preservation, and in excluding others from access to it. The land-owners shooting pheasants may be said to derive greater benefit from the county council policy than the farmworkers poaching rabbits. But this policy may also be assessed at the level of *causality*, and it is here that the most significant bias is revealed. In pursuing a policy of rural stagnation, the county council may be seen to have perpetually reproduced the very situation with which its members regularly claim to be concerned — a low-wage economy based on the agricultural industry. This has not necessarily been intentional, but whatever their motives, Suffolk's politicians have succeeded in generating an environment policy with clear economic advantages for employers of local labour. Preservation of the *status quo* has necessarily involved preservation of existing restricted labour market opportunities and depressed wage structures. Industry, in other words, does not only represent a possible blot on the landscape, a threat to one's heritage. It also represents a potential source of competition for cheap labour. It is no coincidence that although East Anglia has traditionally been among the most prosperous of Britain's agricultural regions, its farmworkers have remained among the lowest paid in the country (for data see Newby, 1972).

Not only, therefore, have the local authorities in Suffolk shown themselves to be generally willing to align with the local farming/landowning interest on the few occasions (the Ipswich town expansion, for example) when public and acrimonious issues have arisen, but in the routine operation of their established policies, they can be seen to have consistently generated a bias in favour of the agricultural interest, and to the detriment of the rural working-class.

Faced with this evidence on the manifest bias mobilized through local authority rates, housing and planning policies, it was apparent to us that the pluralist explanation of political inaction, based as it is upon the assumption of communality as well as legitimacy was largely inapplicable. Where it did provide a useful explanation of inaction was in relation to the passivity of the relatively privileged groups in the county — the larger farmers, landowners, and middle-class residents — for they clearly had little to complain about. But as an explanation of working-class passivity, the Dahl/Parsons model was considered invalid. If, however, we were to explain the passivity of the Suffolk working-class in terms of a model of political manipulation, then it was equally apparent that we needed to demonstrate, not only that a sectional bias was operating, but also how opposition to this bias was effectively prevented from emerging. Power, after all, involves causality (though not, it should be noted, necessarily intentionally). It follows that any explanation of political inaction which denies the applicability of the pluralist model must therefore demonstrate how the powerful have *caused* the passivity of the powerless. As Lukes (1975, pp. 41–42) puts it, 'In brief we need to justify our expectation that B would have thought or acted differently; and we also need to specify the means of mechanism by which A has prevented, or else acted (or abstained from acting) in a manner sufficient to prevent B from doing so'. Having considered outcomes, we had next to consider cause.

The first point to note here is that the most blatantly sectional policies are often represented by those responsible for them as being self-evidently 'in the public interest'. It is not that political leaders deliberately misrepresent the nature of the policies they pursue, but rather that, from their viewpoint, the public interest and their sectional interests are congruent. Miliband (1969, pp. 67–68) has expressed this well:

... to dismiss their proclamations of freedom from class bias as mere hypocrisy leads to a dangerous underestimation of the dedication and resolution with which such leaders are likely to pursue a task of whose nobility they are utterly persuaded. Men so persuaded are not easily deflected from their purpose by appeals to reason or sentiment or evidence, particularly when matters of great moment are at stake.

Accusations of deliberate self-interest on the part of these men are likely to meet with ridicule, for as they see it, they are giving freely of their time on behalf of their community to develop policies from which everyone may benefit. Thus explaining the county council's planning policy, one member (himself a farmer and landowner) observed: ' The lack of industry does help farmers, but this is an agricultural county. It's always been the county council's priority — you don't build on good agricultural land. It does help farmers, but that's incidental'. Similarly one of his colleagues suggested, 'We are all mixed up with the agricultural thing. I mean, when you boil it down, the towns and villages and what-have-you in Suffolk in the main are dependent on agriculture, so that we really have all got the same ends all the time'.

Clearly, there is a self-fulfilling element in these arguments, for the people of Suffolk only remain dependent upon the agricultural industry for their liveli- hoods to the extent that other industries are prevented from locating in the county. We are not arguing that Suffolk's leaders are cynically hypocritical, but we are arguing that the effect of the dominance achieved by *their* definitions of what constitutes the 'public interest' has been to perpetuate a marked bias in local planning and social service policies. This being the case, we are faced with the problem of explaining how it is that challenges to their interpretations, their policies, and ultimately their power have so successfully been avoided, fended off, or stiffled over the years. How is it that sectional policies have routinely been pursued under the guise of communal benefit with virtually no challenge from those most disadvantaged?

The causal mechanisms which account for the lack of opposition in Suffolk may be found in all three of Bachrach and Baratz's (1970) types of 'non-decision- making' discussed earlier. Thus opposition is sidestepped through use of an ethic of non-politics, prevented through the anticipated reactions of a politically fatalistic working-class, and suppressed through ideological manipulation. Let us briefly consider each in turn.

(a) The effects of a non-politics ethic

Leading local politicians place extraordinary emphasis on what they term 'keeping politics out of local government'. Before the 1974 reorganization, for example, over half of all council members in the East Anglian region claimed to be 'independent' of any political party (the proportion reached 68 per cent among farmer-councillors, indicating the strength of this ethic among those with an agricultural interest). On the East Suffolk County Council, a Conservative chairman and Labour vicechairman worked closely together to lead a council where party antagonisms were virtually unknown, while even since reorganization, despité the increased significance of party discipline and patronage, many members of both main parties continue to emphasize the virtues of 'non-political' local government. At the district level, too, this ethic remains strong. Indeed, on one district council, a small Labour group of seven still holds three of the five committee chairmanships, and resolutely refuses to oppose the policies of the Conservative/Independent majority.

The significance of this entrenched value of non-politics is that it not only derives from, but in turn itself perpetuates and strengthens, the prevailing definition of the political situation in Suffolk as one of genuine consensus. In other words, sectional policies can only be represented as being 'in the public interest' to the extent that there is a general acceptance that local government affairs are apolitical in character. If decision-making can be represented as the implementation of the obvious, and if everybody is assumed to be on the same side, then the task of councillors becomes merely the pursuit of a non-problem-atically defined public interest. Given this basic assumption, it then follows that party divisions, 'doctrinaire' decision-making, and critical opposition are not only unnecessary, but a distinct hindrance. 'It is political now', mused one Conservative county member, 'and it's a bloody nuisance . . . I get on very well with the Labour people, but it does lengthen debates'. In consequence, those few Labour radicals who have refused to accept the normative convention of non-politics, and have instead attempted to criticize the effects of council policies, have generally found themselves labelled as 'troublemakers', 'extremists', and thus unworthy of people's serious attention. Yet as one of them complained bitterly to us, 'To a Conservative, being political is being anything other than right-wing. But to me, doing nothing is just as political as being revolutionary'. It is just this insight, however, which is so conspicuously lacking among many of Suffolk's politicians of both main parties.

The significance of the non-politics ethic is clear. If consensus is assumed to exist, then political conflict may be dismissed as the work of 'politically moti-vated' agitators. Party politics thus become defined as irrelevant, and in the absence of party politics, conflicts of interest generally fail to become manifest. A belief in 'non-political' local government, therefore, not only obscures an essential conservatism, but also effectively blocks the fundamental means by which opposition may come to be voiced. Leading members of the Labour groups on the various local authorities in Suffolk are to all intents and purposes co-opted as junior associates of Conservative élite groups. As one Labour radical on a district council observed, 'These Labour committee chairmen believe they're doing their bit by being chairmen. But they're being manipulated by the Tories without realising it'. Or as one of his fellows on the county council put it, 'They're only going to make someone chairman if he's not going to change anything'. Of course, Labour co-optees have their scruples. They will not be *seen* to preside over Conservative policies. As one explained in relation to the low level of council-house building in his area, 'There doesn't need to be political disagreement. The council ought to build the maximum amount of council houses, and it's the policy we've always pursued. If they (the Conservative majority) said they wouldn't do it, then I and my colleagues would be after them'. But the Conservatives never do say that they will not build. They simply 'cannot' find the money (due to the low rate policy), or 'cannot' find the land (due to the planning policy). In this way, the principles of Labour chairmen are maintained, and they feel able to continue to offer their services. That conflict is prevented from developing in Suffolk's local government is therefore due to a large extent to a prevailing political culture which inhibits criticism, leads to the co-option (and hence co-operation) of potential critics, and facilitates the negative labelling of those who transgress these conventions.

(b) The effects of political apathy

We saw earlier that disadvantaged groups may fail to act out of their antici-pation of any action proving fruitless or costly. According to Parry and Morriss (1974), such cases may be amenable to study only in so far as tentative demands are initially made by subordinate groups as a means of assessing which way the political wind is blowing, these demands only later being withdrawn or aborted. Clearly however, cases of inaction stemming from anticipated reactions will more usually be routinized, for subordinate groups are likely to be only too familiar with prevailing wind directions — in Suffolk they rarely waver. The consequence of this is that inaction may often follow anticipated reactions with no outward and visible sign that 'non-decision-making' has occurred, and in such cases it will appear indistinct from the inaction which stems from political satisfaction, for in neither case will subordinate groups actually do anything. This is significant, for it allows those in power in Suffolk to explain all political inactivity and working-class passivity in terms of a pluralist model of satisfaction of political wants. As a district council chairman put it,

It's because of the type of people who live in Suffolk — they're people of the land, but they're no fools. They're very astute people. But they don't get terribly involved — no, that's not the right way to say it — they feel strongly, and they expect their representatives to know what they're feeling strongly about, almost instinctively without writing it down or without saying it . . . I suppose, being facetious, they choose the right people, and the right people do the right things for them. It can't be like that, but it almost looks like that, doesn't it?

Similarly: 'Suffolk does produce pressure groups when necessary. It doesn't have a great deal of cause, I don't think . . . There's not much militancy in any-thing here — there isn't the cause for militancy here'.

The problem with this explanation — apart from the existence of a plethora of 'objective' causes for 'militancy' (discussed earlier) — is that there are occasions when pluralist democracy is supposed to exhibit 'healthy' opposition and competition among its members. On such occasions in Suffolk, however, it has often proved difficult to excite any participation. Local elections provide one example. It is not simply that so few people bother to vote in these periodic celebrations of democracy, but that, at least until 1974, few people could even be found to stand as candidates. Unopposed elections, of course, create a 'bad image', and this has at times resulted in a political situation, as described by one district councillor, with a distinct Alice-in-Wonderland quality: 'What I don't agree with is what has happened in many cases where people get in unopposed. I'm dead against this altogether, and in fact I used to try to get people to oppose me at one time — sounds silly, but I think it's right'. It is almost as if Suffolk's politicians see the inactivity of the majority as simply too good to be true, and thus, paradoxically, attempt to stimulate some opposition!

The same story emerges from a consideration of the recent formulation of the county's Structure Plan, and the attempts made there to encourage 'public participation' in a debate over future planning policies (including, of course, the vexed question of future industrial development and population growth). According to a leading member of the Planning Committee:

I think the public response to our consultative document is representative. Of course, there's an awful lot of people who don't care — a very good response is something like three or four per cent. But the response you get is from those who do bother . . . Although you only get a small percentage replying, you're giving everyone the chance to comment and to be listened to. We get the more intelligent types who are interested in the county replying. The type who says, 'Roll on 5 o'clock, when do the pubs open?' doesn't really care.

The question, however, is why 95 per cent or more of the county's population seem not to 'care' about a planning exercise with profound implications for their housing and employment prospects. The great majority of those who responded to the plan urged greater conservation, and even a council planning official admitted that the planners were hoping to provoke some response from both the Labour Party and the public against the planning policies which have for so long gone unchallenged.

The problem, however, is that inaction is for most people (and, indeed, for the Labour Party) in Suffolk, a standard and routinized response to a situation of continuing objective deprivation and political exclusion. For most of the time, they neither expect nor are expected to play any part in policy-making, and when the structured opportunities to 'participate' are offered them in order to maintain the image of a 'healthy' pluralist democracy, they react as they have always reacted — by doing nothing. Most people in Suffolk recognize, consciously or implicitly, that local politics is not their game. It is hardly sensible, then, to query why they do not join in on the odd occasions when they are called upon to do so, for most of the time they are kept uninformed of the rules and excluded from the field of play. 'There's a tendency in this backward, feudal area for some people to think that "them" above know better', explained one Labour councillor. 'So many people just accept things as they are, and think "they" know best'. Or as another observed, 'People are brought up differently in the country I suppose. They're timid and thankful of small mercies'.

(c) The effects of particularistic power relations

This leads us to consider the third area of 'non-decision-making' identified by Bachrach and Baratz (1970): The situation where inaction results from the prior manipulation of the beliefs, information, and values of subordinate groups by ultra-powerful local élites. The mechanisms by which this is achieved in Suffolk lie in the particularism of the political system. Power, that is to say, is often personalized and essentially non-bureaucratic. The consequence of this is, first, that lower-class solidarism (see Parkin, 1974) is weakened through the individualization of political issues, and second, that the transmission of élite ideologies across the classes is considerably eased.

Take as an example the personal following claimed by many council members. Even since 1974, when the size of electoral wards was considerably enlarged, a personal vote, often cross-cutting party allegiances, remained in evidence in many cases. As one county councillor explained, 'In rural areas the individual carries more weight. If he's well known, irrespective of his politics, a local man has an advantage over a non-local man, especially in Suffolk. It's a personal following'. Such particularism is positively reinforced by the stout resistance of many councillors to any bureaucratic development. On one of the district councils, for example, the attempts of the housing manager to persuade the members to adopt a 'points system' for the allocation of council houses met stout opposition. One explained his opposition thus:

The onus falls on the local representative for who gets housed. He is responsible. When someone gets a house round here, I'm 90 per cent responsible. If I say you're not going to get a house, you don't get one. The people you put into those houses will vote for you, and those you don't will fight you. I've got a moral conscience. I know all my bad housing cases. They are my own personal priority list. I've fought against the introduction of a points system. Those who want to operate a points system can do it, but I won't.

Personal dependence, gratitude, and loyalty are thus positively encouraged. As a result, influence is expected to be exerted at the individual rather than the collective level. Councillors see only individual problems, not political issues, such as the inability of a particular family to get a house, rather than the planning and budgetary policies which produce a housing shortage. In this way, generalized complaints never get raised. The comments of one district councillor exemplify this point: 'There's no pressure group activity at all. I don't believe in being pressurized. People go to see their ward member and stir him up. If they convince me it's sensible, I'll stir things up — but I do stress *sensible* . . . There are no organizations. It's all done on a face-to-face personal level'.

This personalization of power relations not only fragments issues into 'problems', but also eases the transmission of élite ideologies to subordinate groups. A case in point is the notion of Suffolk as a 'community', for we would argue that in the political context of Suffolk, 'community' (and the various associated notions such as localism and anti-urbanism) is a facet of ruling-class ideology. Put another way, ideas of community are consistently asserted by dominant economic and political groups, echoed by subordinate groups, and thus used to foster a sense of fellow-feeling, local attachment, and relative contentment. Identification and solidarism, therefore, is encouraged along the local/non-local, rural/urban cleavage, and in this way, class consciousness based upon economic interests is avoided.

For many of the county's political leaders 'community' implies community of interest. Conflicting economic interests of different classes are simply not recognized: 'All in all, no. I don't think there are any major issues here. I think that everyone fits in very well — a nice friendly area'. The delights of *gemeinschaftlich* relationships, the wholesome goodness of the organic community, are represented by them as real and enduring qualities of life in Suffolk. Essential to this ideology is an entrenched spirit of anti-urbanism. To a large extent rural solidarity is defined in terms of urban hostility. 'Outsiders' provide the focus in terms of which internal solidarity may be generated, and stereotypical 'urbanities', with their perpetual demands for cheap food, their disregard for the countryside, and their ignorance of country folk, provide the ideal outsiders for this function. Urbanites constitute an ill-defined and amorphous 'they' in terms of which 'we' (that is, rural dwellers of all classes) are defined and achieve a collective identity immune to the rupture of mere class antagonisms. The anti-urbanism is not, of course, a deliberately fostered ideology designed to maintain internal cohesion in the countryside. By and large, the rural élite in Suffolk feels a genuine antipathy towards urban values, and the 1974 local government reorganization vividly illustrated the very real hostility shown by rural councillors, not only to newly appointed officers from urban areas, but even to members of their own party representing newly amalgamated urban areas. The hostility to 'outsiders', 'urbanites', and 'newcomers' is thus real enough. But whether intentionally or not, it serves to promote cross-class solidarity by scapegoating external groups. Thus, for example, the shortage of public housing is explained, not in terms of the council's housing and planning policies, but in terms of a weekend cottager invasion, or national government policies. Similarly, development is discouraged, not because it would boost local wage levels, but because it would introduce alien migrants into the local population. Residential origin rather than class thus becomes the most salient criterion of identification, and this in turn blurs class differences and perpetuates working-class passivity.

Before concluding our discussion of the politics of Suffolk, however, we should deal with one possible objection to our arguments. It could be suggested that, if a local élite or ruling class is so dominant that it can successfully circumvent opposition when it occurs, and even prevent opposition before it occurs, then no opposition and no issues should *ever* develop. Clearly this is not the case, for although conflicts have been few and far between, they have nevertheless occurred. Having rejected a pluralist explanatory model, we are therefore left with the problem of explaining how issues arise in a situation of seemingly pervasive political domination. From evidence collected in Suffolk, we may suggest three possible situations in which issues and conflicts may still occur within a context of political and ideological hegemony.

(1) First, conflict may arise as a result of a split within a local ruling group. In Suffolk, for example, many recent *causes célèbres* have concerned antagonisms generated by migrant middle-class complaints about farmers' hedge removal, aerial spraying, ploughing of footpaths, and so on. But despite the publicity which such squabbles attract, and the antipathy of local landowners toward urban 'invaders', the interests of the two are fundamentally in concert. In the words of one landowner and county councillor, 'They simply hate hedge removal and stubble-burning . . . But in some cases a farmer and a retired Londoner are at one — for instance, in not wanting a council estate doubling the size of the village'. We would not wish to underemphasize the significance of conflicts between these two groups over preservation. The professional and managerial middle-class in East Anglia accounts for nearly 50 per cent of all council members, and its political voice is a strong one. Nevertheless, it is also apparent that among the more privileged sections of Suffolk society (including both locals *and* newcomers) the local/newcomer, rural/urban divide is generally less significant than the horizontal class division based upon the conflict of interests between middle-class residents and landowners on the one hand, and the local working-class on the other. Despite the occasional reactions therefore, the hegemony noted earlier is more usually strengthened rather than threatened by the growing political power of the county's immigrant middle-class. Indeed, the conflict takes place, not between those who wish to develop and those who wish to preserve, but between preservationists and 'ultra-preservationists' (see Rose *et al.*, 1976). In similar fashion, local protests from Suffolk's middle-class over rate increases indicate only local property-owners' concern that an extraordinary low rate could perhaps be even lower. Such 'conflicts' are examples of disagreements over the extent to which a given policy should be followed. They are in no way a challenge to the policy itself.

(2) The second situation in which conflict may occur is less of a 'phoney war', although again it in no way indicates any weakness of the local ruling élite. This is where an outside agency attempts to impose a policy on the county against the will of those with power locally. There have been several examples of this in Suffolk in recent years — indeed, most local 'issues' have been generated through outside intervention. (It is worth noting here that such 'interference' by 'outsiders' may provide further grounds for hostility to 'outsiders' in general, and urbanites in particular, and thus paradoxically strengthen the vertical ties, and hence the established power relations, within the county). The proposed expansion of Ipswich, for example, was instigated by the government, and supported by the (urban) County Borough of Ipswich. It was strongly opposed, however, by the East Suffolk County Council, local preservation bodies, and the

National Farmers Union and Country Landowners Association, all of whom were concerned to restrict development in the face of this threat to the *status quo* from outside the county. Similarly today, the county council is violently opposed to the Electricity Board's plans to build a large power generating station on the Suffolk coast, and in this it has the support of local preservation and agricultural/landowning organizations (it should be noted here that the proposed development would also create considerable local employment opportunities). It has also registered its disagreement (in common with its preservationist and agricultural allies) with a proposal in the recently finalized East Anglian Regional Plan that a new town should be developed in the north of the county, while a few years ago it fought a proposal from the Ipswich Water Undertaking to construct a reservoir to the south. All of these issues received considerable publicity. But all are the result of outside instigation, be it in the form of the Government, the Electricity Board, the Regional Planning Team, or the Ipswich Water Authority. Fundamental conflicts are rarely generated from *within* the local political system. Furthermore, where conflicts do arise as a result of outside intervention, they invariably produce a swift and close alliance between the traditional trinity of the county council, the preservationist lobby, and the agricultural/landowning interest against the external threat.

(3) The third and final situation in which conflict may occur locally is where the dominant political grouping is content that it should. Hacker (1965, p. 135) has summarized this point well: 'The élite is content to let the public blow off steam on certain question. This is acknowledged to be necessary, for democracy must have issues to squabble about. If attention is focussed on fluoride in the water and progressivism in the schools, then eyes will be deflected from more important matters'. Curiously, the two examples given by Hacker are both pertinent to Suffolk. Thus one 'contentious' issue currently exercizing the minds of many county councillors and their constituents relates to a proposal for a sixth-form college in Ipswich, while the question of adding fluoride to the water supply has provided the local press with a ready story for many years. Similarly, problems of aircraft noise from American bases in the county (outsiders again!) occasionally make the local press, while at the district level, councillors have argued heatedly over whether or not council meetings should open with prayers, and over appointments to local school governorships. From all this, we may venture to suggest that the political significance (in terms of its effect on the overall pattern of resource distribution) of any given issue varies in inverse proportion to the publicity and attention which it receives. We should perhaps also note that the conservative editorial policy of the local press in Suffolk usually ensures that, even where substantive political issues are raised (such as attacks by some county Labour members on the low rate policy, for example), they are rarely or only minimally reported.

The situation which we are positing is thus analogous to that described by Madgwick and his colleagues (1973, p. 156) in relation to the farming interest in Welsh rural politics: 'No other class is coherent enough to operate as a group . . .

The views of the élites tend to confirm both the existence of some stresses and tensions and the absence of widespread and overt class hostility'. Issues, in this sense, are those defined as such by a politically dominant rural landowning élite. Fundamentally threatening opposition is stifled before it can emerge — the co-option of Labour leaders ensures that — and what Parkin (1974) has termed 'exclusion practices' are operated against a subordinate mass of politically defined 'ineligibles'. The pervasity of particularism ensures that grievances are never generalized while the deep-rootedness of a community ideology is usually sufficient to reinforce vertical solidarity and identification.

Conclusion

For too long community studies have been the last refuge for abstracted empiricism. Their lack of theoretical relevance has been quite rightly deplored. Yet this need not continue. We have shown in this chapter that there is a body of theoretical concepts that can be used to analyse rural areas. Power is both the central and the most difficult (and therefore 'contested') of all sociological and political concepts. We have also shown how an understanding of its operation and its very definition can be furthered by studying rural areas through community studies. Indeed because of the 'localness' of many, if not most political decisions in rural areas the mechanisms through which power operates are more, rather than less, open to empirical investigation. For these reasons alone community studies will retain their usefulness.

And yet, of course, we feel that our conclusions have relevance well beyond local communities in East Anglia. We are confronting here some of the key issues faced by *any* analysis of political and economic structures in *any* advanced industrial society. Just what are the explanations of political stability? The answers to this question involve far-ranging analyses — and have often been sought empirically in large factories and big cities. We have shown here that it is also possible — and we believe it to be imperative — to come to understand the operation of one of the *most* successful ruling classes still extant. We have treated the lack of discontent, the quiescence, the absence of rancour as problematic in its own right. Dogs that do not bark in the night are in some ways even more interesting than dogs that do. Are they contentedly asleep as the Parsons/Dahl pluralist model would suggest? Or are they muzzled as the Bachrach and Baratz two-faces-of-power approach maintains? Or have they been doped as some Marxist models would lead us to believe? As has emerged in our argument above these three models do not, as most commentators seem to have concluded, have to be taken as mutually exclusive. There is in all advanced industrial societies a certain minimum consensus, yet as we have shown above there are many procedures and mechanisms that work to prevent the articulation of the interests of non-powerful groups — in this case the rural working-class. We maintain that it is possible to refer to 'objective interests' in any political and social system and hence to cut through the dense thickets that usually surround the problem of 'false-consciousness'. Though we would not expect that all would agree with our analysis it does seem to us to provide a useful *entrée* to the study of power everywhere.

Finally, we have had a frankly propagandist aim in this chapter. We wish to support Giddens' programmatic statement made in his important paper from which we quoted earlier. He wrote (1976, p. 721) that 'the differentiation between sociology (as the study of social structure) and political science (as the study of government or political power) which has grown up over the years and become institutionally sanctified, should be abandoned'. If as he says, 'It should be one of the major tasks of sociology to create a theory of the modern state and to explore its significance for problems of social theory in general' (1976) then what we have done here is to explore the significance of *local* political power and *its* significance for social theory. We hope that the theoretical issues have become clearer, yet we would be the first to acknowledge that the real work has hardly begun.

References

Abrams, P. and McCulloch, A. (1976), *Communes and Alternative Life Styles* (London: Cambridge University Press).

Ambrose, P. (1974), *The Quiet Revolution* (London: Chatto and Windus).

Anderson, C. (1958), 'Rural sociology', in Merton *et al.*, *Sociology Today* (New York: Basic Books).

Arensberg, C. M. (1961), 'The community as object and as sample', *American Anthropologist*, **63**, 2, 241–264.

Arensberg, C. M. and Kimball, S. T. (1949), *Family and Community in Ireland* (Cambridge, Mass.: Harvard University Press).

Bachrach P. and Baratz, M. S. (1970), 'The two faces of power', in P. Bachrach and M. S. Baratz (eds.), *Power and Poverty* (New York: Oxford University Press).

Bailey, F. G. (1969), *Gifts and Poison* (Oxford: Blackwell).

Bailey, F. G. (1971), *Stratagems and Spoils* (Oxford: Blackwell).

Banfield, E. (1956), *The Moral Basis of a Backward Society* (Glencoe, Ill.: Free Press).

Bell, C. (1974), 'Replication and reality', *Futures*, **June 1974**, 253–266.

Bell, C. and Newby, H. (1971), *Community Studies* (London: Allen and Unwin).

Bell, C. and Newby, H. (1973), 'The sources of variation in agricultural workers' images of society', *Sociological Review*, **21**, 2, 229–253.

Bell, C. and Newby, H. (1974), 'Capitalist farmers in the British class structure', *Sociologia Ruralis*, **14**, 1/2, 86–107.

Bell, C. and Newby, H. (1976a), 'Husbands and wives: the dynamics of the differential dialectic', in D. Barker and S. Allen (eds.), *Dependency and Exploitation in Work and Marriage* (London: Longmans).

Bell, C. and Newby, H. (1976b), 'Community, communion, class and community action: the social sources of the new urban politics', in D. Herbert and R. Johnson (eds.), *Social Areas in Cities, vol. 2*, (London: Wiley).

Benvenuti B., Galjart B. and Newby H. (1975), 'The current status of rural sociology', *Sociologia Ruralis*, **XV**, 1/2, 3–21.

Beteille, A. (1965), *Caste, Class and Power* (Berkeley, Cal.: University of California Press).

Bloch, M. (1961), *The Feudal Society* (London: Routledge and Kegan Paul).

Blok, A. (1974), *The Mafia of Sicilian Villages 1860–1960* (Oxford: Blackwell).

Brody, H. (1973), *Inishkillane* (London: Allen Lane).

Campbell, J. K. (1964), *Honour, Family and Patronage* (Oxford: Clarendon Press).

Chayanov, A. (1966), *The Theory of Peasant Economy* (London: Irwin).

Coser, L. (1974), *Greedy Institutions* (New York: Macmillan).

Crenson, D. (1971), *The Un-Politics of Air Pollution* (Chicago: University of Chicago Press).

Dahl, R. (1961), *Who Governs?* (New Haven, Conn.: Yale University Press).

Davidoff, L., L'Esperance J., and Newby H. (1976), 'Landscape with figures', in J. Mitchell and A. Oakley (eds.) *The Rights and Wrongs of Women* (Harmondsworth: Penguin).

Davis, J. (1970), 'Morals and backwardness', *Comparative Studies in Society and History*, **12**, 3, 340–356.

Frankenberg, R. (1966), *Communities in Britain* (Harmondsworth: Penguin).

Galeski, B. (1972), *Basic Concepts in Rural Sociology* (Manchester: Manchester University Press).

Galtung, J. (1971), *Members of Two Worlds* (New York: Columbia University Press).

Gamson, W. A. (1966), 'Rancorous conflict in community politics', *American Sociological Review*, **31**, 71–81.

Geertz, C. (1965), *The Social History of an Indonesian Town* (Cambridge, Mass.: MIT Press).

Genovese, E. (1971), *In Red and Black* (London: Allen Lane).

Genovese, E. (1974), *Roll Jordan Roll* (New York: Pantheon Books).

Giddens, A. (1972), 'Four myths in the history of social thought', *Economy and Society*, **1**, 4, 357–389.

Giddens, A. (1974), *The Class Structures of the Advanced Societies* (London: Hutchinson).

Giddens, A. (1976), 'Classical social theory and modern sociology', *American Journal of Sociology*, **81**, 4, 703–729.

Glass, R. (1966), 'Conflict in cities' in the CIBA Foundation symposium, *Conflict in Society* (London: Churchill Press).

Goffman, E. (1968), *Asylums* (Harmondsworth: Penguin).

Goldthorpe J. H., Lockwood D., Bechhofer F., and Platt J. (1969), *The Affluent Worker in the Class Structure* (Cambridge: Cambridge University Press).

Gouldner, A. (1970), *The Coming Crisis in Western Sociology* (New York: Basic Books).

Hacker, A. (1965) (ed.), *The Corporation Take-Over.* (Garden City, N.Y: Doubleday).

Hillery, G. (1955), 'Definitions of Community: Areas of agreement', *Rural Sociology*, **20**, 115–125.

Hinton, W. (1973), *Fanshen* (Harmondsworth: Penguin).

Hobsbawm, E. J. (1968), *Primitive Rebels* (Manchester: Manchester University Press).

Hunter, F. (1953), *Community Power Structure* (Chapel Hill, N.C.: University of North Carolina Press).

Kantor, R. M. (1972), *Commitment and Community: Communes and Utopias in Sociological Perspective* (Cambridge, Mass.: Harvard University Press).

Kantor, R. M. (ed.) (1973), *Communes: Creating and Managing the Collective Life* (New York: Harper and Row).

Kroeber, A. L. (1948), *Anthropology* (London: Harrap).

Landsberger, H. A. (1974), *Rural Protests: Peasant Movements and Social Change* (London: Macmillan).

Lewis, O. (1951), *Life in A Mexican Village* (Urbanaiu.: University of Illinois Press).

Littlejohn, J. (1963), *Westrigg* (London: Routledge and Kegan Paul).

Lowe, P. (1975), 'The environmental lobby', *Built Environment*, **September**, 15–20.

Lukes, S. (1975), *Power: A Radical View* (London: Macmillan).

Madgwick, P. (1973), *The Politics of Rural Wales* (Cardiff: University of Wales Press).

Miliband, R. (1969), *The State in Capitalist Society* (London: Weidenfeld and Nicolson).

Mills, C. Wright (1964), *The Sociological Imagination* (New York: Oxford University Press).

Mishan, E. J. (1968), *The Costs of Economic Growth* (Harmondsworth: Penguin).

Moore, B. (1966), *The Social Origins of Dictatorship and Democracy* (London: Allen Lane).

Myrdal, J. (1975), *Report From A Chinese Village* (London: Picador).

Newby, H. (1972), 'Agricultural workers in the class structure', *Sociological Review*, 20, 3, 413–439.

Newby, H. (1975), 'The deferential dialectic', *Comparative Studies in Society and History*, 17, 2, 138–164.

Newby, H. (1977), *The Deferential Worker* (London: Allen Lane).

Newton, K. (1975), 'Community politics and decision-making: The American experience and its lessons' in K. Young (ed.), *Essays on The Study of Urban Politics* (London: Macmillan).

Nisbet, R. (1966), *The Sociological Tradition* (London: Heinemann).

Nolan M. F. and Galliher J. L. (1973), 'Rural sociological research and social policy: hard data, hard times', *Rural Sociology*, 38, 4, 491–499.

Olson, P. (1965), 'Rural American community studies: the survival of public ideology', *Human Organization*, 349–360.

Pahl, R. E. (1965), *Urbs in Rure* (London: Weidenfeld and Nicolson).

Pahl, R. E. (1966), 'The rural–urban continuum', *Sociologia Ruralis*, 6, 4, 299–329.

Parkin, F. (ed.) (1974), *The Social Analysis of Class Structure* (London: Tavistock).

Parry G. and Morriss P. (1974), 'When is a decision not a decision?', in Ivor Crewe (ed.) in *British Political Sociology Yearbook, Vol. 1: Élites in Western Democracy*, 317–336.

Parsons, T. (1966), *Societies: Evolutionary and Comparative Perspectives* (Englewood Cliffs, N.J.: McGraw-Hill).

Petersen, W. (1968), 'The ideological origins of Britain's new towns', *American Institute of Planners Journal*, XXXIV, 2, 160–170.

Pizzorno, A. (1966), 'Historical marginality and social change', *International Review of Community Development*, December, 55–66.

Polsby, N. W. (1963), *Community Power and Political Theory* (New Haven: Yale University Press).

Redfield, R. (1930), *Tepotzlan* (Chicago: Chicago University Press).

Redfield, R. (1947), 'The folk society', *American Journal of Sociology*, 52, 293–308.

Rees, A. D. (1951), *Life in a Welsh Countryside* (Cardiff: University of Wales Press).

Rose D., Saunders P., Newby H., and Bell C. (1976), 'Ideologies of property ownership: a case study', *Sociological Review*, **November**.

Schmalenbach, H. (1961), 'The sociological category of communion' in T. Parsons *et al.* (eds.), *Theories of Society, Vol. 1*, (Glencoe, Ill.: Free Press), 331–347.

Schmitt, P. J. (1969), *Back to Nature: The Arcadian Myth in Urban America* (New York: Oxford University Press).

Schumacher, E. F. (1973), *Small Is Beautiful* (London: Paladin).

Shanin, T. (1966), 'Peasantry as a political factor', *Sociological Review*, **14 January**, 5–27.

Shanin, T. (ed.) (1970), *Peasants and Peasant Societies* Harmondsworth: Penguin).

Smith M. and Crossley D. (1975), *The Way Out* (Melbourne: Jacaranda Press).

Sorokin, P. A. and Zimmerman, C. C. (1929), *Principles of Rural–Urban Sociology* (New York: Henry Holt; Kraus Reprint, 1969).

Stacey, M. (1969), 'The myth of community studies', *British Journal of Sociology*, 20, 134–147.

Stacey M., Batstone E., Bell C., and Murcott A. (1975), *Power, Persistence and Change* (London: Routledge and Kegan Paul).

Stanworth, P. and Giddens, A. (eds.) (1974), *Elites and Power in British Society* (London: Cambridge University Press).

Stein, M. (1964), *The Eclipse of Community* (New York: Harper and Row).

Stinchcombe, A. (1961—62), 'Agricultural enterprise and rural class relations', *American Journal of Sociology*, **67**, 169–76.

Tonnies, F. (ed. C. Loomis) (1957), *Gemeinschaft und Gesellschaft*. (New York: Harper).

Vidich A. J. and Bensman J. (1957), *Small Town in Mass Society* (Princeton, N.J.: Princeton University Press).

Walton, J. (1966a), 'Substance and artifact: the current status of research on community power structure', *American Journal of Sociology*, **31**, 430–438.

Walton, J. (1966b), 'Discipline, method and community power: a note on the sociology of knowledge', *American Sociological Review*, **31**, 684–*689*.

Weber, M. (1964), *The Theory of Social and Economic Organization* (Glencoe, Ill.: Free Press).

Wild, R. (1974), *Bradstow* (Sydney: Angus and Robertson).

Wild, R. (1975), 'Localities, social relationships and the rural–urban continuum', *Australian and New Zealand Journal of Sociology*, **10 March**, 170—176.

Williams, R. (1973), *The Country and The City* (London: Chatto and Windus).

Williams, W. M. (1964), *A West Country Village: Ashworthy* (London: Routledge and Kegan Paul).

Wolf, E. (1966), *Peasant Societies* (Englewood Cliffs, N.J.: McGraw-Hill).

Wolf, E. (1970), *Peasant Wars in the Twentieth Century* (London: Faber).

Wylie, L. (1961), *Village in the Vaucluse* (Oxford: Oxford University Press).

Yglesias, J. (1972), *In the First of the Revolution* (Harmondsworth: Penguin).

4
Capital, State and Sparse Populations: the Context for Further Research

Thomas M. Davies

In this chapter, I attempt to draw from my own limited knowledge of the very wide field of planned industrialization policy, and from its social impact, elements which can be synthesized to give guidelines for future research in the narrower, but at the same time wider, field of sparsely populated areas. I have tried to show the essential interdependence between the role of the state and the movement of capital to new locations, and how these must be understood if research in the field of social and economic impact is to have any meaning. I have also tried to show the need to carry on this research employing a historical methodology, and also in an international context. Capital is now international, and research must become so speedily if it is to keep up with the developments which will take place in the near future. If at times the text sounds a little (or a great deal) more confident than the evidence would suggest, this is a fault of the style. I have tried to put forward a tentative theoretical framework, unnaturally condensed, together with an indication of some supportive empirical material. I have suggested avenues for further research — explicitly in a number of places, implicitly throughout. The field is characterized by a lack of synthesis and a lack of theoretical structure which makes practically every issue worthy of attention. I hope this chapter, whilst indicating this, will help to focus debate about future research strategies.

What follows is written against a background of a personally unresolved, and perhaps universally unresolved, conceptual problem: that of defining and relating 'sparsely populated areas', 'peripheral areas' and 'remote areas'. There is first a research problem here. It is obvious that these concepts are employed in policy, both within nation states, and now in the EEC and similar supra-state bodies. However, they also have some status as academic concepts. Research which showed the relationship between the policy definitions and the academic definitions would usefully clear the air, and would allow a more rigorous approach to the problem than I shall adopt in this chapter. To give examples of the problems which this unresolving gives rise to, I offer you the following confusions. Norway, Ireland and most of the UK are seen as being peripheral by the EEC bureaucracy in Brussels (Commission of the European Communities, 1973). While resenting this definition, the nation states involved, both in and out of the EEC, employ that perception of peripherality for political ends, mostly economic. Peripheral is a polite word, which ducks the issue of whether these areas are not so much peripheral, meaning sharing a boundary with the centre, as remote. Most of us mean remote when we say peripheral. However, we are also thinking about population when we use the word. Here again, confusion arises. For instance, Glasgow and Edinburgh, while peripheral to Europe, and some would say to the United Kingdom, are obviously not remote, while some would say that the Borders were remote. Alternatively, some areas immediately adjacent to Oslo are not peripheral in some sense, but have little or no population (Hansen, 1972).

I intend to use the word 'peripheral' as a device to allow me to continue, in the sense of 'relatively far from the centre of economic activity'.

The Movement of Capital to the Periphery

The conference held in Aberdeen in 1973 on the topic of peripheral areas provides me with a convenient and rich starting point for this part of my argument. We know that there is a considerable contemporary movement to peripheral areas, internationally, of certain kinds of capital, which takes the physical shape of branch plants, highly capital-intensive, in the extractive, process, energy and port-related industries (Gaskin, 1973). Typical of these are nuclear power stations, chemical plants producing general chemicals, aluminium works, pulp and paper mills, and perhaps in the not-too-distant future, steel mills producing general steels (Lyddon, 1973; Warren, 1973). They represent that sector of industry which has reached the highest level of replacement of labour by capital, and frequently represent the largest capital investments which are undertaken by companies in the production sector.

The amounts of capital involved are often spectacular. George (1973) tells us that the Strait of Camso received a Swedish pulp mill worth 132 million dollars, a Canadian GED heavy-water plant of 75 million, a Gulf oil refinery of 75 million, and a state-owned power station of 17 million. The figures for expenditure in the UK are difficult to obtain, and require a considerable amount of research effort; I suspect that the same goes for most countries. The effort would repay rich dividends. For instance, in the UK in 1970, apart from the almost 100 per cent of aluminium capital which went into the 'peripheral areas', 75 per cent of investment in explosives, 65 per cent of investment in metal mining and quarrying, and 55 per cent in general chemicals went also. 'Peripheral' here is taken to be Scotland, Wales, Northern Ireland and the North region of England. These figures are from the DTI Census of Production, and suffer from all the usual problems of lack of disaggregation and absence of key figures in the interests of confidentiality. However, some sort of analysis of capital expenditure is necessary if generalizations are to be made in future (Department of Trade and Industry, 1971).

I have not yet seen a rigorous disaggregated investigation of the movement of industry internationally, which classified industry according to its capital intensiveness, its market orientation, and its ownership, and by the type of area to which it moves. However, it is possible to hypothesize about this; and I would suggest that here is another area for a research project. For instance, we could classify plants into (a) large-scale capital-intensive resource-based branches of multinational firms; (b) large-scale relatively labour-intensive branches of multinational firms; (c) small-scale capital-intensive branches of multinational firms; (d) national firms with capital-intensive branches; (e) national firms with labour-intensive branches; (f) small firms, probably with no branches, or one branch, etc. Considerable evidence exists that the pattern of locative behaviour of such plants would differ systematically (Expenditure Committee, 1973).

The market in which such plants, and their parent firms, operate, determines the 'shape' of the plant, and plants within the same conglomerate with similar products, but with different markets, will behave differently. For example, large capital-intensive chemical plants producing general chemicals will tend to locate in the periphery, while those producing specialized chemicals for a more demanding market will locate closer to the centre of the market (Lee, 1971). High value-added products tend to favour the centre. Plants producing innovative products also tend to locate in central areas. There is some evidence that some national companies, or at least middle-capital companies, may locate new lines which require more capital than they can supply on the market in the development areas of their national states, employing the capital grants thus received, and the labour creation methods, to subsidize high risk innovations. This is probably not true of multinational companies, who would probably not take the risk of introducing innovations whose risk was so high, and whose capitalization was so problematic.

A further major variable is of course that of ownership. Much has been said about the increasing internationalization of capital, by which is usually meant the increasing speed of US investment across the world. However, most of the metropolitan countries have large numbers of production branches outside their own nation states. This process is increasing, and it is a feature of peripheral areas that the capital-intensive firms should be principally branches of multinationals. National capital will tend to invest in more labour-intensive lines, and will decentralize them to the far periphery only under special conditions, such as the prospect of a fairly captive labour force, particularly female labour, and thus cheap labour. Research is needed on the complicated web of international finance of production plants, their relationship to national bourgeoisies, and the extent of local interest should it vary significantly from country to country, peripheral area to perhipheral area. Only then could an empirical base identifying 'local', 'national' and 'international' interests be established.

It is necessary to have this empirical context into which to place peripheral area experience, because we want to know how far the movement of capital-intensive branch plants into these areas is a universal phenomenon, and how far it can be taken as inevitable. Highly capital-intensive industries are at the vulnerable edge of capital; they are the product of the process which Marx describes: the increasing drive for the replacement of labour with capital, often producing low returns to capital, and coinciding with increasing difficulty of financing such plants, not only for the private sector, but for the state also. Their realization is however essential for the further development of capitalism. Their establishment, therefore, has a certain quality of urgency and inevitability about it.

What Do These Plants Look for in the Periphery?

In the first instance, of course, these plants look for markets, but this is usually on the scale of desired nations or national blocs, given the relatively low cost of transport. It appears to be accepted that these plants are looking for coastal sites, or areas with natural resources such as water, raw materials, crops (Lyddon, 1973) areas with large flat sites, or for deep-water sheltered areas (Gaskin, 1973). Some of them are specifically looking for sparsely populated areas, as the pressure to seek 'socially acceptable' locations for polluting plants becomes greater, a factor recently recognized by the Scottish Council (Development and Industry) in evidence to the Select Committee on Scottish Affairs:

. . . it is becoming increasingly difficult for environmental reasons to obtain sites in Western Europe, or the Continent, for refinery and process industrial development . . . We believe that there is considerable land in Scotland . . . which might be suitable for development . . . and which, by advanced (sic) planning, could be considered in such a way that the minimum number of people could be affected. (Select Committee on Scottish Affairs, 1972; Gaskin, 1973)

Again, we require a rigorous empirical base so that we can distinguish between such plants according to the importance of their locating criteria and the relationship of those criteria to demographic characteristics. Given the considerable research effort already devoted to location decision-making, this may merely require synthesis.

What Sort of Labour Forces are These Plants Looking For?

Professor Gaskin states that a characteristic of these plants is that they demand a labour force which is out of proportion to the labour-market pre-existing their arrival, although these plants usually have a smaller ratio of labour to capital than preceding plants in the same product area. Their demands for labour must be met, and they must be met in two stages.

First, because of the immense capital investment which they represent, they require huge construction forces; these must be recruited, held for some three years approximately and then dispersed. The permanent labour force which is then taken on is usually a fraction of the size of the construction labour force, and is of a rather different skill structure: a very high ratio of supervisory staff to other labour (Sadler et al., 1973); most men trained on the job; and a vital and highly skilled maintenance workforce. Such labour can seldom be found ready-made in the areas concerned, but can be assembled by and for such firms, thus providing a unique production advantage (Holland, 1974). Moreover, the technology of the plants involves extreme sensitivity, and for this reason it is necessary to have very good industrial relations (Expenditure Committee, 1972, evidence of RTZ; Drummond, 1973) and also adaptability in the labour force. Some firms moving to small communities appear to have strong expectations that they will eventually be able to create and hold such a force (Drummond, 1973).

Such, then, are the demands which the plants will make upon the populations of the area in which they locate, and upon those workers whom they attract into the area from the national, or in some cases international, labour markets in which they sell their labour power. The creation of the new labour force by these capital-intensive plants appears to have a 'propulsive' effect upon the labour market, as in-migration of new families creates a pool of wives who often have high expectations that they will work. This potential cheap semi-skilled labour will attract smaller plants such as clothing and luxury goods in labour-intensive sectors.

International comparative research is required about the characteristics of labour demand, from construction force to production force, then to the creation of new labour forces by in-migration, and by increased activity rates, etc. Dynamic studies are required which take into account the extent of seasonality in labour markets, and the origins of recruited members of the labour market. This is an essential background empirical resource for successful social impact studies.

The Role of the State in the Process of Peripheralization

Not a great deal has been said about the composition of the state and its role, in so far as the development of capital and its spatial manifestations are concerned. Current work is drawing away from the heritage of simplistic conceptions of the state which exists, and is beginning to recognize the complexity of the state's structure, through which it works out, by a process of conflict and politics, its twin roles. The new concept of the state includes such organizations as the trade unions, universities, and certain groups of intellectuals outside the universities. The various branches of the state apparatuses represent the interests of different groupings within the ruling class — capital, medium capital, national, international, landed interests, etc. — and have an autonomy of their own, chiefly organized around their political role. The state as a whole nevertheless works in the interests of that fraction of the ruling class which has overall power (hegemony) at any given time (Lebas, 1974; Poulantzas, 1973). The styles of national states vary considerably, even though the hegemony of large capital is present in each nation. Some work has been done on the explanation of this variation, but more is required.[1] One thing appears to be fairly universal; branches of the state apparatus which are concerned with the economic usually have much more power than those concerned with the social, unless those latter have important repressive functions.

There are two identifiable functions of the state; they are not held equally by different agencies and groups within the State. The first and most important function of the state is to enable the development of capitalism; the second is to make acceptable that development (Lebas, 1974). This frequently means disguising the fact that capital has been helped and suggesting that the state has encouraged or, in the case of state capitalist societies, forced, industry to locate in certain areas against their will, in order to help 'society', be it local or national. When a local area's interests are most obviously not helped, then it is the 'national interest' which is used to douse the flames of local political protest.[2]

Central to the question of the role of the state is whether the actions of the state lure these plants into areas where they would not otherwise go, or whether they would go there anyway. The answer to this question is more complicated than one or other of these alternatives.

The Enabling Function of the State

As capitalism develops, and produces more and more capital-intensive investments, it becomes more and more difficult to finance these developments (Expenditure Committee, 1972). In societies where ownership is vested with groups outside the state, the private sector frequently has recourse to the state to provide it with capital.[3] Most of these subsidies come from agencies of the state concerned with sectoral policies rather than spatial policies (Lebas, 1974; Expenditure Committee, 1973), but if the subsidy can be combined with a spatial legitimacy, so much the better.[4]

We know that it is policy of at least one section of the UK state bureaucracy to encourage the development of capital intensiveness in the interests of 'efficiency'. The head of the Distribution of Industry Division in the Ministry of Technology stated before the Select Committee on Economic Affairs that:

. . . on the whole, I think our Ministry would think that a switch to rather more capital-intensive methods of production of the same kind of thing was in the national interest [selectivity in favour of this] . . . in the long run . . . is the only way you will maintain your employment and be able to expand, because if you do not do it, you will go out. (Select Committee on Economic Affairs, 1970).

We also know that agencies of the state have been heavily involved in the introduction of increasingly capital-intensive techniques into the farming industry (Expenditure Committee, 1973). Special agencies have been in existence for some time to cope with this process; and they are now emerging to encourage the new wave of capital-intensive plants[5] in several countries. Another feature of this enabling process is the introduction of new legislation to speed up the process of implementation, for instance the Industrial Expansion Act 1968, which allowed large industrial investments and state-enabling activities to go ahead without separate Act of Parliament.

The 'Distortion' of 'Natural' Patterns

The state, in its role as 'keeper of the peace', introduces a number of measures which have an 'ideological' function. A number of these can be identified in the case of peripheral plants. Sometimes it is difficult to separate out the two functions of state activities. This is true of that function of regional and other state policy in so far as it effects a relationship between peripheral locations and capital-intensive plants. The increasing international movement of flows of materials has weakened the nation's control over its own production and trade (Holland, 1974); the drive to regain control, which can be seen as a political tool of the national bourgeoisie, has led to a new situation.

Nation states compete with each other for the available multinational capital, in the interests of the political stability of the nation as a whole, in the interests of the economic health of those states, and in the interests of national bourgeoisies. As Gaskin (1973) has put it:

It is beyond question that there is a strong element of international competition in almost all regional inducement policies, and this operates with particular force where basic processing industry is concerned. Countries have shown themselves willing to pay large sums of money to ensure that they possess particular kinds of smelting or refining capacity . . .

Some of the major 'carrots' in that part of the game of international attraction which involves basic process industries are peripheral sites, near harbours, preferably with planning permission, with a state agency designed to look after the industrialist's interests, even with laid-on public services, and sometimes with special tariff rates for public utilities. The United Kingdom, ironically, in view of its pride in its own planning history, is in the forefront of this competition in the northern part of Europe (Warren, 1973; Select Committee on Scottish Affairs, 1972). Again, we require systematic research into this aspect of the nation state's activities, so that generalizations can be made about variations in their behaviour.

The Regional Distortion

It is well known that most, if not all, peripheral areas are viewed by their nation states to be problem areas, and most are subject to some kind of spatially defined 'policy' or 'planning'. Many of the subsidies and attractions which I have mentioned above are subsumed under such policies, or are legitimized by them. Two goals are identifiable in the regional policy field. They are shared differently by different agencies, shared differently between countries, and vary with historical and political events. The first goal is social: the provision of employment — the political or ideological goal (Oslislok, 1974); the second is economic: the development of the national economy by the 'rational' distribution of production resources, although this is always, in turn, legitimized by referring to the advantages of development for those requiring employment in the receiving areas. Overall, those agencies within the state which are concerned with spatial policies are subordinated to those concerned with sectoral policies; in the UK, for instance, the Department of Industry carries out most of the UK *de facto* spatial industrialization policy. Within this sectoral/spatial split, echoed to a certain extent by the sectoral/physical split, there is a further subordination of social to economic.

We are all familiar with the tools. However, we need to know how much the social goals disguise how paramount the economic goals are. Are regional policy's handouts a necessary subsidy without which the capital investments concerned would not only not come to the regions, or the nations involved, but would not come into existence at all? Evidence suggests that the last possibility is tenable.[6] Regional policy has other functions for the state: it is used as a protective device for national production (Select Committee on Economic Affairs, 1970, particularly the evidence of Professor T. Wilson). and it is used as a device to prevent the inflationary pressures in the regions from crippling the economy (Oslisok, 1974). This last function suggests also that capital-intensive industries will be preferred in these areas; as the creation of large labour forces in such areas will increase rather than lower the inflationary risks. The separation of regional from sectoral policies is, however, artificial (Downing, 1973) unless one distinguishes between their differing loadings of enabling and ideological functions, a task which future research must undertake.

The State Capitalist Countries

If the hypotheses put forward above are to be employed, then it is necessary to look at those countries in which the state itself owns the means of production. There is evidence from the USSR and from Hungary and Yugoslavia that similar patterns of industrial location exist, and that the state organs which are responsible for spatial policies have rather similar status *vis-à-vis* the sectoral agencies, as in the 'mixed' economies. In other words, metropolitan areas still retain the bulk of productive industry, with some selective decentralization within them; returns to investment are lower in the periphery also and the periphery appears to receive large-scale capital-intensive plants (Dienes, 1972).

Despite more overt adherence to ideologies of social equity, there still appear to be considerable regional differences in income per head, suggesting that cheap labour areas also exist in the state ownership nations (Berkovic, 1969). There is the same conflict between the agencies which encourage economic efficiency and those who use social equity as their goal. There is the same political function of regional policy: keeping the underprivileged states or regions satisfied. All this, then, raises the question of whether the plants which are decentralized go to the periphery because they have to / want to, or because they are more susceptible to state pressure. Comparative research between the eastern bloc and western countries needs to be synthesized.

The Role of the State in Labour Reproduction

Recently, Lojkine, in the course of considerable and detailed empirical work on the Paris and Lyons regions of France, put forward a definition of '*la politique urbaine*', a much wider concept than our 'urban planning', much closer to a combination of regional planning and policy and urban planning and policy: '. . . the ensemble of judicial, financial and ideological mechanisms whereby the state apparatus (central and regional) organises socially and collectively the reproduction of capital and the labour force in a given region'. (Lojkine *et al*, 1974).[7]

We have seen that the incoming plants require construction and permanent labour forces; in other words, they require the creation of a labour market together with the social infrastructure necessary to retain the labour force. It is perhaps here that the state's traditional function has always been seen. But recent studies, using patterns of expenditure as an indicator of the priorities placed upon items within the state (Lojkine, 1974) have shown that the production of the collective means of consumption (roads, public transport, housing, schools, hospitals etc.) has lagged behind that produced for the production side. The time taken to implement state plans for social infrastructure is much longer than that for production infrastructure (Bleitrach and Chenu, 1971). The state appears also to spend the minimum on social infrastructure required to actually retain the labour force, to reproduce it and to keep it quiet.

The Social Effects of the Introduction of Industry into Sparsely Populated Areas

This brings us to the area where the interests of labour market economists and those of Marxist methodology overlap most closely. The reproduction of labour and the part which is played in that by the labour market is a key explaining variable in social structure, both in general terms and with particular reference to industrialization and urban form.

In general terms, Poulantzas (1973) put it thus:

While it is true that the agents (people) themselves must be reproduced, 'trained' and 'subjected' in order to occupy certain places, it is equally true that the distribution of agents does not depend on their choices or aspirations but on the very reproduction of these positions . . . It should not be forgotten that it is the labour market which has the dominant role in distributing agents in the ensemble of the social formation.

In other words, the dynamic process whereby capital demands certain types of labour and the process whereby that labour is assembled, held and reproduced is the essential first variable in explaining the class structure of the society and the allocation of individuals to places within the structure. This process can be seen in microcosm in particular locations.

Elizabeth Lebas, referring to the studies carried out by Castells and his team on Dunkirk; tells us that they see its urban form as the product of the system of 'contradictions' (or inbuilt conflicts) which arise from the reproduction of the labour force in a social structure (Lebas, 1974). In the case of Dunkirk, that structure is dominated by monopoly capital (which can be equated closely with international capital) at the 'imperialist stage'. Warnings must be given here. We must try to avoid assuming that all settlement patterns and their social structure will reproduce the patterns which are currently being identified in France; and we must guard against simplistic assumptions which say that there are not other determinants of class position; the political and the ideological are still powerful secondary explaining variables.

The Polarization Process

This section of the chapter must be even more condensed than the others, because it is the area in which the research team of which I am a member has done most of its work. It is also the area in which social scientists (and through them, planners) have most used ideology to mask reality. Most of what I shall say has been dealt with much more satisfactorily by Tonnie Ecker (1974).

The principal process which can be identified in the impact situation is what we have called the 'polarization' process. This is to be distinguished from other processes which have been conceptualized, notably the 'dualism' model, the 'rural/urban' dichotomy, closely related to dualism, and also to its cousin, the traditional/modern syndrome. These, in turn, relate to the under-developed/developed developmental axis. A recent newcomer is the 'enclave effect'.

The dualism model sees the effect of introduction as producing two societies side by side, with separate structures; this is often employed with the other concepts, so that the new society is seen as 'urban' and 'modern', while the old society is seen as 'rural' and 'traditional'.

Polarization is the process whereby the introduction of industry allows particular sections of the local society to jump on the bandwagon represented by the industry, notably, sectors of the working class such as skilled workers, especially those new to the area, and those sectors of the petty bourgeoisie whose capital is invested in retail consumption. A large, perhaps larger, percentage of the population will not participate, will have their relative life-chances reduced, or may even have them reduced in 'real' terms, as they move further down the queue for the scarce social infrastructure which exists in the area (Allen, 1973). However, the two parts of the society are not separate; on the contrary, they are interdependent, the disadvantaged being shaped by the dominant groups on the bandwagon. Nor will they demonstrate differences in values in any systematic way (Horowitz, 1972; Tipps, 1973); indeed, the newcomers may well feel more associated with the local 'culture' than those who see it as a symbol of their mis-fortunes (Donahue, 1957; Horowitz, 1972). Nor will their experience of rural or urban labour markets differ, as has recently been convincingly shown. The polarization effect is not like an 'enclave', a concept derived from linkage studies of the multiplier type, where researchers, having noticed low levels of linkage, have assumed that there is little effect upon the local area.

An example of the kind of thinking which can arise from the dualism model is provided by the paper given by Linklater (1973), in which he said: 'In less developed countries, oil production has encouraged 'dualism', i.e., the formation of subeconomies and sub-cultures which fail to integrate with the whole and create harmful instabilities'. He then goes on to state that he is sure that the Scots are too sensible and well-developed to produce this sort of thing with North Sea Oil. This is to miss the point that the 'dualism' is not a separate phenomenon, but is caused by the introduction of industry. It does not represent the old choice of staying behind while the new get on with the twentieth century. It is just that industrialization requires some parts of the society to accept lower positions.

What are the characteristics of this polarization process? Local people recruited to the construction force may not be taken up in the production force (Furnari, 1973; Sadler *et al.*, 1973) and may emigrate, or suffer dislocation of life-styles. In-migrating people (in many cases returned migrants, a point which must be evaluated) often take key jobs (Hytton and Marchioni, 1973) and make claims upon local services which receive higher priority. Local people, when they do get work, will get the lower paid and unskilled jobs (Lucey and Kaldor, 1969) some may even be worse off than they were before.[8] An obvious split is between the young and the old, though this is not as simple as it may appear (Moore, 1966). Other effects are related to the destruction of that part of the local economic sector which competes with the services which are brought in by the new plant (haulage, mechanical engineering, etc.), and to the growth of those parts of the local service sector which can usefully answer the needs of the new industry, or the spending power of the labour force. Interesting evidence in favour of the idea of a polarization is provided by the Anglesey study, where a negative multiplier was found for those sectors of the labour markets which are most likely to be encouraged by the new sort of plant (Sadler *et al.*, 1973). Further evidence of a polarization process among the petty bourgeoisie in terms of political power, is provided by Ecker (1974).

Discontinuity and Continuity

Identified impact effects have been described as 'new' (Furnari, 1973) and as 'discontinuities', whose effects are 'grave' (Gaskin, 1973), which indeed they are; however, there is a suggestion in much of the literature that what went before was in some way better. Our hypothesis is that it was not better, nor was it worse; it was the same. Every generation of workers, of petty bourgeoisie, and of those elements of the bourgeoisie who continue to inhabit sparsely populated areas, has experienced in some form the penetration of capital and the social structural effects which follow it. Indeed, the present social structure of the so-called underdeveloped areas is as it is precisely because of previous waves of 'development' (Carter, 1974; Fischer, 1973; Steeves, 1972). Some of the sparsely populated areas are the way they are simply because great upheavals of the past, following new economic forms, cleared them of their populations (Carter, 1973). The most startling thing about areas which receive industry is not so much the changes which occur, but the continuity (Poulantzas, 1973). The same people hold power; the same people are dominated. There is some movement of personnel between the classes, but the reproduction of the classes in their relative places goes on through time.

All of the above applies to any situation where industry is introduced. The process of the creation of the new labour force and the polarization which accompanies it is disguised in the areas with dense population, or urban populations, because there are so many other processes going on. In the sparsely populated areas, the effects can be seen easily. The geographical movement of people can be seen; the existing structure of the society can be seen; the inter-dependence between the local and the national, and even the international, can be seen more easily. This is what makes the study of sparsely populated areas so interesting, although of course, the focus itself is policy-oriented, presumably precisely because the state is aware of the importance of these areas in the future.

There are, then, a number of studies in different countries which support the idea of a polarization process. However, to my knowledge little research has been done on the resemblance between these new manifestations of it, and the history of the reproduction of the class structure in these areas. There are other areas of effect which have not been studied on a comparative basis. For example, it seems that the production of one-industry towns (Hansen, 1972) or one-capital towns (that is, towns which are wholly dependent upon highly capital-intensive international capital plants), leads to a captive labour market, subject to the fluctuations of world markets for the product. The dynamic process of replacement of labour by capital proceeds within the firm after its location, and so the number of workers employed tends to reduce, either relative to the product produced or in real terms.[9] In the latter case, this provides the phenomenon of the one-generation town.

The final phenomenon which I want to deal with now is that of spatial polarization. Similar to social polarization, this is the process, sometimes called the growth pole effect, whereby benefits are felt close to the new plant, but dis-benefits occur as one moves further away from it (Gjestland, 1973). Thus, workers on the geographical periphery of the labour market experience the insecurity of being laid off during seasonal contractions of the work force (Mackay, 1973); they receive the worst paid jobs. Fischer (1973), indeed, tells us that this state of conditions is not new for the marginal rural labouring class. His historical study, describing early industrialization, characterizes them thus: '. . . poorer than their land-holding neighbours, more dependent on market fluctuations which could put them suddenly out of work and earnings . . . prone to migration (within fairly narrow spatial limits), easy to upset and uproot . . .'. The petty bourgeoisie of remote settlements experiences a falling-off in trade as workers spend their new wage packets in the central settlement, etc.

The Role of the State in Neutralizing the Effects of Polarization

We have already briefly discussed the role of the state as an enabling agent in the total process of subsidizing the movement of capital-intensive firms to the periphery; we have also described some hypotheses relevant to its role in the creation and reproduction of the labour force. The second role of the state, that of political peacekeeper, or ideology creator, is more relevañt, when its relationship to polarization is discussed.[10]

Polarization can have difficult political consequences; locally based petty bourgeoisies get restless about the degree of control they have over their own circumstances (Lojkine *et al.*, 1974) and can be joined by dissatisfied members of the bourgeoisie. They may well be able to recruit help from dissatisfied members of the local working class (Horowitz, 1972). Labour troubles may arise from unionization, and from the newly arrived workers' experience of relative earnings differences. The in-migrants may also be dissatisfied with the level of collective consumption which is made available to them. The different organs of the state may intervene to patch over these problems, to divert attention away from them, or to shoulder the blame for them, thus alleviating any questioning of the structure of social relations which might result. They work closely with the private sector in this field, public relations being highly developed by large private companies.

We saw briefly the role of the state in providing an acceptable, some would say barely acceptable, level of housing, public transport, schools, etc. Where does the finance for this come from, and who carries it out? Much of the social infrastructure is given to the local state apparatus, which is seen to represent 'local' interests more closely than the central state apparatuses (Poulantzas, 1973). Finance is channelled from the central state for these purposes. Frequently, it is necessary for the local state apparatuses to be restructured in peripheral areas so that they can carry out these new tasks to the satisfaction of the central state or of the companies involved (Allen, 1973). Nevertheless, we have seen that long delays can take place between plan and implementation.

Ironically, one of the reasons why this is particularly acute in peripheral areas is because it is the local authority and local state organizations who appear to suffer most from competition for labour with the incoming plants (Mackay, 1973). Planning plays a particularly important function here. When local authorities do not have planners, they will often call upon a consultant to provide them with a framework of rationality, often technocratically phrased, which will allow them to legitimize their actions, and which will also allow them to retreat behind technical failure, should there be unexpectedly obvious contradictions in the local situation which give rise to discontent (Poulantzas, 1973). Larger planning agencies will already have personnel responsible for this (Carter, 1973). Such agencies and/or personnel often also have the unenviable task of suggesting that, when things go wrong, there are alternatives which can be put into play. Thus, such ideas are put forward as the encouragement of local entrepreneurial flair and cottage industries, ideas which have their roots in the interwar reaction against state interference in declining industries; the encouragement of better linkages to the local area from plants which could never really have better linkages; and the restructuring of other sectors in the host area so that they can 'benefit' from the newcomer, which will have similar polarizing effects.

Behind the whole thing lies a fiction: that the institutions in society shape the social relations in society, rather than that the social relations throw up the institutions; this allows the emergence of 'the planners' as a perceived powerful group of people. It would seem, however, that their power is relatively low in terms of their ability to implement plans which go against the logic of capital development in their areas (Gaskin, 1973; Mlinar, 1971). Their willingness to take the blame for the activities of others is so masochistic as to make one suspect that they are sometimes aware of the unpleasant consequences of the 'real' causes being perceived.

The main content of the ideology of the planners, and all others who manufacture it — politicians, trade unionists (Furnari, 1973) and the companies themselves — is that receiving areas will be saved from decline or from under-development (Gaskin, 1973). Perhaps, as a result, there has been a remarkable lack of evaluation of planned industrialization (Allen, 1973). Various reasons have been put forward for this (Expenditure Committee, 1973). Perhaps the most important one is that there is no indication of what it is that is declining, and what is going to be developed. That said, there had been remarkably little attempt to evaluate even in terms of the simple indicators which exist: unemployment reduction (Law and Howes, 1972; Moore and Rhodes, 1972); job creation; prevention of out-migration; increased activity rates; multiplier effects, etc. This has now changed, and our own group is perhaps an indication of how far it has changed. Does this indicate a need to construct a new ideology as the old one wears thin? After all, the old one was concerned with local interests; evidence from the new sorts of industry coming to the sparsely populated areas would suggest that this can no longer be upheld. Perhaps we are in for a spell of 'national interest'.

Summarizing, then, we can say that there is sufficient evidence to put forward the following framework for consideration by future research. International firms are increasingly selecting peripheral areas, some of which will be sparsely populated, as locations for large capital-intensive branch plants. This selection of peripheral areas will increase in the future and will be vital to the future development of capitalism. The state performs a vital role as an enabler of this process. Such projects are difficult to finance, and the state has to intervene with subsidies, either directly, or in the form of infrastructure or spatial subsidies. The state also has to bear the responsibility for creating the labour force for these firms. There is some evidence that the effects of the introduction of such firms upon the social structure of the area is less than satisfactory, leading to a polarization of elements of the social structure, but that this does not alter the relationship between classes. The state's role as ideology creator, as a disguiser of both the reality of its intervention as an enabler, and of the social effects of industry, is most fully worked out through the agencies concerned with social and physical planning. Research which takes place in this general area of concern, must take into account the interdependence of all these factors if it is to make meaningful statements, and not to become another element in the process which disguises the reality of major dynamics in world society at this time.

Notes

1. I am thinking here particularly ᵤᶜ the work of Nigel Despicht at the University of Sussex, soon to be presented as a Ph.D. thesis.
2. Expenditure Committee (1972) '. . . this is a case of a development area grant not being justified on social grounds — that is, reduction of local unemployment — but being justified in terms of the national interests expressed as balance of payments savings and other factors . . .'.
3. Expenditure Committee (1972). Particularly the evidence of the Treasury representatives, and those from IBM, the latter admitting that the capital grants freed scarce capital for the finance of new products. Expenditure Committee (1973) where the aluminium companies argued that capital items, including special fixed interest long-term loans, and the lowered electricity tariffs which they received were essential for the investments to be initiated. The Department of Trade and Industry representatives admitted that they saw themselves as 'lenders of last resort' in such cases.
4. Expenditure Committee (1973). The representatives of the Burroughs computer company when asked about the significance of regional grant systems, said that it depended upon how much capital goes into the product; if 80 per cent of the product is capital, which it was in the case under discussion, '. . . then it is very important'.
5. Select Committee on Scottish Affairs (1972). The Scottish Council (Development and Industry) made a very strong case for such an agency for Scotland, particularly the Oceanspan target area; comparisons were made with the French agency for the Rhône Delta developments, by Professor R. E. Nicoll.
6. But see Holland (1974), who argues that capital grants are unimportant for multinationals whose system of transfer pricing is much more significant.
7. I am indebted to Elizabeth Lebas for the translated notes upon which my references to the French work are based; any inaccuracies of interpretation are entirely my own.
8. This effect has been found in several countries in the Third World, during evaluative research associated with the 'Green Revolution' programme at the United Nations. See the chapter by Andrew Pearse in this book, especially his designation of the 'Talents-Effect' after the parable of the talents in the Gospel of St Matthew: 'Unto everyone that hath shall be given, and he shall have abundance; but from him that hath not shall be taken away even that which he hath'.

9. From figures produced for a West Norway aluminium town, the ratio of output in the aluminium factory to the number of men required to produce it is as follows:

1948	1950	1952	1954	1956	1958	1960	1962	1964	1966	1968
1.77	0.78	0.62	0.62	0.67	0.54	0.51	0.45	0.42	0.33	0.38

See Gjestland (1973); also Hansen (1972).

10. Rimlinger (1971), not operating a Marxist methodology, puts the role of the state in its 'welfare' function thus: 'Even a highly individualistic society, one that stresses individual responsibility, may legitimise social protection (welfare) for the common interests in social and political stability or in economic productivity'.

References

Allen, Kevin (1973), *Conference on Large-scale Developments in Remote and Rural Areas: A Concluding View*. Paper given to the Aberdeen Conference on Large-scale Developments in Remote and Rural Areas, March.

Berkovic, E. (1969), 'Differentiations of personal incomes', *Yugoslav Survey*, 1, **February**, 81–91.

Bleitrach, Danielle and Chenu, Alain (1971), 'Le Role idéologique des actions d'amenagement du territoire — l'example de l'aire metropolitaine marseilleise', *Espaces et Societies*, **decembre**, 43–55.

Carter, Ian (1973), *In the Beginning was the Board: Thoughts on the Ideology of Regional Planning*. Paper given to the Joint Conference Committee's Conference: 'Planning and the Individual', London Business School.

Carter Ian (1974), 'The Highlands and Islands as an under-developed region', in Emmanuel De Kadt and Gavin Williams (eds.), *Development and Sociology* (London: Tavistock).

Commission of the European Communities (1973), *Report on the Regional Problems in the Enlarged Community*, COM (73), 550 final, **3 May**.

Department of Trade and Industry (1971), *Census of Production, 1970*, Minimum List Heading Tables (London: HMSO).

Dienes, Leslie (1972), 'Investment priorities in Soviet regions', *Annals of the American Association of Geographers*, **62**, 3, 437–454.

Donahue, George (1957), 'Socio-economic characteristics of part-time and full-time farmers in the Twin Cities area', *Journal of Farm Economics*, **39**, **November** 984–992.

Downing, John (1973), 'Community policies of resource allocation', *Built Environment*, **April**, 204–206.

Drummond, Gordon G. (1973), *Management Problems of Establishing a Large Plant in a Remote and Rural Area*, Paper given to the Aberdeen Conference on Large-scale Developments in Remote and Rural Areas, March.

Ecker, Tonnie (1974), *Social Change in Rural Areas: A Critique of Some Commonly Held Assumptions*. Paper given to the European Society of Rural Sociology Conference, Reading, September. Available as Working Paper 17 from Research Unit of Studies in Regional Policy Implementation, C/o Social and Environmental Planning, School of the Environment, Polytechnic of Central London.

Expenditure Committee 3(1972), *Sixth Report: Session 1972/3: Public Money in the Private Sector*, HC 347, I and II.

Expenditure Committee (1973), Session 1973 / 74, *Trade and Industry Sub-Committee, Regional Development Incentives*, HC 327.

Fischer, Wolfram (1973), 'Rural industrialisation and population change', *Comparative Studies in Society and History*, **15**, 2, **March**, 158–170.

Furnari, M. (1973), 'Industrialisation without development: a comment on an Italian case study', *Sociologia Ruralis*, **XIII**, 1, 15—18.

Gaskin, M. (1973), *Trends in the Movement of Large-scale Industry to Remote Areas*. Paper given to the Aberdeen Conference on Large-scale Developments in Remote and Rural Areas, March.

George, Roy E. (1973), *The Effects of Introducing Large-scale Industry into Small Isolated Areas of Canada*. Paper given to the Aberdeen Conference on Large-scale Development in Remote and Rural Areas, March.

Gjestland, Dag (1973), *Storbedrift i et Utkantdistrikt*, Institutt for Sosiologi, Universitetet i Oslo og Norsk Institutt for By-og Regionforskning, Oslo.

Hansen, Jens Chr. (1972), 'Regional disparities in Norway with reference to marginality', *Institute of British Geographers Transactions*, **57**, 15–30.

Holland, Stuart (1973), 'Multinational companies and a selective regional policy' in Expenditure Committee Trade and Industry Sub-Committee, *Minutes of Evidence Session, 1973 / 74 on Regional Development Incentives*, Expenditure Committee (1973) (see reference).

Horowitz, Irving (1972), 'Qualitative and quantitative research problems in comparative international development' in Manfred Stanley (ed.) Social Development: *Critical Perspectives*, New York: Basic Books.

Hytton, H., and Marchioni, M. (1973), *Industrializzazione senza sviluppo: Gela: Una Storia Meridionale* (Milano: Franco Angeli Editore).

Law, David and Howes, Roger (1972), *Mid-Wales: An Assessment of the Impact of the Development Commission Factory Programme*, University College of Wales, Aberystwyth, Economics Department.

Lebas, Elizabeth (1974), *Sociology of Regional Planning and Policy: Theoretical and Methodological Problems*, Paper given to the International Sociological Association's Conference, Toronto, August. Available as Working Paper 14 from Research Unit of Studies in Regional Policy Implementation, c/o Social and Environmental Planning, School of the Environment, Polytechnic of Central London.

Lee, Clive H. (1971), *Regional Economic Growth in the United Kingdom since the 1880s* (Englewood Cliffs, N.J.: McGraw-Hill).

Linklater, Peter (1973), *Oil Production and Inducements to Change*. Paper given to Aberdeen Conference on Large-scale Developments in Remote and Rural Areas, March.

Lojkine, Jean, Orlic, Françoise, and Skoda, Catherine (1974), *La Politique Urbaine dans la Region Lyonnaise 1945-1972* (Paris, The Hague: Mouton).

Lucey, Denis I. F. and Kaldor, Donald R. (1969), *Rural Industrialisation: The Impact of Industrialisation on Two Rural Communities in Western Ireland*, (London: Geoffrey Chapman).

Lyddon, Derek (1973), *Large-scale Development in Remote Areas: The Central and Local Government Planning Context*, Paper to the Aberdeen Conference on Large-scale Development in Remote and Rural Areas, March.

Mackay, G. A. (1973), *The Economic Impact of a Large-scale Plant on a Remote Area: The Invergordon Smelter*. Paper to the Aberdeen Conference on Large-scale Development in Remote and Rural Areas, March.

Mlinar, Z. (1971), 'Social values and decision-making in town planning in Yugoslavia', *New Atlantis*, **2**, 2.

Moore, Barry and Rhodes, John (1972), *Evaluating the Effects of British Regional Economic Policy*, (Cambridge: Department of Applied Economics).

Moore, Wilbert E. (1966), 'Changes in Occupational Structures', in Neil J. Smelser and

S. M. Lipset (eds.), *Social Structure and Mobility in Economic Development* (New York: Aldine)

Oslislok, J. S. (1974), *Present Situation and Future Outlook of the EEC's Regional Policy*, Exposé given at OCIPE's Symposium on Community Regional Policy, Brussels, January.

Poulantzas, Nicos (1973), 'On social classes', *New Left Review*, 78.

Rimlinger, Gaston V. (1971), *Welfare Policy and Industrialisation in Europe, America and Russia*, (New York: John Wiley and Sons).

Sadler, Peter, Archer, Brian and Owen, Christine (1973), *Regional Income Multipliers: The Anglesey Study*, Bangor Occasional Papers in Economics No. 1, University College of North Wales (Bangor: University of Wales Press).

Select Committee on Economic Affairs (1970), *Report: Economic Planning in Scotland*, Report and Proceedings, Vol. 1, HC 397 (1968/9); Vol. 2, HC 267 (1969/70).

Select Committee on Scottish Affairs (1972), Session 1971/2, *Land Resource Use in Scotland*, HC 511.

Steeves, Allen D. (1972), 'Proletarianisation and class identification', *Rural Sociology*, 37, 1, 5–26.

Tipps, Dean C. (1973), 'Modernisation theory and the comparative study of societies: a critical perspective', *Comparative Studies in Society and History*, 15, **March**, 2, 199–226.

Warren, K. (1973), 'The location of British heavy industry: problems and policies', *Geographical Journal*, 139, **February** 76–83.

Part II

Rural Sociology in the
Underdeveloped World

5
Peasant Studies: an Overview

Eduardo P. Archetti and Svein Aass

In many respects the growth of peasant studies in recent years has been the product of the important role played by peasant nations in the postwar struggle for political independence and economic development. Because of this background the 'new tradition' in this field is peculiar to our epoch. On the other hand it is also a continuation of a more 'ancient tradition' concerning itself with peasant problems such as the use of historical studies (for example those of Maurer in Germany and Bloch in France), the practical tradition of some countries where different social scientists tried to combine observation, analysis and politics (for example Haxthousan, Kowalevsky and Chayanov) and studies carried out by scholars working within a colonial framework (Boeske, for example). More recently peasant studies have received a great impetus from social anthropologists, who have defined it as a main focus of their inquiries.[1] But, whether old or new, peasant studies are practised by non-peasants; just as peasants are ruled they are *studied* and peasant studies are not a result of any self-understanding on the part of the peasants themselves.

The growing interest in peasants has resulted in a vast amount of books, monographs and articles, and in recent years several periodicals have been specifically devoted to this kind of investigation — *Études Rurales, Peasant Studies Newsletter* and *Journal of Peasant Studies*. It is almost impossible to comment on all the literature written on the subject, and this may not even be necessary as different bibliographical commentaries have already been published elsewhere (Geertz, 1962; Friedl, 1965; Shanin, 1973). Moreover, books or readers concerning peasants in general, peasant economy and peasant political movements have been recently issued (Potter *et al.*, 1967; Wolf, 1966a, 1969; Stavenhagen, 1969, 1970; Shanin, 1971; Landsberger, 1969, 1974; Hilton, 1973; Galeski, 1972; Firth and Yamey, 1964; Mendras and Tavernier, 1969; and Amin and Vergopoulos, 1974). Therefore in this article we will try to present and to discuss in a rational way some of the main themes and points of view on peasant studies, covering only briefly authors, monographs, regions, historical periods and various kinds of social and political movements. The main issues we will relate to here are: the question of defining peasants and the methodology implied in different research strategies; the characteristics of peasant economy and economic processes, with special attention to Chayanov's influential theory; and, finally, the political mobilization of peasants and forms of peasant political participation.

The Question of Defining Peasants

From Redfield and Kroeber onwards, to rephrase Bertold Brecht a little, 'so many questions, so many definitions': a vast attempt to reach for the 'concept of peasant'. The question to be asked, however, is whether such conceptualization should be the aim of peasant studies.

There seems to be rather substantial agreement on cutting off peasants as a general phenomenon from primitive agricultural producers and in some way or other accepting the existence of the State as a crucial criterion in this. This seems to be implied in the classical definitions of both Redfield and Kroeber, that peasants are part-societies with part-cultures and with a structural dependency on towns (Redfield, 1956; Kroeber, 1948). According to Wolf (1966a) the existence of the State means that there are *classes*; thus peasant societies can be regarded as *class societies*. However, not only do we need a definition of peasant *societies*, but on the level of the immediate producers we need a definition of 'peasant'. Wolf's early opinion (1957) is that a peasant is: (1) an agricultural producer, (2) that he has control of land, and (3) that his production is subsistence *oriented*. Thus, bearing in mind the fact that the peasant lives in a class society, he has to produce a rent fund that is expropriated by the 'centre' (the State or the non-producing classes) either directly or indirectly (exchange).

What is common to these definitional exercises is a scientific search for a general model that is trying to isolate those elements common to peasant societies and peasants in general. There is nothing wrong with definitions as they save us repetition in fixing those traits that are repeated in different times and places. 'Peasant' as a definition, as a type, as a generalization, falls somewhere in between a definition of a 'worker' taken in a complete general form and, for instance, a 'worker' under specific historical and social conditions.

'Worker' as an abstraction concerns only the most general features of the labour process, that is the worker himself, the object and the instruments of labour. 'Worker' under specific social conditions can be subsumed under the general definition but is also something more. For example in the modern wage worker we have a producer, means of production and object of labour, but these elements are combined in a given way which makes him into a social type that cannot be grasped from the general definition alone. Similarly we can see that definitions of peasants are general as to their form but at the same time specify to a certain degree the content of the phenomenon at hand.

The social setting is specified (State, classes, market) as well as the fact that the labour process to a large degree is familial. On the other hand the definitions do not explain peasants as a *social* type in the same way that a wage worker can be understood in terms of capital, labour power and the opposition between the use value and exchange value of the latter. The point here is that we need to arrive at a concept of peasants specific to concrete societies and stages of historical development just as a wage worker in the general sense and peculiar to a capitalist mode of production. A peasant in, say nineteenth-century France and a peasant in Java in the fourteenth century can both be classified according to the general definition, but they both represent specific social types and as such we need concepts which permit us to grasp their social specificity. General definitions of peasants have retained a high degree of validity because for a very long period of time, and covering the most diverse and distant societies, production has been predominantly carried out by domestic groups in agriculture. Thus one easily concentrates on this common feature to the exclusion of the social and historical differences. The latter, however, is what gives production a social content and which gives meaning to notions such as 'French peasant' (Marx's 'sack of potatoes') and 'Javanese peasant'.

Apart from the above considerations, the development of typologies represents an alternative way of theorizing on peasant problems. Mendras (1967), for example, has criticized the approach that tries to grasp the 'peasant'.[2] Instead he proposes to have as an object of research the *peasantry*, in which certain essential characteristics are retained, but which allows for different types of peasantry to be observed in different areas and in different historical periods. Mintz (1973, p. 92) comes close to Mendras's position in calling for the need for middle-range definitions of peasant and peasant societies, 'definitions that fall somewhere between real peasant societies "on the ground", so to speak, and the widest-ranging level of definitional statement, adequate to describe all of them'. The elements which must be included in such middle-range definitions are: the internal composition of the peasant sector, the relationship of the peasantry to other non-peasant rural groups, the use of the concepts of 'traditional culture' and 'small community' in defining the peasantry and the significance of history for the development of a typology of peasant societies (Mintz, 1973, p. 92).

But above all, as a field of research peasant studies have facilitated the convergence of several social science disciplines. Methodologically these studies have been characterized by a combination of micro and macro perspectives, the former being represented by the anthropological tradition and the latter by history, economics, sociology and political science. The combination has resulted in several studies on entire peasant societies (Kula, 1970; Stahl, 1969; Bois, 1971; Shanin, 1972; and Blum, 1971), and comparative research, for instance, on peasant social and political movements (Wolf, 1969a, Moore, 1966; Mousnier, 1967; Wallerstein, 1974; Landsberger, 1969, 1974; Stavenhagen, 1969; Wertheim, 1974). The need to combine these two perspectives is due to the fact already stressed that peasant communities do not constitute self-sufficient units of analysis as they are encapsulated in a larger system, in other words, the existence of a class society (Wolf, 1966b; Redfield, 1956; Bailey, 1969). Nevertheless micro and macro analysis is not a pure juxtaposition of different fields, each of them defined solely in terms of numerical magnitudes of geographical scope. Microterms and macroterms can tell us where to find boundaries related to the different social networks, for instance where the process of familial allocation of resources finishes and the local or the regional market with a new set of networks and social actors starts, but by themselves they do not permit any understanding of the dynamics of a social formation. In this sense 'micro' and 'macro' stand for analytical tools which are needed in the process of scientific work. In real life peasants reproduce themselves as a totality under a given set of conditions which are largely determined by the way the labour output and input is socially channelled.

We will try to illustrate this point by three concrete analyses which by themselves constitute landmarks in the tradition of peasant studies. These cases show clearly that a set of social relations and different process of production and reproduction at various levels enables the peasants and their families to appear as social actors in a social formation. With them we hope to demonstrate that a 'universal' peasant society does not constitute a unit of analysis given once and for all. We postulate that the main target of peasant studies must be to produce concepts and theories by means of which historical reality can be grasped.

(a) Studies in a Mexican Community

We will begin with the relevant data from the study of Chan-Kom, a community located in the tropical ecosystem of the low lands of Yucatan, Mexico, carried out by Redfield and Villa Rojas in 1931 (published 1934). The soil quality and the effect of rain and sun permits an adaption based on slash and burn techniques. A plot is used for two years and then left in fallow for a long period. The main tools used are digging sticks and axes: felling is carried out with the axe and planting with the digging stick. The main foodstuff is corn although this is complemented by other productive activities. The families have access to communal land but there is no private property in land. This means that the peasants cannot sell land to other members of the community nor to outsiders. The authors point out that the way peasants produce does not favour the development of a strong feeling for individual ownership. Land is cultivated for only one or two years out of seven, and therefore during most of the time any piece of land outside the village is covered with bush. It is common that what a man owns, and feels he owns, is the temporary result of his labour: the clearing, the planting and the harvesting but not the land. What is commonly sold, they report, is a cleared field or a standing crop. Land has no price, it is an instrument of labour and has not been produced by labour itself. Only the product of work has value.

All productive tasks are carried out by families with a labour division along the line of sex and age. In the economic process the co-operation with others or communal activities are almost non-existent. Therefore we must not mix together the labour carried out by the families themselves with the social relations of production. At one level relations of production depend on political membership, for being a member of the commune defines the right to have access to the basic means of production, namely the land. Nevertheless the lack of sufficient land compels the inhabitants of Chan-Kom to search for additional land outside of the *ejido*. This land is owned by the Mexican State, the peasants in exceptional cases paying a symbolic rent to the Government. The peasants are engaged in exchange relationships with the regional markets and in this network money is used. The other exchange networks — with peddlers, local merchants and other producers — are to a large extent governed by the laws of barter. In transactions with peddlers products are bought with poultry and maize, with the local merchants maize and money are used, and finally exchanges between peasants are effected through the use of poultry, pigs and maize.

The process of production is guaranteed by the fulfilment of religious ceremonies. As we mentioned above the land is used exclusively by the *ejido*, meaning that political status is of crucial importance, but we also see that religion dominates the relations established between men and nature. The woods, the virgin forest, the maize, the honey and the wild animals belong to the Gods (*yuntzilob*). Only through ceremonies performed jointly by the local priests and the producers are the land and its products transferred from the Gods to mankind. The social relations of production and the overall productive and consumption processes, like in many other peasant communities at different times and in different regions, depend not only on the social reproduction of the family labour force but on the political and social relations as well as on religion and ideology.

(b) Studies on Peasant Life in China

The agrarian social structure in China and the situation of the Chinese peasantry will give some information on the way a class society is generated from the productive system and reproduced through political and ideological systems. We can illustrate this process by briefly referring to some of the main ideas and data presented by Fei (1939; 1946; 1953). In his book on peasant life in China (1939) he describes a village where almost 80 per cent of the households are engaged in agriculture on irrigated rice fields, and practising a domestic silk industry. He clearly shows that the economic viability of the households heavily depends on the balance between the two activities, not only in terms of income but also in terms of the distribution of the labour force: that of the men is devoted to rice cultivation and that of the women to production of silk. All the agricultural work is done by human labour and the only two existing air pumps for irrigation are not used because there is no social need for saving the use of labour power. These peasants are tenants, paying a fixed rent (almost half of the rice produced annually) to the absentee landlords. The social relations described were largely predominant in Chinese society.

He also shows that fluctuations in prices do not affect the total amount of rice produced. This amount is fixed according to the customary consumption rates and the existing rent level. He also calculates that there is no economic viability for a household with rice production alone, because taking into account the expenses in many of the different households the potential income which could be provided by selling rice in the market does not cover the amount of money needed. This deficit is covered systematically by selling the silk produced domestically. In this kind of economy credit is scarce, small loans circulate among relatives and larger sums are borrowed from peasant financial-aid societies or from usurers in town.

Two-thirds of the land of the village is owned by the gentry. The peasants make a clear distinction between two kinds of property in land: they 'own' the surface soil and the landlords 'own' the subsoil, and in doing this, Fei remarks, the tenant is protected from any direct intervention by the owner of the plot he cultivates. What is bought and sold is the subsoil, in other words the plots with the tenants on it.[3] The economic basis of the gentry therefore is the extraction of a surplus product through the rent system. They are living in the towns and their privileges have to be protected by political power. Fei points out that this political power is reinforced through the maintenance of the extended family and the clan system. In the clan system the families gain independence, while the extended kinship unity is preserved through clan property. Common clan property implies a certain degree of security and permits that the corporate unit maintains its power in a wide and unstable system. Fei asserts that in the villages the rules of partible inheritance incite the rapid decline of this type of social organization and that it is therefore essential to the gentry to keep away from them. Hence the town constitutes the residential unit of the gentry.

However, the power of the landowners is encompassed by the power of the monarch. It is in relation to this kind of power that the gentry fulfils a very important role for the peasants: the influence of the gentry appears as the only rampart against various kinds of potentially limitless expropriation. In this sense the gentry is an effective mediator between the rulers and the ruled. An increasing tax burden sets up limitations on the capacity of the tenants to pay the customary rent to the landlords. Nevertheless the gentry have common interests with the rulers as official agents, but in their private capacity they are closely related to the peasants. Fei points out that never in the history of China have the gentry organized their own government, and as a class they never rejected a monarch who was able to take power and who, at the same time, recognized their prerogatives and privileges. In doing this they tried to protect the interests of their kin and of their local dependent people.

In a penetrating article Feuchtwang (1975) has demonstrated that this social formation generates its own means of ideological reproduction through a given religious system. In a set of religious symbols and ceremonial activities the social structure we have described above is reproduced by means of ancestor worship, at the level of the family, and by means of a hierarchical god-structure which covers the residential units, neighbourhood organizations, administrative cities and monarchical power. At each level there is a rupture in terms of symbols apprehended and used which is largely overlapping with the hierarchical differences in terms of class structure. One instance is the fact that the worship of Heaven is a prerogative of the emperor. Feuchtwang shows that the ideological structures at the same time reproduced the relations of domination and protection which constitute the basis of the power of the landlords.

(c) Studies on the Peasants of Languedoc

In his work on the history of the peasants of Languedoc, Le Roy Ladurie (1969) has shown the importance of establishing a specific analysis of a peasant society limited in space and time as well as the necessity of specifying the nature of the links between the peasant 'cells' and the overall society. Le Roy Ladurie's object of study is rural society in Languedoc in Southern France particularly in the period from the end of the fifteenth century to the beginning of the eighteenth century. Inside this limited period he delineates a specific movement within the agrarian régime which he terms a 'great agricultural cycle' and which goes from 'consolidation' to 'division', passing through the phases of 'departure', 'expansion', 'maturity' and 'decline'. Altogether this covers eight generations.

Rural society in Languedoc is characterized by the existence of private property in land, a concentration on cereal farming, the existence of rural classes such as farm labourers, independent small and middle peasants, *fermiers* as well as an aristocratic element and urban classes with important interests in land, rent payment and fiscal exactions. With these traits in mind Le Roy Ladurie shows the changes in the various phases in the agricultural cycle and how each phase corresponds with changes in all spheres, including economics, kinship and ideological changes in the individual peasant 'cells'.

The history of landed property departs from a situation of a relative concentration due to a favourable man/land ratio. In the sixteenth century and until around 1680 a process of division and parcellization is predominant. After that time a new process of concentration and selection takes over. To each of these stages there correspond different levels in wages for farm labourers, in rent and taxes to be paid. At other levels there are changes in religious patterns, crime types and rates, moving from social rebellion to attempts to 'invert the world instead of transforming it' on the one hand, and from aggression and personal crime to passivity and theft on the other. Finally, in the domain of the family the phase of expansion is simultaneously a period of 'important and powerful lineages'. In the phases of down-turn 'the main victim of social adjustment is demography': the number of mouths to feed is simply reduced. This is done by putting off the date of marriage, reducing premarital and extramarital conception and even some restriction in births.

All these changes take place in a setting of essential continuity; characterizing the period and its accompanying agricultural cycle as a whole is a basic stability in production technique. This technological inertia is in turn connected with the overall nature of French society at the time: the triumph of the 'feudal' forces and catholicism thus contrasting with the history of England in the same epoch as one of dynamism and burgeoning capitalism. The technological weakness and the inability of the rural economy to raise its productivity and thus increase production is the main reason why the processes of demography as well as that of landed property take a cyclical form. In this case we can see that the Malthusian theory is valid as a *special* law of population, that is historically valid within the limits of the peasant society in question. Population and population growth here is an important productive force in the specific sense that the pressure of population really is upon the means of subsistence and not as in capitalist society upon the means of employment, where, in other words, 'the means of subsistence are pressing against the population, which is not large enough to consume them' (Engels, to Danielson, Jan, 9, 1895).

The Malthusian economic laws traced by Le Roy Ladurie as shaping the special character of peasant society in Languedoc disappear when science and the development of productive forces later make it possible to overcome the stumbling-block of productivity. With the rise in industry and towns, the expansion in commerce and means of communication, Languedoc is transformed into the modern landscape of monocultural wine-growing. In this process 'the farmers of Languedoc ceased being peasants in the sense of self-sufficient family producers: they became modern wine-growers buying their subsistence and producing entirely for the market'. Concomitantly a new special law of population arises whose impact can be summed up in the expression '*l'exode rural*', and the economic law of diminishing returns is eventually replaced by that of 'permanent over-production'.

Comparative Conclusions on the Mexican, Chinese and French Studies

The works of Redfield, Fei and Le Roy Ladurie illustrate the main approaches to peasant studies: the 'anthropological' one where special emphasis is placed on the 'community' and where social networks are studied focusing on the members of the *ejido*; the 'sociological' one where analysis of peasants and other classes is used in order to characterize the mechanisms of social, political and ideological domination in a way that the analysis of the 'community' is added to the analysis of different classes at various levels; and finally the 'historical' approach where peasants are studied over a long period of time in a limited geographical area. We have called the three studies presented 'landmarks' and we feel that this is the case although the works of Redfield and Fei are sufficiently old to be labelled as 'classics' as well. In spite of quite a lot of scepticism towards Redfield's method, the 'Chan-Kom' study proves the fruitfulness of an interpretive ethnography in the study of human relations, in developing an implicit understanding of the meanings and motives behind the social intercourse. For his part Fei has perhaps been the most successful so far to link a microstudy to an understanding of the total social logic of one of the greatest and least understood of national societies, that of traditional China. *Peasant Life in China* thus still represents a challenge to contemporary peasant studies.

The conditions of social reproduction and social change can only be tackled if we are able to combine these different types of analysis. Moreover, the combination of the different approaches will permit the constitution of a specific field where social anthropologists, historians, sociologists and economists can interact and in this manner transcend the limits set by each individual discipline. The question of different research techniques peculiar to the historical development of social science can be surpassed only if we are able to conduct studies in this manner.

Peasant Economy and Economic Processes

In order not to enter into a too detailed presentation of the views on peasant economy we will leave out the many secondary additions and minor divergencies in the various works carried out by the most prominent scientists.

We propose to concentrate on some comments about those features that seem to be generally accepted as constituting the essence of peasant economy. By this we mean 'the family as a unit of work and consumption' (Firth, 1964; Shanin, 1973–74; Wolf, 1957, 1966a; Thorner, 1962; Kerblay, 1971; Mendras, 1967; Franklin, 1969; Warriner, 1964; Meillassoux, 1973; Tepicht, 1967a and b, 1971; and Galeski, 1972).

On this basis a consistent theory of peasant economy has been developed by Chayanov (1966). In Chayanov's microtheory the main assumption is that a peasant economy constitutes a specific economic system, where land, labour and means of production are combined following the natural process of family development. In a capitalist economy, he observes, the labour force can be defined objectively under the form of variable capital and the combination with a given amount of constant capital is determined by the existing rate of profit. On the contrary, for a peasant the labour product provided by his family is the only possible category of income and, the social phenomenon of wages being absent, the capitalist category of profit is not present. The main question Chayanov is trying to answer is what are the internal mechanisms which could explain the rationality of this special unit of production and consumption.

In the equation of labour and consumption we have on the one hand the size of the family and on the other the existing ratio between working and non-working members. The combination between labour and land and instruments of labour is possible through the drudgery of effort; in other words the achievement of a given function of production depends on the degree of self-exploitation of the labour force of the family. The core of Chayanov's theory is the necessary balance between family consumption and self-exploitation of labour. Chayanov shows that in the case of decreasing prices for agricultural products the peasants do not decrease production, on the contrary they try and maintain the level of consumption through an intensification of production. The typical behaviour of a capitalist enterprise in a crisis situation is precisely the opposite: to decrease production as well. Chayanov writes (1966, pp. 224–225):

We took our farm to be a commodity one and, consequently, one entering into a certain system of the economy which coexists with it, through credit and commodity circulation . . . (but) we have counterposed and continue to counterpose, the family to the capitalist farm; we have done so at the organization and production level — the labour farm contrasted to the farm based on hired labour. In this respect, these are two completely different economic machines which react differently to the same economic factors.

One of the main consequences of this approach is the interaction between the productive and reproductive functions. Fixing as the main variable the *natural* process of development of the family cycle, the relations of reproduction also become relations of production. This accounts for the relevance of Chayanov's theory of demographic differentiation: the development cycle would affect the ways each unit of production relates to the market, the size of the plot and the need for additional workers in special situations. Nevertheless the viability of any domestic group cannot be studied independently of the limits set by a given level of technological development and ecological constraints. There is no *natural* viability, but there is a *social* viability which depends on the interaction between the internal life of each cell of production and the external system. Only through this process can the question of social reproduction be tackled.

Chayanov's microtheory has a wide scope of application, for historically it can be used to explain the economic activity of households in a host of societies. Still, the applicability of his theory to a peasant economy stems not so much from it being a theory of a specific peasant mode of production as from its invariant nature. At the micro level it is really a theory of family labour independent of historical and socioeconomic conditions. If we take the developmental cycle as a natural process the main stages are common to family development in a very wide range of societies; that is, following Fortes (1958), there is to be found a phase of expansion, a phase of fission and one of replacement.

The concentration on invariant natural processes is both justified and at the same time represents a major weakness in the theory. It is justified to the extent that the peasant economy is based on a group where natural processes play an important role in determining the composition of the producing unit. At a more general level this is true for all 'traditional' and peasant societies and is only one way of stating that social and historical evolution means a transition from societies where natural conditions dominate to social forms where historically created elements predominate. The weakness lies in the reduction of the model to solely natural processes. Even though the character of labour in a peasant family depends on age and sex as well as upon natural conditions and the differences of season, labour always has a social character. This essential dimension is entirely lost in the concept of the family labour farm which leaves out all specific social and productive relations.[4]

Contrary to what Kerblay (1971) asserts, namely that the 'peasant economy' of Chayanov represents a specific mode of production, the theory of peasant economy is an analytical concept in the sense that the changes in the setting in which the peasant economy is operating does not change the nature of the peasant economy itself. However, rather than expressing an economic and technical reality, the concept of a mode of production expresses an economic and social reality. Thus the economic element does not simply have to do with the technical organization of material production: one has to consider particularly the relations between producers and non-producers in relation to production. There is no 'general' peasant production, as it is implied in Chayanov's concept. This is an additional reason why we cannot reduce peasant economy to the invariant elements of the domestic 'cell'. In spite of the fact that all peasant economies consist of individual households, the productive and economic relations in which peasant societies are operating are of a very different nature. Thus the peasant economy in the various types of peasant societies can be subsumed under specific and distinguishable modes of production.

How the predominant social relations change the social content of the peasant economy can be seen in the case of the important invariant element in

Chayanov's theory, that of 'subsistence' or the 'needs of the family'. These are supposed to be culturally limited and are implied to be very modest since a basic assumption is that a peasant economy does not accumulate. Instead of expressing a trait specific to peasant economy, however, this only translates the fact that all peasant *societies* (whether some kind of feudal, *parcellaire* or asiatic form) are societies where the use-value of products predominates (even where commodities are produced). When the national economy comes to be dominated by a capitalist type of production, a thirst for surplus-value arises in quite a new way out of production itself and the family labour farm starts to follow the movement of money accumulation; in other words it can be subsumed under the law of capitalist development and accumulation. And this will happen even though we still can assert in a general way that the production of a family farm under capitalist development is *oriented* towards the fulfilment of the needs of the family.

In the case of peasants, then, we have to distinguish between:

(1) 'Peasants' as agricultural producers using a simple technology and their family labour force. As a *type* we can encounter 'peasants' as the dominant producers in many pre-capitalist societies. 'Peasants' are thus to be found in many different modes of production. The specific dominant productive relations in the various modes of production make 'peasants' in each mode of production into a specific *social* category.

(2) A specific peasant mode of production in the sense indicated above. Marx has pointed out that in order to find this mode of production fully developed the peasants must have the ownership of the land they cultivate. This form of landed property presupposes that the rural population predominates numerically over the urban population and the capitalist mode of production appears very fragmented. Marx asserts that this mode of production excludes a rapid development of the productive forces, social forms of labour, social concentration of capital, large-scale cattle-raising and the progressive application of science. Finally he argues that where this mode of production is the prevailing form the general laws of credit are not suitable, because the formation of capital being very low, the formation of loanable money-capital is also weaker (Marx, 1971: pp. 802–813).

(3) 'Peasants' under conditions of developed capitalist production at the level of the national economy. 'Peasants' here is a simple descriptive term for agricultural producers who from the point of view of political economy have less and less in common with 'peasants' but who still must be regarded as such from the point of view of the invariant model of the 'family labour farm'.

We are not saying that Chayanov was not aware of the crucial role played by macro factors in the process of social reproduction of the family farms. In his research he explicitly delimited some boundaries (1966, p. 73):

In the present work, investigating the internal organization of the peasant farm, we cannot deal with the conditions that determine the level of labour productivity, since they

factors determining peasant labour

depend not so much on on-farm factors as on general economic factors affecting the farm's existence. Soil fertility, the advantageous location of the farm in relation to the market, current market situation, local land relations, the organizational forms of the local market, and the character of trading and finance capitalism's penetration into the depths of the peasantry — these are the chief factors determining peasant labour productivity and pay. By their very nature, all these factors lie outside the field of our present investigation.

Moreover, he mentions (1966, p. 68) that the direct relation between the size of the family and the size of the plots depended on the technological level reached by a concrete society, a given normative system regulating inheritance and 'social relations of production'. He admitted that in a farm where the function of production depends on labour-saving technology, the pressure of the biological development of the family undoubtedly does not influence the amount of land for use. If this is the case the farmer can send the surplus labour to work elsewhere and in the high season hire additional labour (1966, p. 68). Regarding inheritance patterns he points out (1966, p. 68) that if there is a non-partible system the natural developmental cycle does not affect the allocation of land following the different stages:

In all probability, in another agrarian régime less flexible than that of the repartitional commune the influence of the biological factor of family development in size of land for use would not stand out so prominently and be so evident as in our material.

Finally, as Daniel Thorner (1962) has observed, the reproduction of the social relations of production based on family labour and the control of land varies tremendously according to changes in the ratio of land to population. Chayanov's microtheory could be applied only in countries which are thinly populated, where the demographic pressure can move the frontier, making it easy to obtain more land and in this way allowing the absorption of the surplus labour.

In several articles Tepicht (1966, 1967a and b, 1971) has extended Chayanov's analysis by arguing that the peasant economy is characterized by its social properties more than by a given degree of technological development. Tepicht argues that the peasantry's patriarchal features, the combination between land and labour being more important than the use of capital and the main productive aim being to increase the global income of the family at the expenses of the revenue per worker, are features present in peasant societies whether the technology is human, animal or mechanical. Therefore even if we are able to find the predominance of peasant units of production in some specific historical conditions (for example, in the case of the dissolution of feudalism in some European societies), we cannot speak of the peasant economy as a mode of production generating and therefore dominating a social formation. The peasant economy is merely a 'sectorial mode of production' which is articulated and does not articulate others and which is dominated and does not dominate others. He defines a peasant economy as having a large variable capital and a small constant capital with a particularly small constant capital of industrial origin, weak integration in the social division of labour, lack of specialization, and productive relations overlapping the structure of the household. Because constant capital is reduced to a minimum, the mutual substitution of land and labour play a decisive role in the process of reproduction, whereas in industrial agriculture what counts the most is either the substitution capital for land or capital for labour.

Political Processes and Political Participation

Even more than in the case of peasant studies in general, the renewed interest in studies of peasant political actions is connected with the important political role played by peasants in the shaping of the modern world. Not only have peasants been the majority partner in the many new states created after 1945, but modern revolutions have consisted mostly of 'peasant wars of the twentieth century' (Wolf, 1969a). As Moore (1966, p 453) has pointed out: 'The process of modernization begins with peasant revolutions that fail. It culminated during the twentieth century with peasant revolutions that succeed'. Understanding how peasant rebellions have changed so much in their outcome depends on an understanding of how the limits of peasant consciousness have changed as the social and political environments of peasants have been transformed (Wolf, 1969b; Shanin, 1966; Hobsbawm, 1959).

It has been asserted that the limitations of peasant consciousness have resulted in only isolated and spontaneous political actions and that the revolutionary role played by peasants in the last century can be explained by outside factors that have been able to overcome these obstacles (Lenin, 1962; Mao, 1927; Hinton, 1966; Hobsbawm, 1959; Wolf, 1969a and b; Landsberger, 1974b). Hobsbawm (1959) for example, has referred to the 'primitive' or 'archaic' forms of political and social agitation which characterize much peasant political activity. Such movements are 'primitive' in the sense that they are *pre-political*; the people involved have not yet found, or are only starting to find a specific language in which to express their aspirations about the world. Thus the typical reactions to poverty, harvest crises, involvement in the network of a monetary economy, evictions from land, increasing demands for rents, tithes and taxes are social banditry, secret societies and millenarian movements. These phenomena represent an endemic peasant protest against oppression and poverty, a cry for vengeance, a vague dream of eradicating some curbs upon them, a righting of individual wrongs (Hobsbawm, 1969). Nevertheless this kind of action is properly regarded as social as much as individual protest, for the poor often protect the bandit and regard him as their champion. All in all, however, social banditry is a modest, unrevolutionary protest which does not produce a higher level of organization and articulation of demands by the peasants.

Secret societies are meeting places of all sorts of tendencies, with their own code of behaviour and rituals. They constitute 'parallel' systems of authority providing some security for their members and likewise offer the possibility for individual revenge and promotion. Their ideology emphasizes equality and the restoration of social justice to the poor. Their values are largely religious, a reinterpretation in popular terms of the prevailing religious system or merely the place where dissident sects or new religious values develop, and who on many occasions are more politically oriented. In countries like China, Vietnam and Indonesia they played an important role at an early stage of the nationalist struggle (Chesneaux, 1973; Chesneaux, 1972; Bianco, 1975; Kartodirdjo, 1968). Chesneaux (1973), for example, has shown that secret societies were involved in all the peasant uprisings and rebellions in Chinese history.

Millenarian movements represent a hope for change in the world, a change which is perceived as being total, irrevocable and imminent. These traits imply that the millenial ideology of salvation could be conceived as revolutionary, in the sense that a transition from an unjust and corrupt present into a new situation is not a gradual process (Worsley, 1957; Pereira de Queiroz, 1969; Chesneaux, 1973; Kartodirdjo, 1968; Cohn, 1957; and Talmon, 1966). The case of millenarianism as protonationalist movement in many Third World countries shows how such primitive movements are often a response to the introduction of capitalist and foreign commercial institutions in a pre-capitalist rural setting and the subsequent disruption of traditional society. As such they have been used by modern political movements to spread their range of influences. This quasi-modern aspect of millenarianism illustrates how the only really primitive aspect of millenarianism is external (the religious form) and that it offers no fundamental structural obstacles to modernization. Their deficiencies simply stem from the limited knowledge on the part of the actors involved about the world.

The problem remains, however, that in some areas agriculture has become completely capitalized without the eruption of serious countermovements on the part of the peasants, while elsewhere peasant rebellions have contributed to bringing down the entire social structure. Spontaneous peasant uprisings seem to characterize those societies where the social relations of production imply the presence of landowners and peasant-tenants (Hilton, 1973; Bloch, 1933; Mousnier, 1967). In the case of feudal Europe, for example, although the peasant class was internally stratified and differentiated by age and sex, the social division which mattered most was that between lord and peasant. The main struggles along these dimensions centred around tax payments and the status of free men.[5] The demand for land, for the division and redistribution of big estates, is, as Hilton (1974b) has pointed out, a modern equivalent of later demands for estate confiscation was the struggle for communal rights and access to communal lands. Specific demands for a return to 'the old communal life' were most common in the early phases of the process of feudalization, at a time when the peasantry had become socially homogeneous through the reduction in social status into serfs. The launching of communal actions were the natural result (Landsberger, 1974b).

At a later stage, when the leading elements in the peasantry were on their way to becoming parts of the rising entrepreneurial class, the demand for rent abolition and peasant proprietorship in land became predominant (Hilton,

1974a). At the same time the opposition inside the peasant communities increased to the point where struggles broke out between the rich 'labourers' and the poorer '*manouvriers*' of the village (Bloch, 1930; Soboul, 1956). As many writers have pointed out, it was not easy for peasants to engage in sustained rebellion. The tyranny of work weighs heavily upon peasants and the work is performed in isolation — although kinship ties and mutual aid, as well as personal control over the land, might act as a buffer against economic crisis (Wolf, 1969b; Marx, 1963; Hinton, 1966; Hobsbawm, 1973). The limitations on peasant political consciousness have been likened by Hinton (1966) to the situation of a man trying to survey the sky while imprisoned at the bottom of a well. This view of social relations leads in turn to an impetuousity of action and when the peasants did act, they were not prepared for decades of protracted struggle.

To pass from peasant rebellion to fully fledged modern successful revolutions the peasants have had to have leaders from other classes. In the modern revolutionary processes we encounter the peasants taking part in political movements characterized by wide-ranging goals, being at the same time anti-capitalist, anti-imperialist and anti-colonialist, and by a high degree of social complexity. In these social movements the peasants fight shoulder by shoulder with intellectuals, various other groups of the national bourgeoisie and urban workers, and they are to a great extent organized into radical and militant political parties.

In relation to the political participation of the different groups of peasants it is necessary to look at the given system of tenancy, the way a surplus is expropriated by means of rent and various types of taxes, the relations with markets, the internal solidarity of the communities and the religious ideology and social organization. At first glance it seems that all types of peasants tend to be present in these upheavals and successful revolutions — whether tenants or owners or squatters, whether tenants who pay rent in kind or in money or in work, whether peasants who sell a small part of the harvest or others who commercialize all they produce, whether Catholics or Orthodox or members of various sects. Faced with these tremendous variations in economic, social and ideological characteristics, it has been necessary to conduct comparative research in order to identify the decisive features common to all the great modern peasant upheavals. Along these lines the analysis has been concentrated to two different phenomena: identification of the peasant group that can most easily be mobilized, and the characterization of the macro and systematic conditions.

Regarding the first question two factors have been emphasized: the autonomy of the producer and the status of middle peasant (Alavi, 1965; Wolf, 1969a). The notion of autonomy fundamentally concerns the relations in the productive system between producers and non-producers. An autonomous peasant is thus one who is able to wield the technical conditions under which the process of work is carried out. According to Wolf, sharecroppers can be considered autonomous where all the processess of work are carried out without the interference of the landowner. According to Alavi, however, the condition of being poor or middle or rich peasant, depends on the relationship of the producers with the land and the labour market: the poor ones are landless tenants, mostly share-croppers, the middle ones own the plots they cultivate themselves with the aid of the labour force of their families, and finally the rich are the ones who own their holdings and are able to systematically hire rural proletarians. Both agree on the fact that some kind of autonomy must be present among a group of peasants who are able to enter into sustained rebellion and both find such characteristics among the middle peasants. Nevertheless we feel that Wolf's approach more inclusive than Alavi's because he does not reduce autonomy to the ownership of land. Only a group of peasants possessing the value of not being under the strict control of the landlords, can become a 'tactically mobile peasantry' and this holds for a land-owning middle peasantry as for sharecroppers enjoying a real autonomy in the decision-making process. These groups constitute the leverage of peasant rebellions and the poor and dependent peasants can join the movement only when a new balance of power has been established challenging the power of the landlords (Wolf, 1969a).

Nevertheless neither a deteriorating economy, nor absentee landlordism, nor various threats to the 'traditional' way of life of peasant communities, nor a rapid process of proletarianization by themselves explain peasant political participation. Moreover this does not mean that the problem of mobilization could be regarded as 'solved' once we have found poor and middle autonomous peasants. Various empirical studies show that not only is there no such phenom-enon as an inner 'revolutionary temperament', but that there also is no 'revolu-tionary' group of poor and middle peasants in the abstract. Wolf (1969a) argues that the peasants mobilize only when they suffer from the impact of three great crises: the demographic crisis, the ecological crisis and the crisis in power and authority. The demographic crisis affects the balance between population and land resources. The ecological crisis implies a rapid change in the ecotypes: with the growth of markets and cities land becomes a commodity, the rural producers are obliged to sell their crops in order to make a living, the payment of taxes increases, and because of the impact of all these factors the peasant cannot allocate resources in the traditional way, an optimal combination of land and labour. Finally the combination of these two crises converges in the crisis of authority. The commercialization and capitalization of agricultural activities weaken the power of the traditional élites (Wolf, 1969a and b).

Barrington Moore (1966) has attempted to solve the puzzle by pointing to the tripartite relationship between commercialization of agriculture, the gentry and the peasants, particularly the relationship between the latter two. According to him the shortcomings of most hypotheses trying to explain the occurrence of peasant uprisings is that they focus too much attention on the peasantry itself. Therefore before looking at the peasantry it is necessary to look at the whole society. With these considerations in mind Moore suggests that certain types or agrarian societies are more apt than others to produce peasant rebellions. For one thing a centralized agrarian bureaucracy is more subject to peasant insurrection than a decentralized and segmental society such as the caste system of India or intermediate 'feudal' systems. Secondly, a revolutionary movement is likely to develop and become a serious threat where the landed aristocracy fails to create a really powerful commercial impulse within its own ranks. Then it may leave beneath it a peasant society damaged but intact. Further, where the peasants have revolted, there are indications that new and capitalist methods of pumping out the economic surplus of the peasantry through market relationships have been added, while the traditional ones lingered on or were even intensified.

It has been often observed that the natural political processes among peasants are 'personalism', 'factionalism' and 'patron–client relationships'. As a general phenomenon this is perhaps connected with the fact that productive and social relations in peasant communities are simultaneously personal relations, either between a tenant and his superior, between kin, between friends and between neighbours. As the bonds of kinship are more or less converging with the process of work or dominant productive relations, the widespread use of kinship terms in peasant political ideology is already 'political' in the sense that one attempts to use a familiar, even though inadequate, language in order to come to grips with specific problems whose nature, paradoxically, is to an important degree directly in contradiction to the content of the language employed.[6] We are not going to discuss deeply all the implications of the processes of peasant personalist politics. Suffice it to say that it is necessary to keep in mind a basic distinction between factionalism and clientele politics. Factions are coalitions temporarily built up in a situation of conflict for scarce resources, either economic or political, or when the existing horizontal ties are collapsing. In this sense they are only processes which do not produce permanent alignments along the line of class or corporate political groups (Nicholas, 1965 and 1966). On the other hand the phenomenon of patron–client ties arises in a given structural set where the peasants depend on the allocation of land or labour, basic resources controlled by a landlord. The power of the landlords as a class, as we have shown in the case of China, is a mixture of legal privileges, the use of coercions and the consensus of the clients. Regarding the peasants, it has been emphasized that in such situations demonstrations of esteem, deference, loyalty and political passivity are the most common responses (Wolf, 1966b; Foster, 1961; Erasmus, 1968; Galjart, 1964).[7] Such relationships are often overlaid by religious ties (Geertz, 1960; Jay, 1963, 1969; Wertheim, 1956, 1964, 1973).

Finally we would like to add that there is a difference between peasant demands when the balance between labour and land is difficult to achieve and the modern peasant-farmers' organizations where claims are centred around a better combination between land and capital or between labour and capital. Peasants tend to imagine an ideal society in utopian terms: a society composed of small-scale producers, all equal but enjoying great freedom in the decisions regarding the process of work and relations with the market. In the peasant-farmer economy, the amount of capital being the key aspect of the social reproduction of the units of production, the demands tend to be concentrated in terms of higher and stable prices, tax, credit, subsidies. The main aim is to create the economic and political conditions for a self-sustained process of capital accumulation. When this moment has arrived the incorporation of independent rural producers as a group into a revolutionary process seems, to be almost impossible.

Prospects

On several occasions in this article we have indicated the important and rapid growth in peasant studies in recent years. Still, many research goals remain to be achieved.

Chayanov's (1966) theory, for example, remains the only available theory of peasant economy, due to the lack of interest, until recently, in the economic basis of peasant societies. The continued pre-eminence of the 'theory of peasant economy', however, can only be justified through a careful test of Chayanov's main hypotheses. A careful investigation of peasant budgets, for example, will permit us to discover the conditions under which peasants behave in accordance with Chayanov's economic laws and under which they do not. The question of external factors for economic reproduction must not be taken as *ceteris paribus*; on the contrary such factors must be systematically introduced into the analysis of peasant economies. We expect that future economic research on this subject will enlighten such questions as the dissolution of traditional peasant economy and the crisis of peasant producers.

Peasant studies have to a large degree been preoccupied with the peasantries of the Third World. In this connection there has been a discussion of how to classify the peasant societies in question; are they capitalist or feudal or is a new term of 'peasant' economy or society needed? We suggest that a major task must be to describe and explain the exact nature of the productive relations in the contemporary peasant societies of the Third World in terms of the more global concepts of 'capitalism', 'feudalism' and 'peasant' in order to reach more appropriate and specific combinations of notions pertaining to the conditions in the peasant communities. The concept of a 'colonial' mode of production as developed independently by Alavi (1965) and Rey (1973) seems to be a case in point. Regarding social and political participation one might suggest more concrete research on the effect of social differentiation on conditions and processes of mobilization. At the same time a careful consideration of ideological values and political traditions will permit an examination of the conditions under which there is or is not a lineal relation between class and political participation. In this sense the book by Berger (1972) on French peasants must be seen as an impressive achievement.

Finally the constitution of a specific peasant field of studies can be achieved through a more open and systematic co-operation between the different branches of the social sciences. This would mean that one could expect, say, a more historical perspective from an anthropologist, and likewise concern for anthropological theory in an historian and, when this is possible, an attempt to reach for the ideological world of peasants. Until now the division of labour in the social sciences has hindered real theoretical integration at various levels. The study of peasantries is bound up with the study of complex societies and the relevance of history. It therefore invites us to combine creatively micro and macroanalysis across time and space. We hope that future research will opt for such an orientation and thus facilitate the rise of a real peasant science, an 'historical and political economy of peasants'.

Notes

1. Recently Le Roy Ladurie (1972) has defined the combination of anthropological theory and historical research on peasants as one of the main tasks for the future.
2. The same has been done by Wolf in several brilliant comparative analyses (1955, 1957). Dalton (1972) argued that there is no general category of peasants and that on the contrary, regarding different socioeconomic stages, we find several kinds of peasantries.
3. Fei is describing an eroded system: the clientele ties were weakened owing to the economic crisis which affected the economic position of the gentry. The landowners were compelled to sell their lands to the new bourgeoisie. In the village the tenants do not know who is the owner of the plot they cultivate, they only are able to report the name of the bureau where they pay the annual rent.
4. Even among hunters and gatherers where 'nature is humanized' and 'human society naturalized' we meet nature and society as parts of a social interaction. The predominance of pure 'nature' in these societies is tantamount to a primitive societal stage, and we encounter nature as mediated through social processes (Lee and De Vore, 1968; Godelier, 1973).
5. The discussion involving Porschnev, Mousnier and Mandrou of the social content in the revolts of the *Nu-pieds* in France, is relevant as an illustration of this remark (Porschnev, 1963; Mousnier, 1962; Mandrou, 1959).
6. Wolf (1967) argued that the political patterns of behaviour among Latin American peasants depend very much on nuclear family ties, kindred and political coalitions which are formed by an alliance of key nuclear families with the support of their kindred and ritual kin. Alavi (1973) has clearly demonstrated that primordial loyalties, like those based on kinship, precede manifestation of class solidarity. Then the complex process of class solidarity is mediated through this basic alignment.
7. Cotler (1969) has developed the concept of the 'closed triangle' as an important condition for the growth of horizontal ties among peasants, because they are tied vertically to the landlords. The presence of brokers under a process of erosion of the social and political system permits the reinforcement of class solidarity among peasants. This model has been used for explaining the modes of political action and participation of Bolivian and Peruvian peasants (Alberti, 1970; Whyte, 1970; Dandler, 1969).

126

References

Alavi, Hamza (1965), 'Peasants and revolution', in R. Miliband and J. Saville (eds.), *The Socialist Register* (London: Merlin).

Alavi, Hamza (1973), 'Peasant classes and primordial loyalties', *The Journal of Peasant Studies*, **1**, 1.

Alberti, Giorgio (1970), 'Los movimientos campesinos', in R. G. Keith *et al., La Hacienda, la comunidad y el campesino en el Peru* (Lima: Moncloa Editores).

Amin, Samir, and Vergopoulos, Kostas (1974), *La question paysanne et le capitalisme* (Paris: Anthropos).

Bailey, F. G. (1969), *Stratagems and Spoils* (Oxford: Basil Blackwell).

Berger, S. (1972), *Peasants Against Politics* (Cambridge, Mass.: Harvard University Press).

Bianco, L. (1975), 'Peasants and revolution: the case of China', *The Journal of Peasant Studies*, **2**, 3.

Bloch, Maurice (1930), 'L'individualisme agraire', *Annales*, **5**, 1, 1–34.

Bloch, Maurice (1933), *Les caractères originaux de l'histoire rurale française*, (Oslo: Institutt for Sammenlignende Kulturforskning).

Blum, Jerome (1971), *Lord and Peasant in Russia* (Princeton, N.J.: Princeton University Press).

Bois, Paul (1971), *Paysans de l' Ouest* (Paris: Flammarion).

Chayanov, A. V. (1966), *The Theory of Peasant Economy*, D. Thorner, R. E. F. Smith and B. Kerblay (eds.) (Homewood, Ill.: Irwin).

Chesneaux, Jean (ed.) (1972), *Popular Movements and Secret Societies in China* (Stanford: Stanford Press).

Chesneaux, Jean (1973), *Peasant Revolts in China: 1840–1949* (London: Thames and Hudson).

Cohn, Norman (1957), *The Pursuit of the Millennium* (London: Secker).

Cotler, Julio (1969), 'Actuales pautas de cambio en la sociedad rural del Perú' in J. Matos Mar *et al., Dominación y cambio en Perú rural* (Lima: Instituto de Estudios Peruanos).

Dalton, George (ed.) (1967), *Tribal and Peasant Economies* (Garden City, N.Y.: The Natural History Press).

Dalton, George (1972), 'Peasantries in anthropology and history', *Current Anthropology*, **13**, 3/4.

Dandler, Jorge (1969), *El sindicalismo campesino en Bolivia: los cambios estructurales en Ucurena* (Mexico: Instituto Indigenista Interamericano).

Erasmus, Charles (1968), 'Community development and the *encogido* syndrome', *Human Organization*, **27**, 1.

Fei, Hsiao-Tung (1939), *Peasant Life in China: A Field Study of Country Life in the Yangtze Valley* (London: Kegan Paul).

Fei, Hsiao-Tung (1953), *China's Gentry* (Chicago: The University of Chicago Press).

Feuchtwang, Stephen (1975), 'Investigating religion' in Maurice Bloch (ed.), *Marxist Analysis and Social Anthropology* (London: Malaby Press).

Firth, Raymond (1964), 'Capital, saving and credit in peasant societies: a viewpoint from economic anthropology', in Firth Yamey (1964).

Firth, Raymond, and Yamey, B. S. (eds.) (1964) *Capital, Credit and Saving in Peasant Societies* (London: Allen and Unwin).

Fortes, Meyer (1958), 'Introduction' in Jack Goody (ed.), *The Development Cycle in Domestic Group* (Cambridge: Cambridge University Press).

Foster, George (1961), 'The Dyadic Contract: A Model for the Social Structure of a Mexican Peasant Village', *American Anthropologist*, **63**.

Franklin, S. H. (1969), *The European Peasantry* (London: Methuen).

Friedl, Ernestine (1965), 'Studies in peasant life' in B. Siegel (ed.), *Biennial Review of Anthropology* (Stanford: Stanford University Press).

Galeski, B. (1972), *Basic Concepts of Rural Sociology* (Manchester: Manchester University Press).

Galjart, Benno (1964), 'Class and "following" in rural Brazil', *America Latina*, 7, 3.

Geertz, Clifford (1960), *The Religion of Java* (Glencoe, Ill.: Free Press).

Geertz, Clifford (1962), 'Studies in peasant life: community and society' in B. Siegel (ed.) *Biennial Review of Anthropology* (Stanford: Stanford University Press).

Godelier, Maurice (1973), *Horizon, trajets, marxistes en anthropologie* (Paris: Maspero).

Hilton, Rodney (1973), *Bond Men Made Free* (London: Temple Smith).

Hilton, Rodney (1974a), 'Medieval peasants: any lessons', *Journal of Peasant Studies*, 1, 2.

Hilton, Rodney (1974b), 'Peasant society, peasant movements and feudalism in medieval Europe' in Landsberger (1974a).

Hinton, William, (1966), *Fanshen* (New York: Vintage Books).

Hobsbawm, Eric (1959), *Primitive Rebels* (Manchester: Manchester University Press).

Hobsbawm, Eric (1969), *Bandits* (London: Weidenfeld and Nicolson).

Hobsbawm, Eric (1973), 'Peasants and politics', *Journal of Peasant Studies*, 1, 1.

Hobsbawm, Eric (1974), 'Social banditry' in Landsberger (1974a).

Jay, R. (1963), *Religion and Politics in Rural Central Java* (New Haven, Conn.: Yale University Press).

Jay, R. (1969), *Javanese Villagers* (Cambridge, Mass.: MIT Press).

Kartodirdjo, H. (1968), *The Peasant Revolt in Banten 1888* (Leiden; Martinus Nijhoff).

Kerblay, B. (1971), 'Chayanov and the theory of peasantry as a specific type of economy' in Shanin (1971).

Kroeber, Alfred L. (1948), *Anthropology* (New York: Harcourt Brace).

Kula, Witold (1970), *Théorie économique du système féodal* (Paris: Mouton).

Landsberger, Henry (ed.) (1969), *Latin American Peasant Movements* (Ithaca, N.Y.: Cornell University Press).

Landsberger, Henry (ed.) (1974a) *Rural Protest: Peasant Movements and Social Change* (London: Macmillan).

Landsberger, Henry (1974b), 'Peasant unrest: themes and variations' in Landsberger (1974a).

Le Roy Ladurie, E. (1969), *Les paysans de Languedoc* (Paris: Flammarion).

Le Roy Ladurie, E. (1972), 'Structures familiales et coutumes d'héritage', *Annales*, 4/5.

Lee, Richard, B. and I. De Vore (eds.) (1968), *Man the Hunter* (Chicago: Aldine).

Lenin, V. I., (1962), 'The agrarian program of the Social-Democrats', in *Collected Works, vol. 13* (Moscow: Foreign Languages Publishing House).

Mao Tse-Tung, 1967 (1927), 'Reports on an investigation of the peasant movement in Hunan' in *Selected Works, vol. 1*, (Pekin: Foreign Language Press).

Mandrou, Robert (1959), 'Les soulèvements populaires et la société française du XVII siècle', *Annales*, **XIV**.

Marx, Karl, 1963, *The 18th Brumaire* (New York: International Publishers).

Marx, Karl, 1971, *Capital, vol. III* (Moscow: Progress Publishers).

Meillassoux, Claude (1973), 'The social organization of the peasantry', *Journal of Peasant Studies*, 1, 1.

Mendras, Henri (1967), *La fin des paysans* (Paris: SEDEIS).

Mendras, Henri, and Yves Tavernier (eds.) (1969), *Terre, paysans et politique* (Paris: SEDEIS).

Mintz, Sidney (1973), 'A note on the definition of peasantries', *Journal of Peasant Studies*, 1, 1.

Moore, Barrington (1966), *Social Origins of Dictatorship and Democracy: Lord and Peasant in the Making of the Modern World*, (Boston: Beacon Press).

Mousnier, Ronald (1962), 'Les mouvements populaires en France au dix-septième siècle', *Revue de l' Academie des Sciences Morales et Politiques*, **4**.

Mousnier, Ronald (1967), *Fureurs paysannes: les paysans dans les revoltes du XVII siècle (France, Russie, Chine)*, (Paris: Colmann-Levy).

Nash, Manning (1966), *Primitive and Peasant Economic Systems* (San Francisco: Chandler).

Nicholas, Ralph W. (1965), 'Factions: a comparative analysis' in M. Banton (ed.), *Political Systems and the Distribution of Power* (London: Tavistock).

Nicholas, Ralph W. (1966), 'Segmentary factional political systems' in M. Swartz *et al.*, (eds.), *Political Anthropology* (Chicago: University of Chicago Press).

Pereira de Queiroz, Maria I. (1969), *Historia y étnología de los movimientos mesiánicos* (Mexico: Siglo XXI editores).

Porschnev, Boris (1963), *Les soulèvements populaires en France de 1623 à 1648* (Paris: École Pratiques des Hautes Études).

Potter, Jack *et al.* (eds.) (1967), *Peasant Society: A Reader* (Boston: Little, Brown).

Powell, John D. (1970), 'Peasant society and clientelist politics', *American Political Science Review*, **64**.

Redfield, Robert (1956), *Peasant Society and Culture* (Chicago: University of Chicago Press).

Redfield, Robert, and Alfonso Villa Rojas, (1934), *Chan-Kom, A Maya Village* (Chicago: University of Chicago Press).

Rey, Pierre-Philippe (1973), *Les Alliances des Classes* (Paris: Maspero).

Shanin, Teodor (1966), 'The peasantry as a political factor', *Sociological Review*, **14**.

Shanin, Teodor, (ed.) (1971), *Peasants and Peasant Societies* (London: Penguin).

Shanin, Teodor (1972), *The Awkward Class* (London: Oxford University Press).

Shanin, Teodor (1973–74), 'The nature and logic of the peasant economy', *Journal of Peasant Studies*, **1**, 1/2.

Soboul, Albert (1956), 'The French rural community in the 18th and the 19th centuries', *Past and Present*, 4.

Stahl, H. H. (1969), *Les anciénnes Communautés villageoises roumaines* (Paris: CNRS).

Stavenhagen, Rodolfo (1969), *Les classes sociales dans les sociétés agraires* (Paris: Anthropos).

Stavenhagen, Rodolfo (ed.) (1970), *Agrarian Problems and Peasant Movements in Latin America* (New York: Anchor Books).

Talmon, Yonina (1966), 'Millenarian movements', *Archives Européennes de Sociologie*, **VII**, 2.

Tepicht, Jerzy (1966), 'Agricultural circles in the light of the general problems of agriculture, *Eastern European Economics*, **IV**, 4.

Tepicht, Jerzy (1967a), 'L' agriculture paysanne et le développement d'economie polonaise', *Études Rurales*, 25–26.

Tepicht, Jerzy (1967b), 'Economia contadina e teoria marxista', *Critica Marxista*, 1.

Tepicht, Jerzy (1971), 'Les complexités d' économie paysanne', *Information sur les Sciences Sociales*, **8**, 6.

Thorner, Daniel (1962), 'Peasant economy as a category in economic history', *Deuxième Conference International d'Histoire Economique, vol. 2* (The Hague: Mouton).

Tullis, F. La Mond, (1970), *Lord and Peasant in Peru: A Paradigm of Political and Social Change* (Cambridge, Mass.: Harvard University Press).

Wallerstein, I. (1974), *The Modern World System* (New York: Academic Press).

Warriner, Doreen, 1964 (1939), *Economics of Peasant Farming* (London: Cass).

Wertheim, W. F. (1956), *Indonesian Society in Transition* (The Hague: Van Hoeve).

Wertheim, W. F. (1964), *East–West Parallels* (The Hague: Van Hoeve).

Wertheim, W. F. (1973), *The Dawning of an Asian Dream* (Amsterdam: University Press).

Wertheim, W. F. (1974), *Evolution and Revolution* (London: Penguin).

Whyte, William (1970), 'El mito del campesino pasivo: la dinámica del cambio en el Péru rural', *Estudios Andinos*, **1**, 1.

Wolf, Eric (1955), 'Types of Latin American Peasantries', *American Anthropologist*, **57**.

Wolf, Eric (1957), 'Closed corporate peasant communities in Mesoamerica and Central Java', *Southwestern Journal of Anthropology*, **13**, 1.

Wolf, Eric (1966a), *Peasants* (Englewood Cliffs, N.J.: Prentice-Hall).

Wolf, Eric (1966b), 'Kinship, friendship and patrol–client relations in complex societies' in M. Banton (ed.), *The Social Anthropology of Complex Societies* (London: Tavistock).

Wolf, Eric (1967), 'Patrons politicos entre campesinos latinoamericanos' in CNRS (ed.), *Les problèmes agraires des Ameriques Latines* (Paris: CNRS).

Wolf, Eric (1969a), *Peasants Wars of the 20th Century* (New York: Harper and Row).

Wolf, Eric (1969b), 'On peasant rebellions', *International Social Science Journal*, **21**.

Worsley, Peter (1957), *The Trumpet Shall Sound: A Study of 'Cargo' Cults in Melanesia* (London: MacGibbon and Kee).

6

The Contemporary Peasantry: Class and Class Practice

Joseph W. Foweraker

The lower classes, historically on the defensive, can only achieve self-awareness via a series of negations, via their consciousness of the identity and class limits of the enemy.
Gramsci *Prison Notebooks*, p.273

It is worth remembering that — as in the past, so in the present — peasants are the majority of mankind.
Shanin *Peasants and Peasant Society*, p. 17

Introduction

The objective of this essay is to introduce a measure of conceptual clarity into the discussion of the peasantry. In particular, it is necessary to resolve the question of the peasantry as a class, before beginning to consider the nature of radical peasant politics. Literature on the peasantry has too often attempted detailed discussion of the peasantry, without facing major theoretical problems, and has remained largely empiricist in orientation. The intention here, on the contrary, is to develop the discussion on the basis of recent theory, first to locate the problems, and then to construct a theoretical framework for their resolution. The areas of theory which are most relevant are that of modes of production and their articulation, and of the place of the political instance in the definition of class, and of capitalist genealogy. Moreover, the methodological premise of the essay demands that any approach to the peasantry be historically specific: the intention is to theorize the peasantry which produces within the contemporary world-capitalist system. No attempt will be made to discuss the role of the peasantry in different historical situations; on the other hand, to theorize the question successfully, an historical perspective is essential.

Sources of conceptual confusion

The first problem nearly all writers on the peasantry face is its apparent lack of homogeneity. The peasantry is differentiated by the labour process, property-holding and relation to the market, among other things. Those who take this diverse reality as their starting point do not admit that there exists a peasantry in general. Thus the classical theorists insisted on talking about classes *within* the peasantry, and many discussions bear reverential reference to Lenin's schemes of the peasantry as divided into seven, five, or three classes. Schemes of this sort can largely be reduced to a simple division between 'poor peasants' (who are usually tenants cultivating landlords' land), 'middle peasants' (who are independent smallholders), and rich peasants (very often capitalist farmers, exploiting wage-labour). The modern view agrees that 'beyond a certain point in the socioeconomic differentiation of the agrarian population the term peasantry is no longer applicable' (Hobsbawm, 1973), except that today there is even reluctance to accept a generalized *class division* of the peasantry. By peasantry is understood 'specific forms of agricultural production, worked and managed to a greater or lesser degree by household units' (Hirst, 1976); the only way to generalize about the peasantry is to look for 'different types of agrarian class societies' (Martinez-Alier, 1974). In short, attempts to begin analysis on the basis of the 'observed reality' have led to a plainly empiricist orientation.

Yet a residual 'generality' subsists in many accounts, firstly through the wide awareness of Marx's treatment of the problem, and the occasional attempts to apply the first elements of a theory of class as defined by its relationship to the means of production (thus Hobsbawn, paraphrasing Marx in *The 18th Brumaire* says that 'objectively it can be defined as a "class-in-itself" in the classical sense, namely as a body of people who have the same kind of relation to the means of production as well as other common economic and social characteristics (Hobsbawm, 1973)). But Marx's theoretical treatment is not developed, and so only serves to confuse the discussion yet more. On the one hand, the clash between these elements of theory and the dominant empiricism leads to imprecise descriptive categorizations of the peasantry, as being, for instance, a 'class of low classness' (Shanin, 1971); on the other, Marx's 'small peasantry' has dogged discussions of the peasantry — in a world where it is statistically insignificant (and where, anyway, nearly every peasant with means of subsistence will either work on others' land or employ others to work for him at some time during the agricultural year).

More important in the majority of accounts, however, is that 'generality' which derives from the obvious (and 'observed') differences between the peasantry and the *rest of society*. This has led to different descriptive categorizations of the peasantry as being 'part-society' or 'part-culture' (see, for example, Kroeber 1948). At its most developed the 'part-society' approach contains ideas of political encapsulation and penetration by larger societal wholes, and the extraction of a surplus from the peasant cultivator. In this, it resembles accounts of 'internal colonialism', which, in analogous fashion, describe a colony, separate from the larger society, and exploited by it. These accounts have been criticized for purporting to explain the colony's existence in terms of race or culture ('racial and ethnic entities are treated abstractly and as if their internal class structures are irrelevant to their existence as groups and to their political and ideological practices' — Wolpe, 1972). In short, the class dimensions of exploitation are obscured; primary contradictions are transposed to a secondary level. Similarly, the descriptive idea of peasantry as 'part-society' inevitably obscures the objective relations of exploitation (this 'society' must contain both 'exploiters' and 'exploited'), and so this attempt at encompassing the peasantry in general will again fail to define the peasantry as a class.

While these attempts at 'conceiving and describing a whole that is both inclosed within other wholes and is also in some part permeated by them' (Redfield, 1960) lie clearly in the empiricist tradition, they yield some important observations. I refer to those discussions which note, repeatedly, the 'subaltern position' of the peasantry, its 'underdog position', and, especially, its 'domination by outsiders' (Shanin, 1971) (or which assert that explanation of productive relations resides finally at the 'socio-political level' — Martinez-Alier, 1974). The most explicit statement to this effect is from Tepicht (1969), who says that the peasantry 'has never been represented in any historical formation where it is present, by a ruling class. In one way or another it remains in a *subordinate* position' (my emphasis). Despite the number of such observations, their formulation is never elaborated so as to further our understanding of the peasantry. Above all it is in no way related to a definition of peasantry through its relationship to the means of production. In short, it is limited by a false problematic, which includes the idea of 'part-society', and which prevents its theoretical development. Yet I believe that the *political subordination* of the peasantry, when theorized within a new problematic, can resolve the difficulties of defining the peasantry as a class. I shall argue for the existence of this class as finally, but not sufficiently, defined by its actual, not necessarily legal, subordination to another class, which, within the peasants' productive system represents the dominance of another mode of production within the social formation as a whole.

Elements of a new problematic

Within the new problematic, political subordination is the key element which has to be theorized in relation to the mode of production within which peasants produce. But it should be emphasized at the beginning that the economic, that is the peasants', relationship to the means of production in that mode of production, is still primary in the definition of the peasantry as a class. This warning is necessary, because it is the political subordination which must be discussed first, in a logical presentation of the problematic.

The problematic derives from a genealogy of capitalism, which contains two major forms of capitalist development — bourgeois capitalism (BC) and authoritarian capitalism (AC) — which are distinguished, on the one hand, by the nature of the insertion of the capitalist mode of production (CMP) in the social formation (SF) as a whole, and, on the other, by the timing and characteristics of State intervention in the process, and the relation of the State to the economically dominant class in the society. It should also be emphasized that these two forms of capitalist development are not different modes of production (MPs) — the internal laws of motion of the CMP are everywhere the same — but they are rather different *economic systems*. Crucial to the difference between these systems is the way in which the CMP is articulated with other MPs, and the continuing importance of this articulation of modes of production (AMP) to the expanded reproduction of the CMP in the authoritarian capitalist social formations (ACSFs). The peasantry is located within this theoretical framework, and the specificity of the peasantry established through the political conditions by which the CMP receives surplus, in the form of rent, produced in subordinate MPs.

Contemporarily, the peasantry produces surplus within modes of production which are subordinate to capitalism, termed sub-capitalist modes of production (SCMPs). It is recognized that these MPs are many, and that they may be differentiated one from the other by their internal structure. There are two justifications, however, for the use of the concept SCMP. In the first place it is employed *pro tem* for the purposes of exploring the general characteristics of AC as an *economic system*, and the place of the peasantry within it. In this way, such questions as 'do the peasantry produce within a feudal mode of production?' can be postponed until the appropriation and transfer of surplus *across* MPs (AMP) — and specifically to the CMP — and its relevance to the definition of the peasantry, is established. (In other words, as we stated above, the political subordination of the peasantry is discussed first.) In the second place, it is my contention that *at this stage* of the articulation of the SCMPs with CMP throughout the world, their 'laws of motion' are becoming more and more similar, and, as I attempt to demonstrate in the later discussion of the *content* of this concept, the relationship of the peasantry to the means of production within these SCMPs is everywhere the same. The logical necessity of discussing the economic system (and the political subordination) first, is then evident, for the nub of the argument is the place of the political subordination in the reproduction of the social relations of production in the SCMPs, and hence in the reproduction of the peasantry as a class.

When analysing authoritarian capitalism I talk about the 'dominance of the political'. This refers to the relative autonomy of the State in relation to the economically dominant class (the bourgeoisie), the necessary intervention of the State to promote capitalist growth, and, more specifically, to guarantee, on the one hand, the dominance of capital over the landlord class, and, on the other, the political subordination (or 'immobilization', meaning a generalized lack of economic and social alternatives) of the peasantry. As will be explained below, the political is 'dominant' because the bourgeoisie is not hegemonic; because for the economic system which is AC to function and expand, the State — initially in the form of institutions of labour control — must intervene to keep labour on the land, and guarantee the appropriation of the product. The dominance of the political only has meaning within the objective structure of AC.

In the same way, the political subordination is an objective relationship, which does not have to do with the motivation of the social agents. Some discussions of the peasantry have viewed certain actions as revolutionary or not in terms of what the peasantry 'want': it has even been asserted that we cannot talk of the peasantry in general because, for a variety of reasons, we cannot know their 'true thoughts' (Martinez-Alier, 1974). These discussions participate in a 'false problematic of the subject' (Laclau, 1975), and conclusions drawn from them are a lottery. By situating my problematic historically I will try to avoid a similar voluntarism.

The historical perspective

Our interpretation begins with the transition to capitalism in Europe. It is during this economic revolution that the peasantry is transformed, and finally 'disappears', for all practical purposes, from certain of the central capitalist countries. This was theorized in Marx by the stage of primitive accumulation, which in its *internal* aspect, achieves a once-and-for-all divorce of the direct producers from the means of production in the countryside. This divorce is theorized in turn as a necessary condition for the development of capitalism: in conjunction with the institution of landed property it forms the 'double mill' which drives labour to the cities, and promotes centralization of capitals. (Expropriation of the peasants takes the form of supplementing one kind of property by another). In this way, Marx successfully theorizes the transformation of the peasantry, and its relation to capitalist development — as he knew it. But as early as 1885 (to Zasulich 23 April 1885) Engels (1934) suggests that the 'historic fatality' of this transformation may be confined to Western Europe. In other words, he opened the possibility for a revision or development of the theory. Such a revision is yet more necessary today, when the expansion of capitalism as a word system has in no way precipitated the 'disappearance' of the peasantry in the 'Third World'.

This revision demands closer examination of the transition to capitalism and consideration of the developments which follow the industrial revolution — within a more general genealogy of capitalism itself. First we must note what exactly occurs in the passage from feudalism to capitalism. Feudalism in its archetypal form had not existed for centuries prior to the industrial revolution. It is experiencing a slow transformation, under the aegis of the Absolutist State — which can be defined as the State of the feudal landlords, in conditions of feudal crisis. In attempting to protect feudal property relations, this State simultaneously establishes the conditions for the development of capitalism. This is not to say that capitalism is suddenly dominant. In the period of transition capital, largely commercial capital, rules, but rules outside the sphere of production. And, in fact, the transformations in feudalism gave considerable economic scope to that fraction of the bourgeoisie engaged with commercial capital, and protected by the State through a system of legal monopolies. Given this scope, the commercial bourgeoisie can practise an *external* primitive accumulation (during what is known euphemistically as the mercantilist era), while the Absolutist State is intervening politically to promote the internal aspect (divorce of the direct producer from the means of production). Both aspects of the primitive accumulation contribute to create the conditions for manufacture, and, finally, the industrial revolution. Thus when the bourgeois (political) revolutions occur they mark the consolidation at the level of State, of the victory already achieved at the level of distribution and production. Thus the transformations in feudalism prepare the way for the specific form of capitalist development which I shall call bourgeois capitalism (BC) — and it is this capitalism (as we know from Marx's (1970) discussion of Wakefield, for instance) which demands the divorce of the direct producer from his means of production.

Bourgeois capitalism is the historical result of the transformation of feudalism 'from within'. When divorced from its means of production the peasantry has no option but to migrate to the cities and sell its labour-power. In short, there is no *free land*. But where free land existed, then feudal forms of property-holding and exploitation had proved far more resilient. In the presence of an 'open frontier' the Absolutist State had to intervene in order to 'immobilize' labour politically, usually by the introduction of serfdom. Without such systems of labour-control it would have been impossible to extract a surplus from the peasantry. In the Russian case for instance, we see the introduction of serfdom, and the flight to the frontier of those who can escape (Trotsky, 1965). Both serfdom and flight lead to the relative unimportance of towns and cities, and a delayed process of social differentiation. This is not a suitable social and economic environment for the emergence of a strong bourgeoisie: on the contrary, most accumulation continues to be controlled by the State within specific systems of labour control. In other words, the conditions are not present for the development of bourgeois capitalism, but, nevertheless, these States will experience the diverse pressures, both military and commercial, deriving from the expansion of bourgeois capitalism. These increase from the time of the bourgeois revolutions, constituting a secular process of 'combined and unequal development'. But the pressures generated by this autonomous process of capitalist development elsewhere do not lead to the dissolution of the systems of labour control; on the contrary, these systems may be reinforced and extended, as we shall see, in order to produce more for the growing 'bourgeois' markets. The peasantry remains on the land, and remains politically immobilized, while first commercial capital, and later capitalist social relations of production begin to dominate the economy. The development which takes place is not bourgeois but *authoritarian* capitalism. Thus AC is 'reflexive' and develops out of systems of labour-control existing prior to the expansion of bourgeois capitalism.

It was said that the bourgeois revolutions were the consolidation at the level of State of a revolution already achieved at the level of production. The bourgeoisie in this case is both (economically) dominant, and (politically) directing, in Gramscian terminology. In other words it is hegemonic, and it is not hard to see why classical Marxist analysis conceived of the State as an 'instrument of the bourgeoisie' (Lenin, 1972). The bourgeoisie secures the State in order to guarantee the reproduction of capitalist social relations of production. In AC, on the contrary, it is the State which oversees the progress of the bourgeoisie. The State develops fast in order to exercize the coercion necessary to exploit the peasantry; its growth far outstrips that of 'civil society'. When with the growth and expansion of CMP the bourgeoisie becomes dominant, it is still not directing. In short, the economically dominant class is not politically dominant — is not hegemonic — and remains genetically weak. Very often it must share power with different classes and class fractions in the *power bloc*. It is not the bourgeoisie but the State which has achieved the 'bourgeois revolution', and the State enjoys far greater autonomy of the dominant class or class fraction than in BC (particularly at moments of crisis). In AC the transition to CMP resembles a period of 'passive revolution' far more than it does the bourgeois revolutions of Western Europe.

In AC, given the presence of free land, the State intervenes to keep labour on the land. It is not surprising that one of the most powerful participants in the power bloc is the landowning class. Examples of AC are Russia in the nineteenth century, Latin America after independence (a more complex case which requires analysis of the formation of the State after the dissolution of the colonial administration) and South Africa in this century. Elsewhere, of course, the presence of *free land* led to quite different developments, as in the United States and Australia — both of them countries which today are noticeably lacking in a peasantry. In these cases no State existed to impose labour control, and then it is the frontier — the very opposite to political immobilization — which is the formative influence in the growth of the economic system. What is crucial for the argument therefore, is that the double mill of expropriation and landed property is as necessary to AC as to BC, but in a very different way. In AC labour is kept on the land. It is politically immobilized so that it may be economically exploited. It is for this reason that AC is characterized in contrast to BC, by a marked dominance of the political. It is this which finally characterizes the difference of AC which has been so widely — if only implicitly — recognized (cf. for example discussion by Samir Amin, 1970).

In the most simple terms, this 'exploitation' depends on political immobilization, and hence the extraction of the surplus was first theorized as a form of primitive accumulation, which continues in tandem with capitalist accumulation proper, in certain social formations. Primitive accumulation we are reminded, can take other forms than expropriation (and it is not necessarily the case that capitalist development and proletarianization go together): 'the most typical methods were, first, plundering of the serf peasants by their lords and sharing of the plunder with merchant capital, or, second, crushing taxation of the peasantry by the State and transformation of part of the means so obtained into capital' (Preobrazhensky, 1965). This concept of a continuous recreation and crystallization of the conditions of primitive accumulation in the present at least established the importance of this accumulation for capitalist development proper. Authoritarian capitalist countries being latecomers could not compete in colonial or imperialist adventures in order to accumulate: bourgeois capitalist pressures thus led to an 'extensive' development through primitive accumulation. (Spain and Portugal were colonial powers, of course, but were indeed 'latecomers' in the transition to capitalism; Spain loses its colonies at the beginning of the nineteenth century, but Portugal continues its 'mercantile' colonialism, while remaining itself dependent on bourgeois capitalism in Great Britain.) Moreover, as AC development began at a stage of general capitalist development which included urban industry and finance capital, capitalist penetration tended to encourage and promote a transfer of surplus from the countryside to the town (in contrast to bourgeois capitalist countries where changes in the countryside were *prior* to urban industry and finance capital). Finally, touching the question of immobilization of labour, the already more highly capitalized technology meant a relatively reduced need for an 'industrial reserve army' in the AC case (Palmeira, 1969).

Except for particular and relatively restricted forms of accumulation, however, as on certain pioneer frontiers, the concept of primitive accumulation is not very exact, or very satisfactory theoretically. When extended to all institutions of labour-control (Palmeira, 1969) it establishes the extraction of a surplus, but again fails to specify the class relations of exploitation. Further, it fails to analyse adequately the way in which labour can be 'divorced' from the land, but kept *on* it at the same time. In short, it is not so much a theory as an historical analogy. This is especially true today, when the content of the concept of political immobilization has been radically altered. What might be called 'immediate immobilization', was needed when all land was far from being monopolized, and labour was scarce. This is what Hobsbawm in effect discusses in his essay on 'neo-feudalism' — an attempt at 'immediate immobilization' in conditions of artificial labour shortage (Hobsbawm, 1969). But in most of the Third World today (with significant exceptions like parts of Brazil) all land is monpolized, and there is surplus labour ('surplus' here being a relative concept which has to do with the effective monopolization of land, prevailing technology and demographic growth). Labour is divorced from the land and 'free' to move. But this freedom is analogous to that of the wage-labourer to sell his labour-power in the market in Dickensian England. It is no freedom at all. The 'immobilization' is still achieved through political subordination, still grossly defined as a lack of generalized alternatives. The peasant stays on the land, even if conditions are harsh, for they are harsher off the land. (Very often, of course, commercial, political and demographic pressures combine to drive him off the land: witness the mass migrations from Ireland and Southern Italy in the nineteenth century, and the problems of 'marginalization' in Latin America today.) Being exploited he is better off. The double mill in AC operates within the *sub-capitalist modes of production* (SCMPs) — that is, *non*-capitalist MPs which are subordinate to CMP. To understand this we need to explore two different areas of theory: that of the articulation between politics and economics, and, in particular, the 'dominance of the political', and that of the articulation of modes of production (AMP).

The AMP, and AC as part of a world system

What we are to consider is nothing less than the expansion of bourgeois capitalism, and the penetration and final dominance of the capitalist mode of production (CMP) in peripheral social formations (SFs). Once the CMP is dominant in these SFs, then the peasantry produces within sub-capitalist modes of production (SCMPs). Posing the problem dynamically and historically allows us to avoid (at least for the moment) the tortuous debates regarding the actual modes of production (MPs), besides CMP, existing in any particular SF. The point is that very different, and complex, SFs were penetrated by CMP, but they can now all be commonly defined at least by the dominance of CMP. Similarly, historically, the peasantry's surplus product was appropriated by different ruling classes in different MPs, but today that surplus (or a large part of it) is finally transferred to CMP, which makes the contemporary peasantry susceptible to study as a 'universal' phenomenon.

The disappearance of the peasantry corresponds in countries of bourgeois capitalist development to the almost total dissolution of SCMPs. But in the periphery the integration into the world market, and the consequent commercial pressures of capitalism, led, on the contrary, to a reinforcement of the SCMPs, as increased exactions were made on the peasantry to supply the new markets. This is Engel's 'second serfdom', and Gershenkron (1962) too testifies to the truth of this response in the Russian case. Certainly in the stage of competitive capitalism, the surplus produced in SCMPs with a high proportion of living labour to 'dead' labour counteracted the tendency of the rate of profit to fall, and AMP was crucial in determining the average rate of profit in the world system (Laclau, 1969). Lenin, in his essay on Imperialism (Lenin, 1964) saw the export of capital 'expanding and deepening the further development of capitalism throughout the world', but even with the implantation of an industrial CMP in peripheral SFs, the SCMPs were not dissolved, but further reinforced.

The reinforcement requires further explanation. Peasantry within the SCMPs produce commodities, or, more strictly 'goods', which are essential to CMP, both raw materials and staples which enter the reproduction of the labour-force in CMP. 'Goods' may be extracted from the SCMP by plunder, or exchange of non-equivalents, or by other means; labour-power may be extracted more or less directly. If labour moves from the SCMP, where its subsistence (or part of it) is guaranteed, to CMP, then from the point of view of the latter, its labour-power may be obtained at a *cost* below its *value*. Similarly, staple goods produced in the SCMPs by so-called cheap labour, and entering the CMP, lower the cost of reproduction of labour in CMP (again, the labour is 'cheap' by the criteria of CMP, which, indeed, gets this 'cheap' labour-power by, for example, enforcing certain conditions of exchange). Surplus-labour, as we know, only has meaning in relation to necessary-labour: by indirectly pumping out increased surplus-labour from the SCMPs, the capitalist can compress the necessary labour time in CMP, and so increase the rate of relative surplus value. It is in terms of mechanisms like these, which will be further elaborated below, that we can assimilate *minifundistas* and even 'middle peasants' to our definition of the peasantry as a class. Given their political subordination they all provide labour-power as a cost below value, either in SCMPs or CMP (see sections on Rent and Dominance of the Political below). And these mechanisms are as important, or become more important, with the dominance in the SF of an industrial CMP. But we should note that the exploitation turns on the preservation of the SCMPs, and the political subordination of the peasantry.

Thus under the given conditions there seems no reason to believe that AMP is a transitory phenomenon, but every reason to think AC a distinct genus of development. In this model the peasant product is economically necessary to the reproduction of the social relations of production not only in the SCMP but in the AC social formation (ACSF) as a whole. (Politically it is necessary to cement the class alliance which forms the power bloc expressed through the AC State.) But it has been argued (notably by Rey, 1973; and Bettelheim, 1972) that the AMP occurs in two stages, beginning with CMP incorporating the commodities produced within SCMPs as part of productive capital. During this first stage when commodity exchange is generalized in the world market (and corresponds to the stage of competitive capitalism), the SCMPs may indeed be reinforced; in the second stage, however, the CMP 'takes root' and destroys all forms of commodity production outside of CMP. Labour-power everywhere becomes a commodity. Rey (1973) in particular argues that for Marx and Lenin finance capital could take root in SCMPs and substitute itself for the production of subsistence goods. Hence, for them, AMP was not a permanent necessity, but only a transitory complement to CMP. What is missing from their analysis, says Rey, is the crucial 'transition' achieved by colonialism, which represents 'finance capital's mission to create the conditions where the exchange of money for living labour of workers can take place'. On the other hand, Rey admits that SCMPs are not 'destroyed so thoroughly' as at the 'parallel stage' in the metropolis; and this is because to expel the peasant from his land was just not possible, and because capitalism had occupied only the superstructure, not developing agricultural production.

Paraphrasing Rey is certainly not the fairest way to present his case, but I think him wrong, if only because he supposes one unique form of capitalist development, and does not admit of a genealogy of capitalism. More seriously, he seems to believe in 'parallel stages' of development (an idea that was discredited with Rostow), and does not develop an objective analysis of the mode of reproduction of the social division of labour in what I term ACSF. He assumes that, as in bourgeois development, the expropriation of the peasantry will finally take place (finally it may, but the transition may be one of several hundred years!). What he cannot explain, is how, in fully fledged monopoly capitalism, the majority of the world's population, whether in colonies or neocolonies, is still producing as peasantry in SCMPs. The peasantry as a whole has not been destroyed, but continues to be 'confined' within a certain 'social space' which is also the SCMPs. (The SCMPs, of course, contain *more* than just the peasantry; we only have to think of the 'marginal' sectors in the cities of Latin America). This is not to say that the relative importance of AMP, or its form, are not changing. In the monopoly capital stage, the pattern of investment in the periphery has shifted rapidly into the production of strategic materials like oil, for example, and into manufacturing production, and allocation of investment funds as a whole has shifted from periphery to centre. At the same time selective areas of agriculture in the periphery have been capitalized, and wage-relations introduced. Investment in these 'select areas' is designed either to guarantee the steady supply and high quality of industrial raw materials, or to promote high productivity production of exchange-earnings crops (or, of course, crops which are costing a disproportionate amount of foreign exchange). All this may mean that the amount of surplus generated in SCMPs which enters CMP is relatively smaller, but it does not mean that it is any the less essential either to the realization of high profits by multinational companies, or to the reproduction of the social division of labour in the ACSFs.

The peasantry therefore is the labour force within SCMPs within ACSFs where the CMP is dominant. It follows that the peasantry cannot be defined as a class by its relation to the means of production in the CMP, *nor merely* by its relation to the means of production in the SCMP. This class must be defined both by the social relations of production in SCMP *and* by its political subordination within ACSF. What interests us now is the way in which this political subordination enters the reproduction of the conditions for the appropriation and transfer of the peasant surplus in the ACSF as a whole, and hence the reproduction of the peasantry as a class. In order to study this we must consider the institutions which 'contain' the SCMPs, and so constitute the principal social and economic bases of AC; relevant too are the forms that the peasant surplus product takes — the question of rent. This is important for the location of the peasantry within the SF as a whole. Rent is the mode of extraction of the surplus in a labour-process dominated by relations of production external to CMP. On the other hand, the rent received by landlords is distributed by capitalist mechanisms, capitalist relations of distribution. Thus the peasantry, as a class, is subsumed within relations of production and distribution belonging to different MPs. This, however, is only possible given its original political subordination. So the first step is to give more thought to the dominance of the political instance.

The dominance of the political

The concept of a *dominance* of the political instance relates both to the specific role of the State in achieving AC development, and, in general, to that political subordination which finally defines the peasantry as a class. This definition does not itself seem unorthodox in the light of recent theory:

a social class is defined by its place in the ensemble of social practices, i.e. by its place in the ensemble of the division of labour which includes political and ideological relations. This place corresponds to the structural determination of classes, i.e. the manner in which determination by the structure (relations of production, politico-ideological domination/subordination) operates on class practices — for classes have existence only in the class struggle' (Poulantzas 1973)

While not concurring in Poulantzas' empiricist conception of class struggle, the point to take is the necessary inclusion of political and ideological relations in the definition of class (without wishing, at this moment, to enter the debate on 'dominance of levels' etc.). And regarding the differentiation of this class it is surely as theoretically valid to talk of *fractions* of the peasantry (which themselves can become the significant social force in specific historical conjunctures), as of the bourgeoisie or petit bougeoisie. In short, the peasantry is no more 'differentiated' or 'stratified' than either of these last two classes, whose theoretical status is never impugned.

The role of the State is evidently important in the creation of this subordination, as much in Russia, as South Africa or Latin America. But in elevating the political more is being asserted than the simple presence of extraeconomic coercion. 'Extraeconomic coercion', in Marx, simply means a coercion which exists outside the sphere of commodity exchange, that is, coercion which differs from that found in CMP (Laclau, 1975). In elevating the political we are doing so *vis-à-vis* the economic, which is understood in the more general sense of 'level of production' (as in the phrase, 'the economic is determining in the last instance'). In short, extraeconomic coercion states that it is not 'capitalist' or 'market' coercion, but, as we have already seen, that 'immobilization' which exists in conditions of near total monopoly of land and abundance of labour does, in fact, resemble capitalist coercion. In other words, this concept is insufficient to the analysis in that it contains an artificial distinction which projects into SCMPs a type of social rationality existing only under (bourgeois) capitalism. The dominance of the political, on the contrary, points to a coercion which is indissolubly economic *and* political; which achieves the reproduction of the social relations of production in SCMPs, and which is vested, in the first instance, in the productive units of SCMPs (*hacienda, fazenda*, plantation etc.) which are themselves, *at the same time*, the institutions of political labour control. Poulantzas (1973) makes a similar point when talking of the enterprise in CMP, but it is readily applicable, and perhaps more appropriate, to our argument:

an enterprise is also an apparatus, in the sense that, by means of the social division of labour within it . . . the enterprise itself reproduces political and ideological relations concerning the places of the social classes. In other words, the reproduction of the all-important ideological relations is not the concern of the ideological apparatus alone: just as not everything that goes on in 'production' is reserved for the 'economic'; so the ideological apparatuses have no monopoly over reproducing the relations of ideological domination.

For us, the institutions of SCMP — principally the large landed estate in its different forms — are, at the same time, ideological apparatuses of the AC State. They cultivate and contain a specific 'culture of repression', which has been extensively investigated (compare, for example, Freire, 1972; Huizer, 1973).

Thus the 'State' which 'intervenes' to create and maintain the political subordination of the peasantry, should be understood in a very diffuse sense (and in some cases it takes many decades for the authoritarian State to achieve any degree of centralization). A static conception of a centralized and hierarchical State will inevitably distort a part of the reality. The State also exists fully in the countryside. In general we would agree that,

State power represents the interests of the hegemonic class or class fraction, not by receiving orders from a private sector, but to the degree that it is capable of finding the objective lines of economic and institutional policy which best secures the dynamics of accumulation imposed by the production structure, which itself creates one class or class fraction as economically dominant. (Meireles, 1974)

But before pursuing these comments on the political into the realm of the production process proper, we must first return to the question of rent.

The question of rent

If other aspects of the discussion on the peasantry are 'undertheorized', then this one is certainly 'overtheorized'. In the first place we must heed Lenin's warning (1967) that

a strict distinction must be drawn between money-rent and capitalist ground-rent: the latter presupposes the existence in agriculture of capitalist and wage-workers; the former, the existence of dependent peasants. Capitalist rent is that part of the surplus-value which remains after the deduction of the employer's profits, whereas money-rent is the price of the entire surplus product paid by the peasant to the landowners.

The failure to make this distinction has marred many otherwise distinguished discussions (cf. Martinez-Alier, 1974). So it is important to emphasize that Marx's original analysis of capitalist ground-rent presupposed capitalist agriculture; in other words it presupposed the disappearance of the peasantry which follows upon (is part of) bourgeois capitalist development. In this development there is a monopoly of land (one half of the 'double mill'), capitalist competition to enter agriculture (given the low organic composition of capital in that sector), and rent is that portion of total surplus-value which accrues to the landlords, and which depends on the legal impediments to free movement of capital created by the monopoly of land. In AC development, on the contrary, while monopoly of land continued to be necessary, there is in general no capitalist competition for land, as in the bourgeois case. This for two reasons. In the first place, except in rare cases where an alteration in the production function reaps huge rewards in increased productivity, the potential rate of profit in the countryside is low (or certainly lower than that existing in industry or real estate). Despite the low organic composition of capital in the countryside, capitalist exploitation of labour is not profitable precisely because it has to complete with the superexploitation of labour in SCMPs — and wages cannot be paid at below subsistence. In the second place, the landlord and 'capitalist' *rentier* most often are one and the same person. As Marx (1964) made clear, this landlord may play according to capitalist 'rules', and make every effort to maximize profit, but he is not, in fact, a capitalist (but produces within SCMP):

the historic process is not the result of capital, but its prerequisite. By means of this process the capitalist then inserts himself as a (historical) middleman between landed property, or between any kind of property, and labour [but] if we now talk of plantation owners in America as capitalists, if they *are* capitalists, this is due to the fact that they exist as anomalies within a world market based upon free labour.

Hence the rent extracted from the peasantry is clearly money-rent in its different forms (money = leasehold; kind = sharecropping; labour = labour-service obligation), and it is equally clear that this rent is *forced* rent — depending on that coercion which is both political and economic.

The different arguments against this position, are all fallacious in one way or another. For instance, it is argued that if land has a *price*, which is understood as capitalized (capitalist) ground-rent, then this ground-rent must exist. But Marx theorized prices as capitalized ground-rent in the case of capitalist production in agriculture, and to assert that prices prove the existence of capitalist ground-rent is to beg the question. Here Rey (1973) is quite correct to condemn 'price of land' as an irrational category which has the function of subordinating the SCMP to CMP, and behind this category always lies the reality of money-rent. In short, 'price of land', is a function of AMP. Then it is argued on a more empirical level, that agrarian reforms are instigated by industrial bourgeoisies in the Third World in order to reduce the relative participation of 'rent' in total surplus-value. The theoretical myopia of this assertion fails to perceive the emptiness of the 'evidence': not only are most agrarian reforms in the Third World very limited, cosmetic exercises, but in most countries at most times a transfer of surplus-value from countryside to city can be clearly demonstrated (Foweraker, 1974).

None of this denies that conjunctures do occur in Third World agriculture where better-placed producers and/or producers on more fertile soils realize a greater-than-average profit. But this usually occurs in conditions of labour-scarcity which demand the introduction of wage relations in the countryside; it is then perfectly correct to theorize this greater than average profit as a differential rent. The classic case where rent of this kind was obviously important is Argentina, and Argentina, of course, is unique in Latin America for the historical absence of a peasantry. But if we are faced with the existence of 'bigger-than-average' profits in the SCMP, then it is precisely that, a surplus-profit (not a differential rent). This follows from the logical premises of Marx's analysis. Differential rent is created, in the first instance, by a rising (or fluctuating) demand, such that less fertile or more distant soils are brought into cultivation. Rising of fluctuating demand in SCMP, however, will induce the landlord (as a 'maximizer of profits') to put more land into production within the unit of production, which is the large landed estate, such that the greater profit he realizes represents an increase in money-rent, and not a differential rent. And historically it is true that any surplus-profit created in this way accrues more to merchant capital than the landlord; that remaining to the landlord is considered a 'bonus', and will probably go to conspicuous consumption.

Thus, in my opinion, Wolf's original definition (Wolf, 1966) of peasants as rural cultivators who pay rent is not so far off the mark — if we consider rent as a mechanism for siphoning surplus, for getting labour-power at a cost below its value. And we do not have to think only of tenants in this connection. *Minifundistas*, by their dependence on the landlords, also contribute to a fund of rent when they are forced to offer their labour-power to the landlord. Even 'middle' peasants — self-sufficient peasant owners — are only autonomous if considered in terms of agrarian structure. Their surplus-product is extracted by market mechanisms of unequal exchange (that is, directly to merchant capital) or by taxes (that is directly to the State); but these are only secondary mechanisms which substitute for rent in the case of the 'middle' peasantry (which is anyway peripheral to the agrarian structure). And this 'middle' peasantry, if unsubordinated, is inherently unstable, tending always to merge into the main configuration of exploiters and exploited. In this way the differentiation of the peasantry by forms of money-rent, by property holdings, is only confusing if we become fixated in the *structure*. The point of this paper is rather to emphasize the analytical advantages accruing to an examination of *process*, which is the process of appropriation of surplus-labour.

Sub-capitalist modes of production

Having located the 'social space' where the peasantry exists, it is now time to give content to the concept of SCMP. Any theory of MPs is, in my view, highly abstract, and can only provide the 'preconditions' for studying 'concrete' realities. MP is a theoretical construct *par excellence*, in that it immediately demands further determination if it is to explain these realities; so when speaking of MPs we are at the first stage of the theoretical construction of the object. Thus it is a clear abuse of the construct to distinguish different MPs which describe distinct, if complex, historical realities — for instance 'colonial MP'. This merely leads to a gross multiplication of MPs, which finally forms the material for a new empiricism. The Manchester workshop, and the New Jersey multinational corporation appear empirically very different, but both appropriate surplus-labour within the CMP (that is, through mechanisms of surplus-value).

Yet there do exist, in the present, different MPs, which have a certain but not total capacity for self-reproduction. But to study these MPs as 'separate' structures tends to lead directly to a formal structuralism, which obscures the process which gives them their economic and political meaning — the real appropriation of surplus. In short, what concerns us now is not the separate existence of MPs (if it ever did) but, precisely, their *articulation*. There are good *a priori* reasons for this, founded in the dominant economic development in the world over the last two centuries, which is the expansion of CMP and the penetration of CMP as the dominant MP throughout the periphery (and outside the socialist bloc). Thus, there are no 'pure' MPs (if there ever were) but only 'exceptional forms' (which are now, however, the norm) which have been 'mangled' by a continual process of dissolution and reinforcement and vice versa; such that appropriation takes place in a different way, very often, than it would have done in 'ideal' conditions (which are the conditions of an MP existing in isolation). Hence it was emphasized at the beginning of this essay that all SCMPs are now 'defined' by the dominance of CMP — and the reproduction of the social relations of production, not only within SCMP but also in CMP (in the ACSF) depends, again, on the *articulation* of these different MPs.

But the question remains of the content of the construct SCMP. Even if it is preferable theoretically to emphasize process rather than structure, structure subsists, in that we must know *what* is articulated in the process of appropriation. In short, there must be a further determination of the construct — but not in a 'structural' way. It is not necessary to pose the existence of forces of production, on the one hand, and social relations of production on the other, and specify the exact 'correspondence' between them. Not only is this an artificial separation, but it diverts attention away from the principal problem which is *what* it is in SCMP which achieves the appropriation of surplus-labour (and, is it common to all SCMPs?). This is, of course, precisely how we define CMP; it is the generalization of commodity exchange including, crucially, labour-power as a commodity which achieves the appropriation (capital is *itself* a social relation of production). But the problem for SCMPs is somewhat different. In general, it is a problem of defining the place of the *political* in the reproduction of SCMPs — and here the concept of the 'economic being determining in the last instance' is clearly insufficient. In our discussion on rent, it was concluded that appropriation takes place in SCMPs by a forced money-rent, which depends on a coercion which is simultaneously economic and political. How is this achieved?

The concept of rent as we have defined it is important to the discussion because this rent is *common* to all SCMPs. Marx in the passage on 'precapitalist forms' of rent (Marx, 1974) notes that this rent always derives from the same conditions, which are landed property in the possession of a ruling class who hold the direct producers in a relation of political subordination; the direct producers in 'effective' possession of the means of production (as they must be ir non-capitalist agriculture); and, as a consequence, surplus-product appropriated on the basis of an 'extraeconomic coercion' through rent, in the form of labour-service, kind or money. This leads Hindess and Hirst (1975), in their discussion of the passage, to conclude that 'precapitalist rent is not in fact conceived as an economic relation at all, but as a relation of political domination'; that the State creates the exploitation, and is a condition of its existence. In short, there is no theory in Marx which gives the relations of production as relations of exploitation, which in turn necessitates the existence of forms of domination as *mechanisms* of exploitation. Production has no social conditions of existence, and the political and ideological instances must be presupposed to constitute the social relations of production. But in the absence of any mechanism of exploitation arising from the system of production, this is tantamount to asserting the dominance of subject by subject (and conflates the level of the political *instance* with the level of political *subject*). Therefore the 'dominance of the political' is not executed over the economic instance or through the structures of the economic instance: the dominance is one of 'political' subject over 'economic' subject. This leads to a further conclusion: that it is the features of the apparatuses of political domination which differentiate SCMPs (in our language) and not the forms of production to which they are applied. If this is the case — if the political and ideological instances are the internal 'determinants' of the MP — then, despite an emphasis on process — we are inexorably forced into a new empiricist problematic (and this is precisely the dilemma which certain critics see as deriving from Poulantzas' emphasis on the political and ideological). In other words, the Hindess and Hirst discussion raises the question we want answered — that of the place of the political in the reproduction of the SCMPs.

After a great deal of discussion Hindess and Hirst point to a distinction which, in their view, must be made before the question can be answered. The distinction contrasts that *domination*, whether political, legal or ideological, which provides the pre-conditions of an MP's development, and that *dominance* which provides the conditions for the existence of the exploitative relations of production, which in turn provides the social foundation for the political instance by creating the division between exploiter and exploited — a division internal to the system of production. But the distinction they make is not analytical (still less theoretical), but historical (but as history is excluded from their book, the distinction must enter as theory). It is, moreover, a distinction which emerges clearly from a closer reading of Marx, especially the key passage which asserts (Marx, 1974) that 'in all forms in which the direct labourer *remains* the 'possessor' of the means of production . . . the property relationship must simultaneously *appear* as a direct relationship of lordship and servitude' (my emphasis) — which is purported to demonstrate a conflation of 'political instance' and 'political subject'. The point to note is that the direct producer *remains* a 'possessor'. After what? after the expropriation of the direct producers (which is in plain contrast to what happened during the phase of primitive accumulation prior to bourgeois capitalist development). Expropriation may, of course, mean not only that direct divorce of petty commodity producers from the land, but, as during the early historical formation of authoritarian capitalism the prevention of a direct combination of labour with land. With the direct producer remaining in 'possession' the property relationship appears, but only appears, as a direct relation of lordship and servitude. In fact, the monopoly of land already achieved provides the conditions for the exploitative relations of production — the 'social foundation of the division of exploiters and exploited'. And this *monopoly* (private property in land) is not merely a juridical relationship (which supports the social relation of expropriation as in CMP), but is also the institutions of political and social control — which today are plantation, *hacienda* etc. Hindess and Hirst (1975) finally make this point, in a different way, by emphasizing that the landlord does not merely have juridical rights, but is also engaged in the process of production, controlling allocation of the means of production and the division of labour. But the point is made late and without sufficient force, which is inevitable given the non-historical nature of the analysis. If the question is approached historically and dialectically (as it must be when considering of AMP in the contemporary period) then there is no necessary conflation — or certainly none in Marx — of economic relations with the political conditions of their existence (Hindess and Hirst, 1975). What are termed domination and dominance are subsumed within the dominance of the political in the historical development, in this case, of authoritarian capitalism.

In this light the commentary on the insufficiency of the concept of 'extra-economic coercion' takes on substance. If there were no monopoly of the land, and the direct producers were producing in isolation, then the exploiter would have to coerce them directly to give up part of their product, by the use of pure political force. But with monopoly of land the conditions for the appropriation are created, and the rent extracted from a tenant, for instance, is most usually agreed before the beginning of the agricultural year. But this is not a wage-relation, and there is no illusion of the 'freedom' of the labourer to sell his 'labour-power'. Thus the coercion is not 'extraeconomic' in the sense that it is removed from the level of production ('no monopoly' above), but is 'extraeconomic' in the simple sense of being outside the sphere of the market. However, this leaves unanswered the question of the place of the political — which we have attempted to locate above. Thus contemporary peasantry are subsumed within sub-capitalist relations of exploitation, by virtue of the dominance of the political in the reproduction of those SCMPs, and in the development and reproduction of AC (ACSF). The mechanisms of subordination are not merely those of political force (though these are employed): subordination is achieved through coercion which is at once political and economic, and confines the peasantry to a precisely defined social space. This is what is meant by 'immobilization'.

The peasantry as a class

We must note that our theoretical construct is only one of a number of possible constructs (there is always an alternative construct). The choice was taken to focus on the process of appropriation of surplus labour and the part the political instance plays in that process in a particular historical development which is the subordination of SCMPs to CMP in ACSF. In attempting a definition of the peasantry within this construct, the relative importance of many other aspects of peasant economy (such as forms of rent, technology of the labour process) was reduced. In other words it is assumed that the units of peasant economy are less significant for this definition than the insertion of the peasantry in ACSF. Such a construct must be judged first by its internal coherence, and secondly by its 'explanatory power'. I shall confine my comments to the latter.

In the first place the very perspective achieved in the construct may immediately resolve certain 'irrationalities' observed in peasant movements, such as the peasant movement in La Convencion (Peru) against the neofeudal landlords (Hobsbawm, 1969) which unified different groups of peasants which exploited one another. The definition of the peasantry as a class in our construct makes this quite comprehensible, and support for our view comes from other observers of the Peruvian peasantry:

I think it would be wrong to infer from the relatively disconnected nature of land invasions in Peru, or from the lack of permanent peasant organizations, or from the failure of the union movement of 1945–47, that Peruvian peasants have been the fragmented units of Marx's 'sack of potatoes'. Marx was, of course, referring to peasant owners in France, not threatened by large estates. (Martinez-Alier, 1974)

This is but one concrete example of a more general theoretical achievement of the construct, which is the resolution of the complexities of the differentiation question. Within the construct, not only is the question of differentiation not a problem, but it is precisely the differentiation which often makes AMP (CMP–SCMP) *politically* possible. In this sense, differentiation *is* the articulation. We may agree with Alavi (1973) — who however understands the dimensions of the question in a different way — that, 'differentiation within local communities is itself an aspect of a class structure which is enforced by the national polity . . . the power of the privileged classes in the local community derives from and contributes towards the national economic and political system'. However, this should not tempt us to an overly categorical or rigid view of the specific function of this differentiation in the ACSFs. If we recall the debate over dissolution and reinforcement, there is no doubt that at certain times or certain places dissolution of the SCMP does occur — to a degree. But the peasantry remains, and the dissolution in ACSFs is never more than partial. Hence what we may theorize is not so much a dissolution as a modification of the relations of production in the SCMPs, to meet the changing needs of capital accumulation in the ACSF as a whole (but particularly in the dominant CMP). Usually these modifications may be understood as maintaining or increasing the rate of transfer of value from the countryside to the city.

For example, the penetration of capital into the countryside usually precipitates increased polarization among an already differentiated peasantry. In the classical formulation, this means more '*kulaks*' and more 'landless labourers'. But at least in the first instance, this penetration is usually commercial (Forman and Riegelhaupt, 1970a and b), and does not necessarily imply an introduction of capitalist social relations of production. On the contrary, the effect may be to drive out the 'middle peasant', concentrate more land in large landed estates, and reproduce in expanded form the social relations of SCMP. In short, the greater the penetration, the greater the exactions on the peasantry (so that none are 'self-sufficient'), and the closer the picture resembles a 'pure' model of SCMP. On the evidence it seems correct that the 'middle peasant' is the first to be affected by penetration of this type, whether in China, India, or North-East Brazil (Alavi, 1965; Forman and Riegelhaupt, 1970 a and b). As for the 'landless labourers', the great majority are far from constituting a rural proletariat: in Mexico, for instance, a country which has experienced a radical agrarian reform, and capitalization of distribution (and production) in the countryside, there are almost four million of these landless 'peasants'.

Nevertheless, there are 'exogenous' influences acting on this process in the monopoly capital stage of capitalism which place in doubt the relevance of this analysis. These influences are best summed in what has come to be known as the Green Revolution. This 'revolution' has been promoted from the centre, speciously to bring high productivity farming to the periphery and so solve the world's food shortage, but, in fact, to create a market for the agricultural chemicals and hardware produced by the monopoly capital corporations (Feder, 1973). The revolution is also associated with the development of new agricultural technology, and changing intersectoral terms of trade (agriculture/industry) — usually engineered by local governments, convinced by 'aid' incentives. The revolution inevitably precipitates a different kind of polarization in the countryside, between capitalist and proletarian. But then we no longer have to theorize the presence of a peasantry, but that of a proletariat. In the great majority of cases to date, capitalist penetration of this kind is very limited (in terms of geographical space) — and highly selective (in terms of produce, soils and technology). But where it is relatively more widespread, then the social and economic bases of the political subordination of the peasantry are, in fact, threatened with dissolution. The traditional bases of AC development can no longer control labour, and in this way it is true that the contradictions of monopoly capital penetration may impel a radical change to a new centralized authoritarianism, whereby coercion and control of labour, both in the countryside and city, may be exercised from the centre. From this perspective it is no mere coincidence that the radical mobilization of the peasantry in Brazil, Peru and Chile, preceded, and, in my view, precipitated the installation of repressive and highly centralized military-authoritarian régimes in those countries. The crisis at the level of the State is material for another essay: we merely wish to mention the role of the peasantry in this crisis. This is the moment when:

huge masses (especially of the peasants and petit bourgeois intellectuals) have passed suddenly from a state of political passivity to a certain activity, or put forward demands which taken together, albeit not organically formulated, add up to a revolution: a 'crisis of authority' is spoken of: this is precisely the crisis of hegemony, a general crisis of the State. (Gramsci, 1973)

The peasantry: class position and class practice

The construct also makes intelligible the political practice of the peasantry (within the overall process which is the real appropriation of surplus), such that we can talk more effectively about 'radical peasant politics'. For this we must distinguish the peasantry as a class, from its *class position*. But our definition of the peasantry allows us to perceive that its class position depends not only on whether it is more or less exploited, but on whether it is more or less *subordinated*. Many writers have noted that there seems to be little connection between the absolute degree of misery of the peasantry, and their 'rebelliousness'. In my view too, the degree of economic exploitation is certainly not sufficient to explain a radicalization of the peasantry. Rather the peasantry may be mobilized and radicalized when the political subordination it suffers is weakened in some way — so that the traditional 'immobilization' through institutions of labour-control is partially or totally destroyed. This can only occur in conjunctures where the peculiar combination of exploitation within the SCMP and the subordination in the ACSF is threatened. Because this is true it is often the simplest comments on the position of the peasantry which can explain most: as Alavi (1965) says of the Hunan province, 'the removal of men who had exercised power on the spot loosened social control in the villages, enabled the peasants to gain more confidence and allowed militancy to develop'. From our perspective it is clear that if this is not a complete explanation of that militancy, it is at least an essential element of the explanation.

The insertion of the concept of class position within that of conjuncture prevents a static or synchronic conceptualization of the problem. Class position rather describes a trajectory which is ascending or descending, and this in itself may help explain how the peasantry plays such radically different political roles (everything from the mass base for fascist movements to the mass base for socialist revolutions). While the construct implies that external influences are primary in determining this trajectory (the peasants are more or less subordinated), a certain centrifugal force within the peasantry (deriving from transformations within agrarian structure, for instance) is in no way precluded. To return to the question of capitalist penetration of agriculture of the kind that introduces capitalist relations of production, it is obvious that this penetration both makes peasantry less 'subordinate' (in our meaning) and creates pressures within the peasantry — which is likely to lead to mobilization as it did in North-East Brazil. Pressures from commercial capital would not have the same effect: in La Convencion it was not in increased labour-services demanded by the land-lords, but rather the increased political autonomy of the peasants (given the high profitability of their coffee crop) which created the conditions for mobilization. A second possible result of commercial pressures is, of course, the expropriation of 'middle' peasants, or peasant (often Indian) communities, as landlords extend the area of land under a cash crop. This too can be an impetus to mobilization — but this immediately introduces a further determination into the model — which is the class position of different *fractions* of the peasantry in the conjuncture.

It is apparent from our construct that the poorest of the peasantry, and especially the great majority who are poor tenants, are the least likely to mobilize. The poor tenant and his family are totally dependent on the landowner (that is, he is most completely 'immobilized') and will only revolt when it has been demonstrated beyond any shadow of doubt that the landowner's power is, or can be, broken (when the political subordination is weakened). All arguments regarding the potential militancy of the poor tenants or sharecroppers, based on the 'apparent contradictions' between them and the landowners, are theoretically null, and empirically very hard to prove. On the other hand, 'middle' peasants, and still more the statistically far more significant *minifundistas*, have, initially, a greater *possibility* for mobilization, in that they are less directly politically subordinate. In other words, some (if not sufficient) means of subsistence do constitute at the same time a slight increase in 'political autonomy'. Yet this possibility will rarely be translated into active mobilization, except where this fraction is threatened with expropriation. At that moment, the fraction is certainly the most militant, and may generate an initial impetus to general mobilization — but, precisely because of its class position, may prove more reactionary at a later stage in the mobilization. In this sense it is certainly true that fractions of the peasantry can take on an important role as a *social force*, a role which is relatively distinct from other fractions of the class.

It has already been noted more than once that capitalist penetration raises the problem of differentiation of the peasantry in an acute form, particularly when this penetration promotes a stratum of rich peasants (or *'kulaks'*) and makes many other peasants landless. Such a conjuncture raises another possible impediment to mobilization, which is the imposition of an hegemony throughout the class by this fraction of rich peasants, which begins to show a 'bourgeois face'. Another way of theorizing this development in terms of our construct, is to pose the possibility of class contradictions *within* the peasantry, appearing as soon as one of the defining elements of the peasantry as a class, that is its political subordination, begins to disappear. As we have already argued, radicalization does not only emerge with the weakening of political subordination, but depends too on the sort of 'centrifugal forces' generated within the peasantry. So it may be that a weakened political subordination accompanied by the raising of higher barriers to the incorporation of the peasantry (and 'rich' peasants in particular) into CMP will mean faster mobilization; contrariwise, it may be that mobilization will be slower to the degree that the *kulaks* are successful in adapting to the new conditions created by the penetration of CMP in the countryside. Finally, the precise explanation, or prediction, of peasant mobilization will depend on the application of the construct to the conjuncture, and a careful assessment of the specific features of that conjuncture. In this way too, the theory itself can be further refined. What is sure is that in authoritarian capitalist States, the mobilization of the peasantry always threatens the political and social conditions for the reproduction of the peasantry as a class, and therefore, precisely because this peasantry is never 'represented' at the level of the national State, this mobilization nearly always has revolutionary implications. Where these mobilizations have occurred recently (Brazil, Chile, Peru, for example) they have led to a rapid centralization of the AC State, and to a greatly increased incidence of control and repression from the centre.

Conclusion

Transition and contradiction

This attempt to theorize the peasantry as a class has tended — if only implicitly — to construct it as an object of contemporary imperialism. 'The imperialist centre/periphery social division of labour is essentially between town (industry) and country (agriculture). This permits precisely a domination by the CMP of formations in the interior of which MPs other than CMP can often predominate' (Poulantzas, 1974b). It is precisely the dominance of CMP in the social formation as a whole which leads to the complex effects of dissolution / conservation referred to above (pp. 138–141). While it is true that these effects will certainly differ on an international scale in response to distinct phases of imperialist expansion (that is precise forms of accumulation of capital and international imperialist divisions of labour), it has been argued here that — in the periphery at least — there is no overall secular tendency in these effects towards dissolution. In other words we cannot speak of a universal *transition* to the CMP (indeed it is only legitimate to talk of phases of imperialism in so far as CMP presents certain particularities in its articulation with SCMPs), and this transition does not appear to be necessary to expanded accumulation in the AC economic system as a whole. In short, contemporarily,

where the mode of production of the metropolis is reproduced in specific form in the very interior of the dominated and dependent formations the effects of conservation, to unequal degrees and contrary to what happens in the metropolis, continue to override those of dissolution. (Poulantzas, 1974b)

However, to argue against a discernible tendency to *transition* is not to deny the *contraditions* existing between different MPs in the social formation, nor their mediation through the class struggle.

The question of transition, or the lack of it, has raised some interesting problems in the analysis of these 'dominated and dependent formations'. Alavi (1975) criticizes Laclau's 'mechanistic' resolution of the problems of two or more MPs *coexisting* in a social formation, 'If there were indeed two separate modes of production in a single formation they would be dialectically related in mutual opposition and contradiction'. There must of necessity be a 'contradiction between coexisting modes of production, one in ascendant and the other in disintegration'. But because the 'other' is not in disintegration Alavi dispenses with these 'separate and antagonistic modes' in favour of one 'colonial' mode of production, whose 'unity is conferred by the unified structure of imperialism, which includes both centre and periphery'. Within this 'unity' he hopes to encompass the effects of dissolution/conservation: 'parallel with that external integration of the structure of the 'colonial economy', the conception of 'colonial MP' must also consider its internal disarticulation [an aspect emphasized by Amin and reintegration under imperialist hegemony'. But Alavi's reasoning is fallacious, and *his* resolution 'mechanistic'. Two or more MPs means contradictions means transition; there is no transition, therefore there can only be a single MP. Having raised the important problem of contradiction, he conflates it unnecessarily with the moment of transition.

Alavi tackles the problems of analysing 'dominated and dependent formations', and, in particular, the problems of transition. There are many illuminating passages which foreshadow aspects of this paper — on political 'immobilization', transfers of value, mutation of SCMPs etc. But finally he is limited by his problematic. I have already criticized the concept of 'colonial MP' on epistemological grounds, and, in practice, it proves an unwieldly instrument of theory. The relationship of Eastern Europe with the centre of capitalist development in the West was analogous to a colonial relationship, Alavi says, so its development — 'reflexive', he agrees — must be characterized as proto-colonial MP; once indigenous industrial development occurs within a colonial MP — such as India — it then becomes a postcolonial MP. These descriptive categories refer to changes in the periphery which are a response to different *periods* in the development of capital and capitalist development, that is the transition at the centre from mercantilism and manufacture to capitalism proper, and from competitive to monopoly capitalism. The response of the periphery to *these* transitions are better theorized, in my opinion, within the objective construct of authoritarian capitalism. On the other hand, transitions at the centre can create or heighten contradictions in the periphery (including those expressed in effects of dissolution/conservation), and in this sense it is perfectly correct to emphasize the existence of these contradictions.

Contradiction and class struggle

Regarding the periodization of capitalism itself, and especially the transition to monopoly capital, it is true that the relative weight of MPs in an AC economic system may change, as may the form of their articulation. (Similarly, SCMPs may mutate, but not always in the direction of capitalist social relations of production). But their 'coexistence' continues to be necessary to the expanded reproduction of the system as a whole. We see this in Alavi's own discussion (1975) of the Green Revolution in India. 'If we look at the development in terms of rates of growth, the change appears to be quite dramatic' but 'the absolute magnitude of the changes must be considered against the background of the enormous size of the Indian countryside . . . there is still a very great deal of ground to be covered before we can see it as having made a qualitative change'. On the basis of the discussion he reaches a conclusion which places the problem in exactly the right perspective:

the issue is not simply whether 'capitalist' relations of production *exist*, nor indeed whether they have completely done away with feudal survivals, but precisely of the relative weight of each, the alignment of classes that represent each MP *vis-à-vis* the other, and therefore the thrust of political conflict and the nature of class struggle.

The contradictions are expressed through the changing relative weights of MPs, the changing forms of articulation, which themselves are mediated through the class struggle. Alavi is in substantial agreement that these changes can, for instance, break down 'conditions of dependence' (political subordination) and so lead to greater peasant militancy.

There is nothing new in the notion that classes in a mode of production enter into contradiction. But we are talking of contradictions existing *within* and *across* MPs, and, given the complex AMP, then the peasantry can engage in class struggle with various other classes.

The peasantry in industrial societies has shown an ability for cohesive political action — and not only when facing traditional landowners in belated battles of a precapitalist type; their common interests have driven peasants into political conflicts also with large capitalist landowners, with various groups of townsmen, and with the Modern State. (Shanin, 1971)

These common interests — which this paper has attempted to demonstrate — are rarely expressed because of the peasantry's 'sociopolitical weaknesses', such that it is comparatively infrequent that the peasantry engages in 'independent class action'. As exceptions to prove the rule Shanin cites Mexico between 1910 and 1920 and China in 1926. More often than not they engage in 'guided political action', which requires an external organizing force to provide the 'missing factor of unity on a wide scale', That is, 'they cannot represent themselves, they must be represented'. And while Shanin does not raise the matter explicitly, what he is pointing to as a prerequisite for effective peasant political action is *class alliance*. It is, of course, precisely the location of the peasantry within the AC economic system (with its complex AMP) which makes class alliance possible.

While it is possible, it is not initially very likely. In the first stage of the expansion of capital, in its commercial form, the dominant alliance is between international commercial interests and the landowners (achieved by exchange mechanisms or by direct force). Even with the penetration of capitalist social relations of production, the interests of native industrialists ('internal bourgeoisie') and landowners are close enough for the alliance to continue: indeed, the landowning class has increasing need for the alliance in order to maintain political control in the countryside. And during all of this latter period the proletariat is probably too weak to provide a 'natural ally and leader' for the peasantry. So that, in the majority of cases, the peasantry does not act politically, or does not do so very effectively. As already noted, it must rely on some external force to challenge the order of political subordination. The peasantry without leadership cannot make revolution (even if it carried a vision of total social transformation). But if the proletariate remains weak (and often equally subordinated) in the periphery, who is to provide this leadership?

The answer is that until now it has nearly always been provided by fractions of the bourgeoisie. Traditionally the peasantry is politically subordinated through property relations which are, at the same time, a system of labour control. But even if these relations are changed, as they are in certain 'radical' agrarian reforms, the peasantry will still act to consolidate the general economic order, and the relations of exploitation — so long as the relations of production remain unchanged. In short, the peasantry can be mobilized towards structural transformation of the countryside without this mobilization leading to social revolution. The classic case is Bolivia where, despite early 'revolutionary' work amongst the peasantry by Trotskyist groups and the left wing of the MNR, the tolerance of the MNR in power (a reformist, 'populist' party) for the reform in the countryside, rendered the peasantry politically immobile following the reform. This pattern of peasant mobilization, through class alliance and the effective containment of the challenge by the bourgeoisie, is equivalent to Gramsci's movement of 'revolution-restoration', and it is the dominant pattern. This is not finally to exclude other possibilities of leadership provided by a revolutionary party (the case of China), or of eventual alliance with the proletariat (which looked possible in Chile, where the agrarian reform threatened total revolution until reversed by US imperialism). But it does mean that contemporary peasant mobilizations, while they always carry revolutionary implications, rarely lead to revolution.

Acknowledgements

In preparing and revising this paper I benefited greatly from my discussions with Harold Wolpe, Ian Roxborough, Ricardo Israel and Ernesto Laclau, and from the opportunities I was given to present some of these ideas to seminars at the LSE, Liverpool and Essex. The work of Octavio Guilherme Velho sparked the first ideas, and some of these were developed with the help of the students attending the MA seminar on Brazil, Chile and Peru in the University of Essex. Final responsibility for everything in the paper remains my own.

References

Alavi, Hamza (1965), 'Peasants and revolution', Miliband and Saville (eds). *Socialist Register*.

Alavi, Hamza (1973), 'Peasant classes and primordial loyalties', *Journal of Peasant Studies*, **1, October** 1.

Alavi, Hamza (1975), 'India and the colonial mode of production', Miliband and Saville (eds) *Socialist Register*.

Amin, Samir (1970), 'La transition au capitalisme périphérique' in *l'Accumulation á l'échelle mondiale* (Paris: Antrhropos), pp. 163f.

Banaji, J. n.d. 'Harris on the peasantry', Oxford International Socialists (mimeo).

Bettelheim, C. (1972), 'Theoretical comments' in *Unequal Exchange*, A. Emmanuel (ed.) (London: New Left Books).

Bradby, Barbra, n.d. 'Destruction of natural economy in Peru: a problem of articulation of modes of production' (mimeo).

Cardoso, F. H. (1974), 'Dependency and development in Latin America' *New Left Review*, 74.

CNRS (1967), *Les problèmes agraires des ameriques latines* (Paris: CNRS).

Diaz del Moral, J. (1967), *Historia de las agitaciones campesinas andaluzas*, (Madrid: Alianza).

Engels, F. (1934), in *Karl Marx and Friedrich Engels: Correspondence 1846–1895* (London: Lawrence and Wishart).

Feder, E. (1971), *The Rape of the Peasantry*. (New York: Doubleday Anchor).

Feder, E. (1973), 'Dependency and the agricultural problem in L.A.' Workshop on Dependency in Latin America (Amsterdam: CEDLA), **19–21 November**.

Fernandes, F. (1968), 'Capitalismo agrario e mudanca social', *Sociedade de Clases e Desenvolvimento*. (Rio: Zahar).

Forman, Shepherd (1971), 'Disunity and discontent: a study of peasant political movements in Brazil'. *Journal of Latin American Studies*, 3, **May** 1.

Forman, S. and Riegelhaupt, J. (1970*a*), 'Market place and marketing system — toward a theory of peasant economic integration'. *Comparative Studies in Society and History*, **XII**, 12.

Forman, S. and Riegelhaupt, J. (1970*b*), 'Bodo was never Brazilian: economic integration and agricultural development'. *Journal of Economic History*, **Spring**.

Foweraker, J. W. (1974), *Political conflict on the frontier*. D. Phil. Oxford (mimeo), **April**.

Freire, Paulo (1972), *Pedagogy of the Oppressed*. (Harmondsworth: Penguin).

Galeski, B. (1972), *Basic Concepts of Rural Sociology*, (Manchester: Manchester University Press), pp. 117ff.

Gerschenkron, A. (1962), *Economic Backwardness in Historical Perspective*, (Cambridge, Mass.: Harvard University Press), pp. 5–30.

Glock, Oriel (1976), *Capitalist Development, Rent and Agrarian Reform: The Chilean Case*. M.A. thesis, University of Essex, **January**.

Griffin, Keith (1968), 'Coffee and the economic development of Colombia' *Bulletin of the Oxford University Institute of Economics and Statistics* **30**, **May** 2.

Gramsci, Antonio (1973), 'Notes on Italian history' and 'State and civil society', in *Selections from the Prison Notebooks* Hoare and Smith (eds) (London: Lawrence and Wishart).

Gramsci, Antonio (1968), 'The sourthern Question', in *The Modern Prince and Other Writings* Louis Marks (ed.), (New York: International), pp. 28–51.

Hindess, Barry and Hirst, Paul Q. 1975, *Pre-capitalist Modes of Production* (London: Routledge & Kegan Paul), pp. 1–20; 221–259.

Hirst, Paul Q. (1976), 'Can there be a peasant mode of production?' (mimeo).

Hobsbawm, Eric (1969), 'A case of neo-feudalism: La Convencion, Peru' *Journal of Latin American Studies*, **1** 1.

Hobsbawm, Eric (1973), 'Peasants and politics', *Journal of Peasant Studies*, **1**, **October**, 1.

Huizer, Gerrit, (1973), *Peasant Rebellion in Latin America*, (Harmondsworth: Penguin) pp. 143–162.

Kroeber (1948), *Anthropology* (New York: Harcourt, Brace and Co).

Laclau, Ernesto (1969), 'Modos de produccion, sistemas economicos y poblacion excedente', *Revista Latinoamericana de Sociologia*, 2.

Laclau, Ernesto (1971), 'Feudalism and capitalism in Latin America', *New Left Review* **May–June**, 67.

Laclau, Ernesto 1975, 'The specificity of the political', *Economy and Society*, **4**, **February**, 1.

Lenin, V. I. (1967), *The Development of Capitalism in Russia*, (Moscow: Progress Publishers). p. 178 footnote.

Lenin, V. I. (1972), *The State and Revolution*, (Moscow: Progress Publishers).

Lenin, V. I. (1970), *Imperialism, the Highest Stage of Capitalism*, (Moscow: Progress Publishers).

Martinez-Alier, J. (1974), 'Peasants and labourers in Southern Spain, Cuba and Highland Peru'. *Journal of Peasant Studies*, **1**, **January**, 2.

Marx, Karl, (1970), *Capital* Vol. 1., especially book VIII 'The so-called primitive accumulation' (London: Lawrence and Wishart).

Marx, Karl (1974), *Capital* Vol III pp. 748–813 and *passim* (London: Lawrence and Wishart).

Marx, Karl (1972), *18th Brumaire of Louis Bonaparte*, (Moscow: Progress Publishers).

Marx, Karl (1964), *Pre-capitalist Economic Formations*, E. Hobsbawm (ed.), (London: Lawrence and Wishart), pp. 109–120.

Mauro Marini, Ruy, (1972), 'La reforma agraria en America Latina', *Transicion al socialismo y experiencia chilena* (Santiago: CESO: CEREN).

158

Meireles, Jose (1974), 'Role de l'État dans la developpement du capitalisme industriel au Bresil'. *Critique de l'Économie Politique* **16–17**, **April**. (Paris Maspero).

Palmeira, Moacir (1969), *Latifundium et Capitalisme: lecture critique d'un debat*, Thèse du 3eme cycle: Faculté des lettres. Paris (mimeo).

Poulantzas, Nicos (1973), 'Marxism and social classes', *New Left Review* **March–April**, 78.

Poulantzas, Nicos (1974*a*), *Fascism and Dictatorship* (London: New Left Books).

Poulantzas, Nicos (1974*b*), 'Internationalization of capitalist relations and the Nation State', *Economy and Society*, **3**, 2.

Preobrazhensky, E. (1965), *The New Economics*, (Oxford: Clarendon Press) p. 85.

Redfield, Robert (1960), *The Little Community* (Chicago: University Press), p. 144.

Rey, Pierre-Philippe (1973), *Les Alliances des Classes*, (Paris: Maspero).

Shanin, Teodor (ed.) (1971), *Peasants and Peasant Societies* (Harmondsworth: Penguin) pp. 15 and 238–262.

Stavenhagen, R. (1971), *Las classes sociales en las sociedades agrarias* (Mexico: Siglo XXI).

Tepicht, Jerzy (1969), 'Les complexités de l'économie paysanne', *Information sur les sciences sociales*, Conseil International des Sciences Sociales, **December**.

Trotsky, Leon, (1965), *The History of the Russian Revolution*, (London: Victor Gollancz), p. 25

Velho, Octavio (1973), *Modes of Capitalist Development, Peasantry and the Moving Frontier*, Ph.D. thesis, University of Manchester.

Wolf, Eric (1966), *Peasants* (Englewood Cliffs, N.J.: Prentice-Hall).

Wolf, Eric (1969), *Peasant Wars of the 20th Century*, (New York: Harper and Row).

Wolpe, Harold (1972), 'Capitalism and cheap labour-power in South Africa: from separation to apartheid', *Economy and Society*, **1**, 4.

Wolpe, Harold (1975), 'The theory of internal colonialism — the South African case'. *Beyond the Sociology of Development*, ed. Oxaal, I. London.

7

Reaching the Rural Poor and the Poorest: A Goal Unmet

William C. Thiesenhusen

Policy-makers and theorists today have no trouble agreeing that if a country's policy goal is 'development' it must attack poverty in a direct and purposive manner. The rhetoric at the fifth Summit Conference of Non-Aligned Nations (Colombo, August 1976) differs hardly at all, in this respect, from the analyses of more detached scholarly observers: better income distribution is as essential as growth itself if there is to be real progress in the less-developed countries (LDCs) (Shaplen, 1976b; Chenery *et al.*, 1974, pp. 3–37). Furthermore, neither can be left to market forces alone: government policy must intervene. Unless that intervention takes the revolutionary path it has in China and Cuba, the lessons and experience to guide it will come from the piecemeal, eclectic course which the attack on poverty is taking, with bewildering variety and a wide range of results, in the contemporary developing world.

For the LDCs the income pyramid is almost invariably characterized by a sector of poverty making up perhaps 40 per cent of the population. This has always included a sub-sector whose poverty tested the ingenuity and goodwill of society because it could be alleviated by job creation, distribution of productive resources, and collective action. For another sub-sector, the basic requirements of a minimum living standard could be met only by income transfers. Yet the most imaginative use of these measures has always left another sub-sector whose poverty has been utterly unresponsive to any technique yet devised by any capitalist society. This paper will concentrate on the first group; the needs of the second group are obvious, and on the third I have nothing to contribute other than to urge that its plight be explicitly and prominently included on the scientific research agenda.[1]

Who and Where Are the Poor?

Given the almost 30-year history of concern with development, it is difficult to realize how few of those who were the earliest to sense the problem envisioned the possibility that a steady rise in *per capita* income in a developing country might leave the majority of its people as badly — or worse — off than before.

It is now dismally evident that the process of development in an LDC often tends to concentrate gains in the hands of an already advantaged stratum of income receivers: landowners, industrialists, businessmen, professionals, government officials, traders, those with foreign connections, etc. These groups fall into three main classifications: those who have wealth because their families were rich, those who occupy key positions at the growth points of the economy, and those who perform brokerage or service functions for the other two.

On the other hand, there are a variety of classifications of seemingly intractable poverty. Most of the categories are relatively large, and some are so large that they encompass the vast majority of people in a country. Each requires distinct solutions which have not been clearly formulated to date.

There are, to be specific, *whole nations — a sub-classification of those we usually call less-developed countries — which in terms of average income have stagnated or dropped in the last ten or fifteen years*. This very likely means that a few within these countries have gained at the expense of the vast majority. How these countries — some 30 of them which are collectively designated as the 'fourth world', with an average annual *per capita* income of under US $150 — can even survive as nation-states, much less progress, without permanently allying themselves with other nations is an unanswered question.

There are, moreover, *backward geographical areas with fairly uniformly low average family-income levels even within economically rapidly growing countries*. They include the Appalachian Mountains region in the United States and North-East Brazil. Size of the area in question and wealth of the country as a whole must figure importantly in dealing with this kind of poverty, but to what extent no one seems to know. There has been at least speculation that an area like the Appalachians as a 'pocket of poverty' can be dealt with only as a welfare problem. That may be so in a nation as rich as the United States, but the vast North-East Brazil is too dominant to be considered a 'pocket' by any geographical tailor. Welfare measures designed and executed in Brasilia are bound to be inadequate for the task. Sub-continents of poverty remain intact today, decades after their plight was first recognized, and as untouched as walled fortresses by the progress that surrounds them. Although not all who live in regions of this kind have been unserved by economic change, by and large those whose incomes have improved have been either traditional élites or resource holders who cannot even be enumerated as residents because they collect their rents or interest or dividends from some other part of the country or the world.

Most countries, and especially the LDCs, have *certain productive economic sectors that contain more poverty than their share of the population*. Agriculture is probably the prime candidate for such a designation, and it is no surprise that the poorest of countries are usually those that are the most preponderantly agricultural. The World Bank has noted that about 85 per cent of the people it describes as living in 'absolute poverty' are in rural areas.

In many countries, under existing institutions, *there is a poor and disenfranchised group that has no real voice and obtains little consideration from political, social, or economic policy decisions. Even where they have been considered by policy decisions, the result has often been ineffectual. For whatever reasons, this group lacks access to the institutions that ostensibly govern and serve its society.* When whole nations have stagnant or declining average *per capita* incomes, it will usually be found that the vast majority of the population falls into this group. In less-developed countries (let us say those in the self-named Group of 77 whose representatives met in Lima in September 1975), a great proportion is in agriculture and/or lives in a backward region and /or is self-employed. (This last point on self-employment is emphasized by Ahluwalia in Chenery *et al.* (1974), pp. 3–37. The original group of 77 now consists of over 100 nations.) The heterogeneity of sources of livelihood for these people on the bottom-most rung of the human ladder (from bootblacks to intinerant labourers) often means that a government finds real difficulty in designing policies to help them even when there is genuine will to do so.

Some policy issues are best addressed not by dealing directly with these variances within the category of poverty, but by asking: 'How did a particular sub-sector of the poor get where it is?' Those who have been left behind in their own lifetimes by the inexorable forward march of technology or in an otherwise dynamic milieu with which they have been unable to keep pace — those who have become, in effect, obsolete — pose different problems from those who were born into their unhappy situation. Both groups may lack the education, vision, and/or energy necessary to extricate themselves. Both may be held down by unyielding institutions. But those who were once in the economic mainstream present a more tractable problem unless personal or group discouragement is so pervasive that it is impenetrable by any means.

The poverty groups within nations may benefit little from national policies and influence them marginally if at all. To the poor in many LDCs — the majority — their national government could as well be on the moon as in the capital city; it would matter little to them. Likewise, cold and cruel as it may sound, many of these countries pursue economic policies that relate primarily or solely to the market economy and would need little or no modification if today saw the total disappearance of all those below the median income level.

In many ways these policies reflect a continuing and fundamental misunder-standing of the problem of poverty, and imply a belief that if the national income can somehow be raised it will *ipso facto* raise the lot of all those contained therein. The truth that groups of people are differentially (and some even adversely) affected by a rising national average income is hardly a revelation to those who care to recall their reading of Dickens. The key in designating a country as rich or poor, developed or underdeveloped, lies not only in averages, but in how many rich and poor people there are as a proportion of the total population ('rich' and 'poor' being only the two simplest of many arbitrary income categories expressed as some function of the cost of living), how quickly mobility is taking place, and how rapidly the total quantum of both groups is changing.

At any rate, the 'poor' make up from five to ten per cent of the populations of DCs and from 20 to 60 per cent of LDCs. Contemporary language of assistance agencies refers to 'the lower 40 per cent'.

The Public Assistance Record: What Is Being Done About Poverty?

Improving the distribution of income came to be explicitly recognized as an aim of the Development Decade by the General Assembly of the United Nations in the autumn of 1970. In 1973 the US Congress, in the Foreign Assistance Act setting forth the legal framework for loans and grants to less-developed countries, instructed the Administration to give highest priority to undertakings which 'directly improve the lives of the poorest of their people and their capacity to participate in the development of their countries'. The International Development and Food Assistance Act of 1975, signed by the President on 20 December of that year, likewise directed a heavy orientation toward the needs of the poor majority. At the World Bank, President Robert McNamara's addresses have been milestones in calling attention to the poor. In his now famous 1972 Santiago speech he recognized the gross income inequalities in most contemporary LDCs. A speech the next year in Nairobi added 'the lowest 40 per cent' to the vocabulary of development analysts as he gave emphasis to the needs of people 'who have neither been able to contribute significantly to national economic growth nor to share equitably in economic progress'. In that document McNamara sketched a programme designed to raise the production of 100 million small farmers by five per cent a year by 1985. With optimism he said that as early as 1975 it would be possible to reverse the widening of income disparities in the poor countries. He foresaw eradication of absolute poverty by the end of the century, together with the elimination of malnutrition and illiteracy (Lelyveld, 1975).

But the two years between Nairobi and his 1975 message apparently made him less confident as to the nature of the solution and humbled him to the task at hand. 'The closer we get to the core of poverty in the countryside,' he said, 'the more difficult, complicated and time-consuming the task becomes.' Assessing that year's progress, he was sobered:

Indeed, in many respects, the outlook now appears worse than it did twleve months ago . . . For the poorest countries — those with *per capita* incomes of less than $200 — the situation is particularly grave . . . In 1974, *per capita* incomes of one billion people living in these nations declined an average 0.5 per cent. For the hundreds of millions of them already severely deprived, it meant hunger and illness, and an erosion of hope. (McNamara, 1975, pp. 3–4, 13)

His Manila speech, given in October 1976, seemed equally pessimistic.

Dorner (1975) also sees little reason for optimistic evaluation of the anti-poverty programme sponsored or otherwise supported by the World Bank, USAID, the Regional Banks, or the United Nations Development Programme. Too often these programmes were either: (1) meant to reach the poor but diverted or dissipated in the process, perhaps reaching some other recipient group; or (2) not aimed at poverty groups at all in anything but a rhetorical sense. Commenting on the Bank's 1974–78 lending programme, Dorner (1975, p. 2) concludes:

The $4.4 billion earmarked for agriculture represents about 20 per cent of total lending planned by the Bank over the five-year period. This is approximately the same percentage for agriculture as in the previous five years, 1969–73. How much of this new lending will actually reach and benefit the small farmer? The World Bank's past performance on this score is not encouraging. Only $1 billion out of a total of $25 billion lent during the Bank's first 25 years of existence went to small farmers — a mere four per cent.

Some of those in poverty have enjoyed a modicum of improvement in absolute income levels, and there has been some slight progress toward egalitarianism in some countries in the last several decades. But the most usual result is that the entire income spectrum is raised without changing the ordinal positions of those on the income ladder. A recent time-series study for eighteen countries reveals very little relationship between rates of growth of income and changes in the share of the lowest 40 per cent of income earners (Ahluwalia in Chenery *et al.*, 1974).

The unfortunate situation as it exists today is cautiously summarized by the United Nations:

In a number of developed as well as developing countries, economic and social policy discussions reflect a new and growing emphasis on distributional objectives. National or macro-growth policies have generally failed to remove, or in some cases even to reduce, wide disparities in the level of living or the quality of life. These disparities persist even in conditions of mass poverty . . . Their intractability retards the achievement of an adequate level of living for all people, threatens national unity in some countries, and everywhere impedes the development of human resources for development. (United Nations Department of Economic and Social Affairs, 1974, p. 3)

Nevertheless, the plain fact is that the rich are not choosing to redistribute much wealth or economic power and the poor have been too weak, powerless, and unorganized to force them to do so.

There is no standard descriptive model to test the success of programmes meant to aid development. One highly conjectural manner of conceptualizing how such programmes relate to a 'more equality' target would be to visualize their differential impact on each income quintile in a typical less-developed country (deciles or quarters could just as easily be used, since precise data are not at hand).[2] Pertinent government development programmes of the 1950s largely concerned savings and investment, while in the 1960s trade was emphasized. (There is little if anything in Secretary Kissinger's 1976 Nairobi initiatives, some major points of which were rejected by the United Nations Commission on Trade and Development (UNCTAD) itself, to indicate that US policy has progressed beyond this point. Rejection of some of Kissinger's key suggestions occurred some three weeks later at the close of the meeting — see *New York Times*, 7 May 1976.)

Speaking very generally of these policies of recent decades, in most of the less-developed countries the top quintile was benefited more than the second. The third quintile often gained something, but the bottom two either received nothing or were adversely affected. That this is true should not be surprising.

Investment and trade policies both favour those groups who have resources initially. A group gets little direct benefit from low interest, investment tax credits, export subsidies, import duties, protection of infant industries, etc., unless it has a certain quantum of resources to invest or with which to generate a tradeable product. This immediately reinforces the position of the investor and the trader in the upper twenty per cent or so of the population. If, say, the middle quintile or the one above that is to benefit, it must be connected in some meaningful way with those who have the resources — perhaps it sells its labour to the 'haves' in a market where skill is important and thereby benefits when the upper groups enjoy some measure of prosperity. On the other hand, it may be buying food and clothing for its own use at prices so inflated that its gains on the factor market are neutralized by its dealings in the product market, a situation fairly common in the upper part of the middle quintile. The bottom 40 per cent or so includes, along with some unemployables, a vast pool of self-employed, unemployed, underemployed (the *lumpenproletariat* is included within these three latter categories and 'sub-proletariat' might be a better description for it (see Wolfe, 1976). If this lower 40 per cent has any connections at all with the sectors above it, they are likely to be highly exploitative in nature. It is a sector kept alive by certain marginal employment, the necessity at least to subsist, a few welfare measures (including income transfers), and repression.

Changing the way income and resources are distributed is more complex than simply adding to investment or increasing trade. Both of these latter measures are specific, determinate, and thus easy to measure. Perhaps most important, their income repercussions almost always agree closely with the interests of the dominant classes.

It is obviously too simplistic to assume that egalitarian measures always work against the interest of controlling upper and middle groups in the society and influential outsiders, although that interpretation is often made. Even when there are general expressions of support (on at least an intellectual basis) for better distribution, there is little agreement as to how to bring it about. Long before the United Nations made its proclamation, many writers of the 1960s had already seen the problem of growing inequities, called attention to them, and predicted that something would have to be done to revise a development policy whose effects on social and economic relations were to protect the current holders of resources. They foresaw irresistible pressures building among the 'have-nots' to force the 'haves' to a more realistic, if not more benevolent, policy.

In the final analysis, significant numbers who had been in the middle class entered the upper-middle class, and in many countries some who were at the top of the poverty class entered the bottom of the middle class. Meanwhile, top groups became wealthier pretty much in proportion to the resources they already controlled. A few from the second and even the top quintile spoke out for the poor. But if the middle quintile benefited, it tended to be not because of any wholesale benevolence of those at the top, but because of its own increasing restiveness. Those occupying this quintile made it clear, in the words of Falstaff, 'I am poor as Job, my Lord, but not as patient'. In the 1960s this restiveness was never mobilized into mass rebellion. Except for those who were completely voiceless and effectively repressed, nearly everyone was gaining something in an absolute sense and little meaningful political change occurred or could have been expected.

The 1970s have not as yet brought any astounding new and fresh insights on how much of the bottom 40 per cent of the population can be brought into the mainstream. But a few modest speculations can be stated more confidently now than at the beginning of the decade:

(1) There is little reason to expect a shift in the balance of power that will give the poor a bigger share of the national wealth at the expense of the ruling élites (despite the pious outpourings of intellectuals and liberals on the urgent need for such a change). The only arguments that will be persuasive for such a shift will depend on showing those who have the power that they will either have their power enhanced thereby, or will lose it and its accoutrements entirely if it is not shared to some extent.[3]

(2) Repression will continue to be used in place of reform whenever those in power can do so without fear of losing internal legitimacy or arousing debilitating international condemnation.[4] Military governments, which have proliferated in the early 1970s, will tend to be quite durable and may even be the most efficient — though certainly not the most humane — way to bring about reforms to the upper poor (the only ones who have enjoyed even a modicum of help from anti-poverty programmes). Unfortunately, the reforms may have as a consequence the side-effect of leaving others worse off than before.

(3) There will, in response to more audible and clearly enunciated outcries for social justice and reform, be more and more eloquent proclamations by ruling classes as to the need for distributive equity and broad egalitarian societal goals.[5] It will thus become more difficult than ever for the press and for social analysts to determine where rhetoric ends and accomplishment begins.

(4) To the extent that reformist goals can be met with public policy, the lowest twenty per cent or so of the population (excepting those who receive some income transfers) will not be affected and probably the quintile of income receivers above that will be little touched. We are only slowly recognizing how abysmally little our existing knowledge and the current technology of public assistance — agrarian reforms, taxation, infrastructural development, more schooling, credit earmarked for the poor — do for the bottom twenty per cent of the poor and, for that matter, how little the entire bottom 40 per cent has been helped.

Some say that we should be more optimistic than these arguments would indicate. While there has been waste and inefficiency and, more seriously, we have fallen short of any hope of substantially alleviating poverty, a few at the top levels of poverty have been helped. I feel it is unjustifiable to feel joy in the face of such minimal accomplishments when sweeping change was the enunciated goal of almost every aid programme in the 1960s.

This argues for analytically separating 'the poor' in terms of the origins of their poverty. In order to develop a technique for helping the poor, we need to examine the disadvantaged groups in each country to attempt to determine why they are mired in such deep poverty.

In most cases people are poor because they do not have income-generating resources; those that exist are firmly in the hands of a small élite. Giving the poor more resources and other means of production to use to generate incomes is one technique for coping with the problem of poverty. Land reform is the most obvious of these policy measures, and it is far from being an alternative that is exhausted, at least in most of Latin America. But given the rapid rates of population growth (which are common in LDCs and which add more to poor categories than to rich ones) even if all available land were to be distributed in some more or less equitable fashion (as individual, co-operative, or collective rights), a large core with little or no attachment to land would remain in most countries.

In every society there are the lazy and the profligate; in every society there are the old, the infirm, the chronically disturbed, the orphaned, and the social misfits who must be dealt with in other ways. But the question remains: What does society do with ablebodied, willing-to-work products of a population explosion of fifteen or twenty years ago who cannot by any known technique be provided with the jobs that will let them earn an honest living? This group must find a productive niche in society if our talk about egalitarianism and development is to be more than rhetoric. This group constitutes the 'poorest of the poor'.

Social research to date gives us few clues for coping with this mass of humankind. My plea is not for abandoning the policy search — the contrary is true. But we must in the process admit that liberal reforms have helped and probably can only help only the upper poor. At the other poverty extreme, welfare measures must be designed to help those who are poor because they cannot work. But to help the rest of the poorest of the poor — the 'critically' poor[6] — we do not know how in any practical, politically feasible sense. Of course, mass income transfers would work, but they are not politically or economically possible.

Reaching the Poor: Services with Basic Institutions Unchanged

During the 1960s and early 1970s it was thought that the problems of the landed peasant could be at least partly eliminated if he could be reached with public programmes. Programmes of this nature never reached the fastest growing and poorest segment within farming (the migrant worker or the worker with only tenuous rights to a piece of land), and indeed were never designed to do so. Research even casts some doubt on how much help established small-scale farmers have had from these auxiliary assistance programmes. Given our earlier paradigm, it seems probable that the middle quintile was by and large missed, and the upper 40 per cent received the bulk of the assistance.

In reporting on the small farmer in El Salvador, Jackson (1974, p. 22) notes that 'credit is only received by 6.3 per cent of the plots and agricultural extension reaches only 3 per cent of small farmers'. In El Salvador, 93 per cent of the farmers occupy about nineteen per cent of the land. Soles (1974) reports for Colombia that the Caja de Crédito Agrario, Industrial y Minero was founded in 1931 to serve as a source of institutionalized credit for *campesinos* who did not qualify for loans from commercial banks; now it accounts for about half of all official credit. Soles indicates that these loans are small enough so the *campesinos* should be able to benefit from them. They do not even approach the size of loans made by the private and cattle banks, and interest rates are lower. Yet while total loans increased by US $9 million between 1966 and 1967, the *campesino's* share decreased by over US $6.6 million and the share of better-off borrowers increased by over US $17 million. For a detailed examination of loans by purpose see Soles (1972).

Soles continues (1974, p. 37):

Examination of the Caja's loans for specific purposes also casts considerable doubt upon its claimed *campesino* orientation. Nearly one-half of the Caja's total credit is allocated to livestock, although the vast bulk of Colombia's rural populace are farmers, not ranchers; this credit is not allocated for family livestock purchases but for large-scale cattle-ranching. Non-livestock, or agricultural, loans were over several thousands of dollars. Even crop loans went increasingly in large blocks of credit to the commercial crops — cotton, bananas and cacao.

After presenting more evidence, Soles concludes (1974, p. 39):

(The Caja's) loan programs come down heavily weighted on the side of owners and large-scale commercial renters. While regional data are unavailable as to loans to tenure groups, where such data are available they indicate the Caja's loan program to be even more skewed away from the *campesino* class in the coastal regions.

In addition to the Caja, Soles reports (1974, p. 33) that there are three other

main channels of official agricultural loans in Colombia ... Traditionally they have tended to favour borrowers who possess a capacity for repayment in the form of real goods. Hence livestock enterprises have received 50 per cent or more of all official credit in recent years, leaving only about 45 per cent for the vast majority of Colombian farms.

He concludes that:

... the bulk of this credit has gone to the larger farmers ... INCORA (The Colombian Land Reform Agency) instituted its supervised credit program in 1963, but has never exceeded 5 per cent of total official credit. Its initial focus was on the *campesino*, but later it began to pull back and focus both on larger farms, and on servicing clients located on its own irrigation and parcelation projects.

In reporting on Fómeque, Haney (1971) notes that a branch savings bank of the Caja Agraria was opened in 1946, and in 1952 the regional office for the credit programme was transferred there. Haney could not determine the distribution of the US $84 547 available for distribution in 1966, the year of his Fómeque study, but noted that in practice loans were disbursed to those who have over 3 hectares, and the major portion goes to livestock farmers. He

168

continues (1971, p. 55):

In July 1964, INCORA initiated a supervised credit program in Fómeque... In 1965, the program was extended to other *municipios* in the eastern part of Cudinamarca, and by the end of 1966 the project with its principal office in Fómeque included 329 borrowers in five *municipios* who held nearly US $295 000 worth of loans. As in other parts of the country, most of the INCORA borrowers were recruited from the more progressive, middle group of farmers who had successful borrowing records with the Caja Agraria.

In February 1967, the *municipio* of Fómeque had 124 INCORA borrowers (about 5 per cent of the total number of rural families). The average amount of land owned by the borrowers was about 12 hectares ... Nearly 40 per cent of the borrowers owned 10 or more hectares of land. A number of borrowers were farming part of their land — conditions which are supposed to disqualify them for supervised credit ...

In another paper, Soles (1973, pp. 5–6) analyses data on credit for other Latin American countries:

The older 'peasant-oriented' institutions are often criticized for not serving the peasants. Mexico's Banco Ejidal has been accused of 'creating more problems than it solved' (by driving many *campesinos* into debt); it is very doubtful if the Caja Agraria is in fact '*campesino* oriented' — though it now claims to again be moving in that direction; and Bolivia's Banco Agrícola though also specifically directed by law to serve *campesinos* now pleads with the government to be allowed to do anything but.

The 'new' *campesino* credit agencies recognize that credit funds *per se* are not productive and hence have also emphasized the use of modern technical inputs and practices — in short, the 'package approach' of supervised credit and extension activities.

However, these programs and agencies often regress toward either serving the larger farmers or simply have not been effectively serving many *campesinos*. INCORA's supervised credit program, after an initial flurry of expansionist activity in Colombia's countryside, is now seen to be reducing its activities to concentrate on the few *campensinos* it has already settled on its irrigation and parcelation projects. The largest of the ACAR programs in Brazil (in Minas Gerais) reached only 5 per cent of the small farmers — which is at least better than the 2 per cent reached by the SCICAS program in Guatemala. INDAP, on the other hand, in Chile apparently did provide credit for a substantial proportion (47 per cent) of its potential clientèle through a program of credit in kind (e.g., loanings bags of fertilizers instead of money) to *organized groups* of *campesinos*. Credit to organized groups of *campesinos* also appears as one of the key mechanisms of the Puebla Project in Mexico.

About Puebla, Díaz Cisnero (1974, p. 496) concludes, '. . . the existence of institutional problems has prevented the project from reaching the vast majority of *campesinos* inhabiting the region'. But on balance he concludes that 'the strategy in current use there represents a realistic alternative to effectively help the *campesino* family to improve their material conditions and general wellbeing'.

Haney (1971) reminds us that credit is not the only public service programme which may miss its target in trying to eliminate poverty. He describes the marginal situation of the majority of Fómeque's farmers (pp. 58–59):

A reassessment program completed in 1967 increased the theoretical property taxes of the *municipio* by more than five times. But in context of the existing local political structure, peasants will have little incentive or justification for paying the additional taxes. With little or no peasant representation in the local government, there is no assurance that the additional revenue will be channeled into the much needed improvements in rural infrastructure . . .

Fixed costs account for a high percentage of total local government expenditures. In 1964, the combined costs of administration, justice, public order, and tax collection comprised 27 per cent of the total disbursements by the local government. Most of this outlay goes to support a local bureaucracy which, by and large, is indifferent toward the felt needs of the peasantry. In general, peasants have no opportunity to air a public problem before a local government official; they are not treated with justice in legal confrontations . . .

Reaching the Poor: Technological Change with Institutions Unchanged

Technological changes in agriculture — new knowledge, new forms of organization, new physical inputs, new infrastructure — have positive income effects on those who have resources, and there is often some spillover to the upper end of poverty groups. So far there is little evidence that they touch those in middle- and lower-poverty groups except perhaps adversely.

What repercussion they have in specific countries depends largely on the institutional milieu, especially initial resource distribution.[7] For example, the most likely consequence is an accentuation of income (and hence class) differences when the land tenure pattern is inequitable (bimodal, as, for example, in the *hacienda* system); this is less probable when land is distributed in a fairly egalitarian manner (unimodal, as in the family-farm system).

Green revolution technology may affect income distribution through the factor market in that (1) it might cause some agricultural workers to be more fully employed than formerly, while others would be adversely affected (unemployables would not be touched); (2) some farmers might completely or partially be denied access to the new technology, thus increasing the income gap between the rich and poor. I need spend little more time on (2) since it was alluded to in the last section. The point is clear: to be optimally effective, green revolution technology requires more fertilizer, better seed, and better regulated water. This means more credit, which the poor may not have or be able to obtain.

More generally, the success of the green revolution rests on how well the non-farm sector can provide inputs: the seed–fertilizer revolution is distinguished by its increased dependence on purchased inputs. If bottlenecks in the distribution of these inputs affect the quantity delivered and the timing of their delivery, income will be affected. The chances for the large-farm sector to obtain seed and fertilizer may be greater than that of the small-farm sector simply because the large-scale farmer has more expertise in dealing with complex bureaucracies. And if there is a problem with an input shortfall, the large-scale farmer can use his personal vehicle to pick up seed, fertilizer, and pesticide at a more distant location, an alternative usually not open to small, undercapitalized farmers. Griffin (1972, p. 47) believes that:

Perhaps the most important reason for the bias of the 'green revolution' is the bias of government policy. For many years research, extension and investment programmes in agriculture have been devoted to raising output (preferably exportable output); their primary concern has not been to increase the welfare of the rural population and improve the distribution of income and wealth (see also chapter 8 by Pearse in this book).

This does not mean that those with small farms are always denied green revolution inputs. Rochin (1971) found that *barani* (rain-fed) smallholders in Pakistan 'have adopted dwarf varieties of wheat in a remarkably short time'. In Hazara they heard about it on the radio, saw it growing in demonstration plots, and were quick to purchase the inputs when available.

Alternatively green revolution technology might affect income distribution through the product market in that it might cause prices for a commodity to drop. Non-adopters would lose because they would not be able to make up in quantity what they lost in price. They would either retreat further into subsistence cultivation or take advantage of high land prices to sell out. Whether they ultimately benefit would depend largely on what happened to them then; if they were able to obtain better jobs after they liquidated their land assets, they would ultimately benefit, but this is unlikely in a labour-plentiful economy where the displaced smallholder is likely to be unschooled and without skill. Adopters would likely gain and, unless markets were exceedingly oligopolistic, so would consumers.

If the resultant agricultural product is exported rather than consumed locally, income effects will depend on who gets the foreign exchange that is generated. Will the government get a share? If so, how will it be used? What will happen to the share retained by individuals? Will it make up an income stream for the already rich with little 'trickle-down' effects on the poor? Will it be invested in towns or in the countryside? Will it be used for conspicuous consumption? Will it be sent out of the country and hoarded abroad? If benefits flowing to the rich are taxed away, the poor could benefit, but LDCs do not have a good record of either taxing the rich or spending public revenue in such a way that the poor would be helped.

Effects through the labour market are most likely and should be explored somewhat further. The employment problem in rural areas of less-developed countries is serious and becoming more so (Thiesenhusen, 1971, 1974a). Some feel that the green revolution technology may be exacerbating what is already a bad situation. The most direct way that income distribution can be affected by the green revolution is if rural workers — who are already crowded at the low end of the spectrum of income receivers in most LDCs — lost their jobs or find fewer days of work than presently because of it.

In summarizing one seminar on the green revolution in New Delhi, Das (1972, pp. 2266–2267) indicates that determining the income impacts of technology on various tenure groups is not an easy task:

While in UP (Uttar Pradesh), the neglected group may be the sharecroppers on large estates, in Maharashtra it may be the marginal farmers on hill-side slopes. Landless labour might have gained in Punjab, whereas sharecropper dispossession in Tamil Nadu may have worsened the position of agricultural labourers there.

Barker *et al.* (1972) discovered that with the introduction of the new technology in the Philippines, the structure of employment in rice farming changed while total demand for labour remained fairly constant. The reduced labour requirements for mechanized land preparation were more than offset by increased labour requirements for weeding and harvesting or more possibilities for double-cropping. It remains to be seen whether the labour peaks created for these operations might be so steep that mechanical processes will ultimately be substituted for hand-work or day labourers substituted for resident workers. At any rate, chances are good that as accentuated peaks and valleys appear in the structure of employment less resident farm labour will be needed. When labour requirements were more or less evenly spread throughout the agricultural year, resident farm labour was called for which related the labour force to the landlord in a traditional patron–client dyadic contract. Landlords frequently provided live-in workers with a house, some land, and/or other perquisites while the worker provided his labour. When the rhythm of work is changed so that some labour-use peaks get very steep and troughs appear in other seasons, there is no good reason to support permanent workers full time on the farm. Frankel (1971, p. 198) discusses this point with reference to India:

The rapid progress of agricultural modernization tends to undermine traditional norms of agrarian relationships based on the exchange of mutual, if noncompatible, benefits and services that have historically provided a justification for inequalities between the propertied upper and middle castes, and the landless low castes and Harijans.

What this means is that where a patron–client relationship exists, it may well break down. This may be applauded as one more necessary step toward development, but in some countries where the system had overtones of landlord benevolence or *noblesse oblige*, the change is liable to be a wrenching one for many workers.

Tenants, especially in Asia where they are more common and poorer than in Latin America, face a very special problem as green revolution inputs come to be used and farming becomes more profitable. As land values rise with increased crop values, rents rise. Certainly landlords do not allow benefits of the green revolution to flow entirely — often not even in part — to renters. They are successful in raising rental payments because of the competition from many potential tenants for rental property. Some owners are simply reclaiming the leased property and working it with hired labour and/or machinery. Of India, Frankel (1971, p. 197) states rather bluntly 'Certainly, (landlords) do not hesitate to raise rentals in line with appreciating land values and/or to evict even tenants having longstanding cultivating possession of the land'.

There are other ways in which the green revolution may have an effect on labour use, and they involve substitution of machines for hand labour:

(1) The green revolution might shift land away from high labour-use crops to crops that are not so labour-intensive. This is not to say that all shifts are unwarranted or should be foregone.

(2) The technological opportunities presented by the several green revolution crops vary in their potential for creating employment. Rice farmers may move toward the structural labour-using forms of Japan; because wheat is more amenable to mechanization, wheat farmers may adopt the capital-intensive structural form of the United States (Saito, 1971).

(3) Even where double-cropping is not possible, modern grain varieties may require precision seedbed preparation that hand labour cannot provide and larger machines may be used.

(4) Even seemingly small changes in technology and institutions may result in enormous changes in labour use. This is especially the case where there is a super-abundance of labour. (One example of this latter kind is documented by Collier *et al.*, 1973, Sinaga and Collier 1975.)

There is still hope of increasing jobs and hence bettering income distribution via the seed–fertilizer revolution. The truth is, however, that upon close analysis some innocuous changes, or those which by any superficial analysis seem as though they should be labour absorbing, turn out to be the opposite (for a more detailed discussion see chapter 8 by Pearse in this book).

Reaching the Poor Through Reform: Institutions Changed

Even the efforts to introduce direct institutional change (in contrast to the earlier examples of directing assistance programmes at groups within the existing institutional system and introducing technological change into the existing system) have not reached those without some prior resource foothold. The example of agrarian reform in at least non-socialist countries during the period after the Second World War is a good one. Why it has not reached the poorest of the poor and who it benefits or is likely to benefit requires some understanding of prereform claims on the peasantry on the land.

Each LDC has sub-classes of peasantry recognizable to each other by a relationship to the land which has been dignified by local or national nomenclature. Status is incurred by this relationship, and while those with no relationship to the land, living, say, in Santiago, may call all peasants '*campesinos*', those with even a passing knowledge of agriculture will be able to run down a status list that usually tops out with '*mediero*' (sharecropper) and ends with '*afuerino*' (seasonal worker, migratory labourer or day labourer), with various, sometimes quite complex, combinations along the line.

Some sub-classes in any country are more apt to benefit from agrarian reform than others. The existing smallholder is unlikely to get more land and this seems, on the surface, no more than just. If not all can be accommodated anyhow, there seems little to justify granting more land to those who already have some. But within the smallholder category there are those heads of households who have plots so small (*minifundistas* or *comuneros* in Latin America) that they are unable to scratch a living and must work on estates for the bulk of their income, perhaps leaving their land to be tended by other family members. They are as poor — maybe poorer — than the other group of labourers which has next to no chance to obtain land in a reform, the day labourers. Indeed, because their plots are so tiny they must be considered in the itinerant labour classification; they are day labourers with the added burden of reduced mobility to seek more remunerative employment elsewhere.

The migratory day labourer constitutes a group least apt to benefit from any reform. He is unorganized and has no prior, enduring ties to one farm, such as a usufructuary plot, a contract, or often even an established or continuing work pattern.

The resident farm labourer, who has these claims and can be considered at least in a middle-poor category, is more apt to receive land in a reform. He is more often organized (and if not, organizable). Especially in the case of 'top down' liberal reformers, the resident labour force of an estate is a propitious target group. It already possesses some tools and implements, may have certain proprietary interests on the land because of its longevity or that of its ancestors in the area, is handily located, and has more managerial experience; among the peasantry, it poses the least risk for those who must concern themselves with maintaining production goals.

In Table 7.1, which depicts only a few of the many peasant tenure types in several Latin American countries, the labourers in 'A' would probably benefit from a reform (in some countries they are benefiting). Labourers in 'B' would not. Indeed, when the resident labour-force gets land, it may systematically deny it to the 'poorest of the poor', the migratory labour-force, which, in most countries, is the numerically fastest growing portion of the peasantry. From the standpoint of the beneficiary this is reasonable: heirs need to be accommodated and, if post-reform organization is communal, more members are perceived of not only as potentially disruptive interlopers on an established farm, but as unnecessary claimants to a share of joint profits. From a national standpoint the result may imply a paradoxical result of reform: after land redistribution, income distribution may be as skewed as before.

Pearse (1975, p. 149) reports that in the Bolivian reform distribution 'followed the existing pattern', presumably with those who had strongest claims to demesne land getting most. While it was not explicit in Law 16 040 (the agrarian reform legislation of Chile), preference in land assignment under the Frei government was given to those who had worked on a permanent basis on the farm being allocated for at least three of the four years prior to expropriation (Barraclough and Affonso, 1973, p. 2). Even enunciated efforts to include poorest rural workers — as in Peru and in Chile under Allende — have come to little. In analysing the progress made in the Allende reforms, Barraclough and Affonso noted that in only eighteen months, November 1970 to June 1972, the

Table 7.1. Two generic types of peasants in several countries of Latin America

	Country	Local term	Lives on estate (*hacienda, estancia, fundo, fazenda*)	Cash wage	In-kind payment (like pasturage, food)
(A) Farm labourer who is paid for work on landlord's property by land usufruct	Brazil	*condição colono camarada*	x	x	
	Chile	*inquilino*	x	x	x
	Colombia	*cuidandero recomendado arrendatario viviente concertado terracero*	x	sometimes	sometimes
	Costa Rica	*péon*	sometimes	x	sometimes
	Ecuador	*huasipungero*	x	sometimes	x
	El Salvador	*colono*	x	x	x

Guatemala	*colono*	x	seldom	sometimes
Peru	*colono arrendire allegado*	sometimes	sometimes	sometimes
(B) Farm labourer who is paid for work on landlord's property in cash and/or rations and not land usufruct				
Chile	*afuerino*		x	
Colombia	*jornalero peón*		x	x
Ecuador	*yanapero*			x
El Salvador	*jornalero*		x	
Guatemala	*cuadrillero peón trabajador*	seldom	x	
Peru	*enganche (system) yanacona*	x	x	x

Note: x denotes 'usually'. Systems often vary from region to region within countries.

government expropriated and incorporated 3282 farms. They calculated this at 21 per cent of the productive agricultural land of the country, estimating that 75 000 had directly benefited from the 1967 law (on which Allende as well as Frei built his programme. The authors found this progress praiseworthy — since other peaceful 'reforms' such as those in Colombia, Ecuador, and Italy had not affected more than five or ten per cent of the agricultural land. Yet the direct beneficiaries were seldom the migratory farm labourers: 'The position of the most backward agricultural groups, such as the Mapuches (the Indians who live on reservations in the South), the *comuneros* of Norte Chico, the *afuerinos* (day labourers) and the poor *minifundistas* continues now as in the past . . . (Lopez *et al.*, 1968, p. 93).

Assessing the progress made under the Peruvian land reform law of 1969, Lastarria and Havens (1976, p. 28) report that the agrarian reform under the Military Government

affected the vast majority of the large landholdings in Peru. However it has affected only 25 per cent of the total agricultural population. Significant sectors have been neglected by the reform activity, particularly the landless peasant, the part-time day labourer and the large small-farm and *minifundista* sector.

That so few non-resident *hacienda* or plantation farm labourers have been incorporated in the Peruvian reform process comes as no great surprise; it is continuation of a trend described in 1974 by Horton (pp. xxvii–xxviii) who noted that:

One of the major disappointments of the reform is its impact on employment. Neither striking increases nor declines have been reported, and it seems likely that the net effect is a small positive one . . . Reform enterprise members are by no means interested in increasing membership or non-member employment at the expense of profits. On most of the estates visited the trend in pre-reform employment was downward. The reform has greatly diminished this trend, but there is little evidence of a marked increase in employment.

After a careful examination of a number of cases of agrarian reforms, Horton (1974, p. 166) concludes that

In no case did members or managers consider it rational to cut back or delay mechanization in order to employ more field hands. Nor were cases found where members cut the number of days each worked in order to take on more outside labourers.

In the Philippines only tenants on rice and corn farms above a certain acreage have been affected by the agrarian reform, often called the number one priority of President Marcos' New Society. While it is generally agreed that more progress has been made in the last three-and-a-half years than the past 30, the similarities to Chile and Peru are obvious in that only groups with some foothold in the system benefit. As Shaplen reports (1976a, p. 92).

The major part of the land problem — the freeing of peasants from bondage as impoverished tenants and sharecroppers — has been only partly solved by the program, which covers merely those areas devoted to the cultivation of rice and corn. Nearly a million and a half hectares (a hectare is about two and a half acres) of these crops, worked by nine hundred and fifteen thousand tenant farmers, are covered under the program. When it is completed — sometime in 1977, the government hopes — over half the land will have been transferred to almost four hundred thousand tenant farmers under permanent lease-hold arrangements. This is no more than a third of the country's total agricultural land; the rest is devoted to other crops, the most important of which are coconut and sugar. Peasants working land devoted to these crops want to bring it under the reform program, too, but no such action is imminent, even though workers in sugarcane fields are, with one exception, probably the worst paid and most underprivileged of all agricultural employees. The exception is landless peasants, who work when and for whom they can — a category that, according to some estimates, comes to perhaps three million people.

Conclusions

Previous papers have catalogued and provided a rationale for the known policies that I believe most LDCs must follow if they are to alleviate poverty and narrow the ever-increasing income and resource gap in rural areas (Dorner and Thiesenhusen, 1972; Thiesenhusen, 1974a, 1974b, 1974c, 1975a). Each country is distinct, and which policies are followed and which take priority depends on political exigencies, the state of knowledge, and the 'art of the possible'. In general, we know that most countries require a land reform early in their development effort followed by programmes which deliver inputs that will increase the ability of beneficiaries to be more productive. Because of land scarcity these programmes will, in the context of contemporary reform laws, reach the 'upper poor'. Others who cannot be reached in this manner must be employed through agroindustries and infrastructure development. Intermediate technology must receive certain favoured status, and a proper climate for peasant reorganization and co-operatives must be fostered. But because of the magnitude of the problem, it is likely that a substantial group of poor will be left behind even given the most favourable of conditions. Some of these can be helped only through income transfers; there may not be another way to incorporate them into society.

The challenge of eliminating or at least substantially alleviating poverty in the coming decades seems almost insurmountable. People form the core of the problem and human beings are not known for predictability or, fortunately, for manipulatability. Furthermore, mainline academics have either neglected the poverty issue or treated it within a narrow disciplinary framework. But if the complex secrets of space science, solar energy, nuclear power, poliomyelitis, RNA, and DNA can be unlocked in the course of one generation, certainly the poverty in which at least two-thirds of the world's people live must be attacked with equal resources and intellectual vigour

(1) How can appropriate institutional reforms and delivery of all the supple-mentary inputs that must accompany them be speeded?

(2) How can meaningful income transfers to the unemployable be implemented?

(3) How can the numerically rapidly growing groups that are not affected by liberal reforms, job creation, collective action, or income transfer be reached?

(4) How, at minimal cost, can the poor who already have some resources be assisted to increase their income?

(5) How can technology be adapted or created to accommodate more 'employables'?

(6) How can the rich within poor countries and the rich countries within a poor world be convinced that without their voluntary — or, if it comes to that, involuntary — help the problems of poverty can never be alleviated?

(7) How can the world community avoid solutions that are discouragingly piecemeal responses to the endless and unsupportable wave of population growth?[8]

Acknowledgements

I wish to thank my colleagues Marion Brown, Peter Dorner, Archibald Haller, Henry Hart, Don Kanel, Bryant Kearl, Jane Knowles, H. A. Oluwasanmi, Arthur Padilla Lira, Kenneth Parsons, Raymond Penn and Edward P. Reed for comments on an early draft.

Notes

1. Dividing the poverty sector into groups for analytical purposes is not a new idea but it is one that has been neglected by those individuals and groups who ask the broad question, 'How can the poor be helped?' Raj Krishna (1974) concludes:

   We already know from other analyses of family expenditure data that at least 30 per cent of the population is poor. Thus, once again, with all-India data, we can safely maintain the view that the poor are more numerous than the idle; the idle are more numerous than the willing; and only a fraction of the idle are willing to work more . . .

   It is clear, first of all, that the elimination of poverty is a much more gigantic undertaking than the elimination of the idleness of those who are available for additional work. Any attempt to identify the two by definition cannot help the policy-makers. Fundamentally, of course, it is poverty that must be eliminated. But the poverty of the employed, the unemployed, the self-employed, and the unemployable requires different treatment. The unemployables need simple income transfers; the self-employed (small farmers and artisans) need additional inputs, credit and knowledge; the employed need more effective unionism; and the unemployed need work and/or means of production. (See also Parsons, 1969)

2. Among the less developed countries, studies on income distribution are beginning to appear using Latin American data for some selected countries which might be interpreted as corroborating, in rough fashion, the observations above. Comparing 1960 and 1970 data:

(*a*) The top five per cent of income receivers have gained the most in *per capita* terms in nearly all countries.

(*b*) In most of them the fifteen per cent below this group have gained in relative terms and have substantially bettered their situation in absolute incomes. In others, this category has just held its own in terms of relative shares.

(*c*) In a number of Latin American countries (dominated by Brazil) groups closer to the median lost more ground in relative terms than any other of the groups on the income ladder, but held their own in absolute income. In a larger number of countries (dominated by Mexico) these groups held their own or gained in relative terms, but less than the groups above them.

(*d*) Those groups below the median lost in relative terms. In the former countries, losses were less pronounced than those of the groups immediately above them; in the latter countries, losses contrast sharply with gains by the groups above them.

(*e*) Absolute income levels of the poorest groups remained practically static while their income shares deteriorated markedly. Deteriorating levels of living are characteristic of this bottom quintile.

(See United Nations Economic Commission for Latin America, 1975, pp. 57–64).

3. As one of President Laugerud's key advisors said before the 1976 earthquake in Guatemala, 'Either the Indian is integrated into the present system, or else they will massacre our children' (*Latin America*, 5 March 1976, pp. 77–78).

At first sight it might seem strange that Laugerud should wish to challenge the political, economic, and social élite which, together with the army since 1954, has been the backbone of the Guatemalan power structure at which he stands. His motives can be traced back to the 1974 elections, in which Laugerud . . . was defeated at the polls, but saved by the army in a fraudulent event . . . The biggest swing against the ruling coalition was precisely among the Indians of the *altiplano*, who have not entirely lost the political awareness and ability to organize themselves that they acquired in the decade from 1944 to 1954 . . . It seemed to Laugerud . . . that it would be . . . sensible to support and develop the co-operatives which already existed in the *altiplano* to a limited degree . . . All these plans now are in ruins. The 'class quake', as it is now being called, caused the greatest damage in the *altiplano* areas where the co-operatives were being developed, while the wealthy *latifundistas* and exporters emerged virtually unscathed.

4. 'Using strategy of rhetoric and repression, the government works skillfully through the official National Peasant Confederation and, when necessary, the army to mobilize the peasant on its behalf and to crush occasional outbursts. "The killing of peasants is a routine event," a respected student of Mexican politics said. "The latest massacres only drew attention because one of them was used as an excuse to overthrow the Governor of Sonora. Otherwise it could not have been newsworthy" (*New York Times*, 'Mexico: Heedless of Peasant Plight', 1 December 1975).

5. It continues to be somewhat surprising — and it perhaps should not be — to hear elected and non-elected leaders speak self-critically of their régimes. In September 1975 President Ferdinand E. Marcos admitted that after three years of martial law in the Philippines, 'we are in fact a nation divided against itself — divided between urban and rural, rich and poor, majorities and minorities, privileged and underprivileged . . .' (Robert Shaplen, 1967a, p. 82).

President Michael Manley says,

'The fact is, we have both a massive urban unemployment . . . in 1972 the unemployment figure was 23.7 per cent island-wide . . . some of the rural parishes had an even higher figure than the national average. Jamaica's problem is like that of almost all other developing countries, with the chronic rural unemployed drifting to the town' (*Tropic* (Miami) 'Conversation with Michael Manley', 11 April 1976, p. 28).

In another story President Manley was quoted as saying that Jamaica is 'being made a time bomb', citing the fact that 60 per cent of the people are under 30 years of age and 30 per cent of these are unemployed (Ralph Blumenthal, 'Political Violence in Slums of Jamaican Capital Has Subsided, But Island is a Time Bomb', *New York Times*, 29 February 1976).

6. The lexicon of adjectives to describe poverty is as rich as it is imprecise. Marshall Wolfe distinguishes between the 'relatively' and 'critically' poor in Wolfe (1976).

The World Bank prefers to make a distinction between 'absolute' and 'relative' poverty:

Approximately 85 per cent of the 750 million poor in the developing world are considered to be in absolute poverty — based on the arbitrary criterion of an annual per capita income equivalent to $50 or less. The remaining fifteen per cent are judged to be in relative poverty — having incomes above the equivalent of $50 but below that of the national average per capita income (World Bank, 1975, p. 4).

Edward Teller claims that three-quarters of the world is 'wretchedly' poor (*Newsweek*, 17 May 1976, p. 15).

7. With historical perspective, Kuznets (1974) believes that technological imperatives bring about institutional change and cultural adjustments and, while modern technology provides the potential for economic growth, lack of appropriate institutional responses can limit or halt it. These adjustments are accompanied by changes in ideology and changes in the conception of man and nature brought about by the innovation. Whether this is true of matters concerning equity, whether it applies in contemporary LDCs (Kuznets' observations were based on the historic Western European and US experiences), and/or whether this is a long-term rather than a short-term view are matters for conjecture.

8. This point relates directly to issues discussed at the United Nations Conference on Human Settlement (Habitat) held in Vancouver, 1–13 June 1976. Extensive press coverage began in all major newspapers on 30 May 1976. See, for example, Gladwin Hill, 'A Look at the Man-Made Mess', *New*

York Times, 30 May 1976; and 'World Seeks Way to Aid Its People', *Milwaukee Journal*, 31 May 1976. See also the following articles in *Science*, 4 June 1976, pp. 941–975: Margaret Mead, 'Habitat', p. 941; Frederick C. Turner, 'The Rush to the Cities in Latin America', pp. 955–962; Richard L. Meier, 'A Stable Urban Ecosystem', pp. 962–968; Roger Revelle, 'Energy Use in Rural India', pp. 969–975. Also relating to this issue is Thiesenhusen (1975*b*).

References

Barker, Randolph, Meyers, William H., Crisostomo, Cristina M., and Duff, Bart (1972), 'Employment and technological change in Philippine agriculture, *International Labour Review*, **August–September**, pp. 111–139.

Barraclough, Solon, and Affonso, Almino (1973), 'Diagnóstico de la reforma agraria chilena (Noviembre 1970–Junio 1972)', separada de la revista *Cuadernos de la Realidad Nacional* (CEREN), 16, **April**.

Chenery, Hollis, Ahluwalia, Montek S., Bell, C. L. G., Dulor, John H., and Jolly, Richard (1974), *Redistribution With Growth* (Oxford: Oxford University Press).

Collier, William *et al.* (1973), 'Recent changes in rice harvesting methods', *Bulletin of Indonesian Economic Studies*, 9, **July**, pp. 36–45.

Das, Amritananda (1972), 'Understanding the green revolution', *Economic and Political Weekly*, **18 November**, pp. 2266–2267.

Díaz Cisnero, Heliodoro (1974), *An Institutional Analysis of a Rural Development Project: The Case of the Puebla Project in Mexico*, Ph.D. thesis (Madison: University of Wisconsin).

Dorner, Peter (1975), 'International assistance for agricultural development: new directions?' (Land Tenure Centre Paper No. 107, University of Wisconsin). A shorter version of this paper is published as 'International assistance for the small farmer', *Challenge*, **May–June**.

Dorner, Peter, and Thiesenhusen, William C. (1972), 'Latin American Rural Development Strategies for the 1970s', paper prepared at the request of the Organization of American States, **August**.

Frankel, Francine R. (1971), *India's Green Revolution: Economic Gains and Political Costs* (Princeton, N.J.: Princeton University Press).

Griffin, Keith (1972), *The Green Revolution: An Economic Analysis*, Report No. 72–76 (Geneva: UNRISD).

Haney, Emil (1971), 'Possibilities for the economic reorganization of *minifundia* in a Highland Region of Colombia', Land Tenure Centre Research Paper No. 43 (Madison: University of Wisconsin).

Horton, Douglas E. (1974), 'Land Reform and Reform Enterprises in Peru'. Report submitted to the Land Tenure Centre, University of Wisconsin, and to the International Bank for Reconstruction and Development.

Jackson, Don (1974), 'Communal Production Co-operatives: The Salvadorean Experience'. *Land Tenure Centre Newsletter*, 45, **July–September** (Madison: University of Wisconsin).

Krishna, Raj (1974), 'Unemployment in India' in Agricultural Development Council Teaching Forum, *Development Processes and Planning*, 38, **March**.

Kuznets, Simon (1974), *Population, Capital and Growth: Selected Essays* (London: Heinemann).

Lasbarria, C., Susana, and Havens, A. Eugene (1976), 'Agrarian structure, agrarian reform and Peru's "Revolution"' (mimeo), prepared for *Latin American Perspective*, special issue on Peru, Lima, **April**.

Lelyveld, Joseph (1975), 'McNamara's style at the World Bank', Business and Finance Section, *New York Times*, **30 November**.

Lopez, Pedro M., *et al.* (1968), *Exposición metódica y coordinada de la ley de reforma agraria de Chile* (Santiago: Editorial Jurídica de Chile).

McNamara, Robert S. (1975), Address to the Board of Governors, World Bank Group, Washington DC, 1 September.

Parsons, Kenneth H. (1969), 'Poverty as an issue in development policy: a comparison of United States and underdeveloped countries', *Land Economics*, 45, **February**.

Pearse, Andrew (1975), *The Latin American Peasant* (London: Cass).

Rochin, Refugio (1971), 'Dwarf wheat adoption by *barani* smallholders of Hazara district: technological change in action (Islamabad: Ford Foundation) (mimeo).

Saito, Kazuo (1971), 'On the green revolution', *The Developing Economies*, **March**, pp. 16–30.

Shaplen, Robert (1976a), 'Letter from Manila', *New Yorker*, **3 May**.

Shaplen, Robert, (1976b), 'Letter from Sri Lanka', *New Yorker*, **13 September**.

Sinaga, Rudolf, and Collier, W. L., 'Social and regional implications of agricultural development policy'. Paper presented at the South East Asia Agricultural Economics Assiation meeting, Balikpapan, Indonesia, 3–4 November, 1975.

Soles, R. (1972), 'Rural Land Invasions in Colombia: A Study of the Macro- and Micro-conditions and Forces Leading to Present Unrest'. Ph.D. Dissertation, Chapter 4, App. 1, pp. 220–237 (Madison: University of Wisconsin).

Soles, Roger E. (1973), 'Agricultural credit in Latin America: persistent problems and potential promises', Land Tenure Centre Paper No. 96 (Madison: University of Wisconsin); reprinted from *AID Spring Review of Small Farmer Credit*, **16**, *Additional Papers*, no. SR116, **June**.

Soles, Roger E. (1974), 'Rural land invasions In Colombia', Land Tenure Centre Research Paper No. 59 (Madison: University of Wisconsin).

Thiesenhusen, William C. (1971), 'Latin America's employment problem', *Science*, **5 March**, pp. 868–874.

Thiesenhusen, William C. (1974a), 'What changing technology implies for agrarian reform', *Land Economics*, 50, **February**.

Thiesenhusen, William C. (1974b), 'El desarrollo agricola de América Latina en la mittad de la década del sesenta', *Desarrollo Rural en las Américas* (San José), 6 **(September–December)** pp. 44–62.

Thiesenhusen, William C. (1974c), 'Food and population growth', *Ekonomi dan Keuangan Indonesia* (Jakarta), 22, **September**, pp. 209–224.

Thiesenhusen, William C. (1975a), 'Development and equality: partners or rivals', *Solidarity* (Manila), 9, **(January–February)**, pp. 7–19.

Thiesenhusen, William C. (1975b), 'Population growth and agriculture', Paper delivered at the Seminar on Population Growth and Programme Change, International Union for the Scientific Study of Population, Liège, Belgium, at the Colegio de México, Mexico City, 15–17 December.

United Nations Department of Economic and Social Affairs (1975), *1974 Report on the World Social Situation*, E/CN. 5/512/Rev. 1, St/E SA/24 (New York).

United Nations Economic Commission for Latin America (1975), 'Human development and social change, E / CEPAL / 981, *Latin American Development and the International Economic Situation*, part 1, Chapter 1.

Wolfe, Marshall (1976), 'Poverty as a social phenomenon and as a central issue for development policy', ECLA/Draft/DS/133, Social Development Division (Santiago).

World Bank (1975), *Rural Development: Sector Policy Paper* (Washington DC)

8

Technology and Peasant Production: Reflections on a Global Study

Andrew Pearse

This chapter is about a study of the social and economic implications of the 'green revolution' — in other words, the large-scale introduction of high-yielding varieties of foodgrain — sponsored by the United Nations and carried out between 1970 and 1974 in the countries mainly affected by the UN Research Institute for Social Development. The importance of the theme is that it concerns a campaign aimed at solving the dilemma of those countries whose growing populations seem to be pressing hard on existing food resources and arable land. These countries face growing food shortages and internal distribution failures causing the hunger of their poorer majorities and economic crises for their governments whose food import bills increase year by year. The so-called green revolution was an international campaign aimed at increasing the productivity of land by means of the introduction of a science-based technology (referred to here for convenience rather than for accuracy as 'the new technology') in the production of foodgrains. The campaign succeeded in bringing about the introduction of the technology on a sufficient scale to give it great socioeconomic significance and to merit the closest inspection as to its implications: hence the study.

Essentially, three related aspects of the process of technological change in the agricultural/rural sector were studied. These were:

(1) the identification of the factors facilitating or obstructing the acquisition and use of a technology based on specially bred plant varieties (mainly for irrigated tropical lands) and the use of manufactured chemical compositions for plant nutrition;

(2) the identification of the economic and social changes which follow the large-scale introduction of the technology to be observed in the agrarian structure, in the level and quality of livelihood of the participants, and in the social structure of the rural society;

(3) and assessments of measures and programmes proposed and carried out by governments in order to manage or modify the processes which are set off by technological change.

© Sage Publications Ltd. This chapter was originally published in *Development and Change*, vol. 8, no. 2, April, 1977. Permission to reproduce it here is gratefully acknowledged.
The author was Project Manager in charge of the UNRISD/UNDP research project known as Global Two, and is now at St Antony's College, Oxford. This article is written in a purely private capacity.

Studies were contracted by agronomists, sociologists, agricultural economists, anthropologists, political scientists and historians. They sought to illuminate and explain the emergent situations at different levels and in different ways. They were provided with an inventory of what seemed to be significant issues but nevertheless gave the characteristic angle to their individual studies according to their sensitivity to local issues, their own situation in the society and their respective disciplines. Each used his own methods of research. No standardized instruments were insisted upon but it was made clear that field studies were required which would approach the livelihood and social relations of the different groups and classes of persons involved in agricultural production, the functioning of agrarian institutions, the operation of units of production and forms of marketing and exchange at the local level, as well as the real performance of governments, private sector agencies and purveyors of the elements of the technology in question. Most of the studies which resulted attempted to look at the introduction of the new technology in the context of one or several primary rural settlements, or better still, in the context of such settlements and their relations with the urban market centres on which they were partially dependent. A number of studies, however, used data gathered by sample surveys of productive units within a more extensive area. While these studies provided aggregate data comparable with regional and nationwide statistics, they were seldom able to provide explanations of the persistence or alteration of the form and content of social and economic behaviour, which, however, becomes evident in the framework of community relations and in the specificity of the locality at a particular point in its history.

While the studies provided useful and varied answers to the questions posed, the message of these reports and the conclusions drawn from the whole experience is that the technology will inevitably play an increasingly important part in agricultural production, but that the main principles of the strategy adopted for introducing the technology are inadequate for the developmental needs of the mainly rural countries concerned and harbour a potential for increased pauperization and social conflict.

The evaluation of policies and programmes, of course, required clearly established and agreed notions about what the objectives of the introduction of the new technology were. This key problem was finally solved by taking the position that governments, scientific institutions and technical assistance or development agencies were able to give their assent to the proposition that the two main objectives of the technological changes contemplated were: (1) freedom from national food dependence through accelerated increases in food production leading toward food self-sufficiency; and (2) freedom from hunger for their populations. While the mandatory nature of these two objectives is generally agreed, the relation which they have to one another, and the order of priorities and means of realization are the subject of disagreement and conflict.

The new technology is built around the use of man-made varieties of wheat, maize and other foodgrains in man-controlled environments. The qualification 'man-made' refers to the fact that the new varieties are the result of a sophisticated scientific process of selective breeding designed to result in stable new varieties of plant having certain desired qualities, most of which are favourable to higher yields and higher production. These qualities include resistance to specific pests or diseases; and increased capacity to absorb nutriment from soil or sunlight; greater structural strength achieved by the reduction of plant height (so that the resulting dwarf character enables the plants to hold up the increased weight of the ear and withstand high winds or rough treatment at harvest time from human or machine handling), and greater tolerance of dry spells or cold temperatures. Other variables which plant breeders manipulate are: the length of the growth period, the shortening of which makes possible more intensive use of the land (in other words, the cultivation of two or three crops in a year instead of one), and photo-period sensitivity which is related to the link between the maturation of the plant and the seasons of the year. Still other qualities which scientists attempt to control have to do with the value of the plant such as its taste, its colour and its nutritive or culinary qualities.

The man-controlled environments in which these more delicate custom-built plants can best thrive are achieved by means of the use of manufactured chemicals, carefully timed and rationed applications of moisture, and appropriate cultivation recipes. The function of the chemicals is to increase available plant nutrient to the optimum level of uptake for these more voracious varieties; to control the onslaughts of pests and disease, intensified in response to the increase in host material; and to destroy weeds which also luxuriate in the surfeit of fertilizer. Cultivation practices themselves are of course a way of controlling the environment, but the high potential yield of which the new grains are capable can only be achieved if such practices as weeding, watering, fertilizing, transplanting and plant-spacing are all carried out in a specially stipulated manner which is more demanding of accuracy and labour time than customary husbandry.

Change from the traditional to the new technology implies a step away from an agriculture adapted to and relying on a particular environment and towards a much higher degree of domination of this environment in the interests of food production. Such a transformation has already occurred and continues to occur in those countries which lie within the direct ambit of the industrial revolution, and it is in these countries where the problems of environmental deterioration are most critically raised. For rural cultivators in the Third World countries, the most immediately visible implications of this transformation is that agronomic dependence tends to replace self-sustaining local production/consumption systems, in two ways:

(*a*) chemicals, machinery and fuel must be obtained by cultivators from the industrial sectors of their own countries or else imported from the countries which produce them, and (*b*) ultimate control over the correct cultivation recipes, recommended 'packages' and other technological knowhow is vested in distant and often foreign research centres and experimental stations.

In a market-dominated society, the agronomic necessity of obtaining production inputs from the industrial sector categorically requires the cultivator so to reorganize his economy as to be assured of producing a standard minimum surplus which can be marketed in order to pay for the purchased inputs and for any interest due on the loan needed to buy them. And while a number of cultivators in any locality would certainly have been producing and marketing regular surpluses and paying for them by means of credit prior to the arrival of the new technology, in all areas where small 'family farms' have been involved, this new requirement is a drastic one for most, so much so indeed that they were unable to meet it.

Indeed a large part of the 'social and economic implications' of the new technology is connected with the requirement which the market society imposes upon the majority of cultivators in the developing countries: that they should become businessmen competent in market operations and small-scale financing and receptive to science-generated information about cropping practices, in place of being 'artisan' cultivators obtaining family livelihood direct from their production, with variable surpluses offered on the market, on the basis of tradition and locally valid practices of husbandry. So the central theme of the research turned about the situation of the peasantries and the agricultural labour force of Third World countries as they are urged to accept ever-increasing incorporation in the market networks and institutions of the larger world systems, and more specifically as cultivators are urged to accept new cultivation 'packages' and to embark on entrepreneurial agriculture based on credit.

Cultivators and labourers figure in the drama in two distinct roles which are nevertheless joined together in the peasant family: on the one hand as producers of most of the developing world's food crops, and on the other as the bulk of the world's poor, amongst whom malnutrition and seasonal hunger are endemic.

Programmes promoting the 'new technology'

The yield-raising chemical genetic technology was welcomed by those countries experiencing scarcity of irrigated land for producing staple foodgrain for their increasing populations. These land-poor countries are mainly in Asia (as will be seen from the accompanying tables) and the crops were rice and what. The new seeds were produced by the International Centre for the Improvement of Maize and Wheat in Mexico (CIMMYT) and the International Centre for Rice Research (IRRI) in the Philippines. Each Centre produced a sequence of varieties which were experimented with and submitted to further selection in the countries for which they were considered appropriate. Further international centres have been set up in the last few years in different plant or climate specializations, but the account given in this paper refers essentially to the products of these two centres (Dalrymple, 1974a).

Tables 8.1 and 8.2 provide a picture of the spread of the technology in Asia, using as indicator that percentage of the total wheat or rice which was planted in HYVs (the 'high-yielding varieties' originating in IRRI and CIMMYT) year by year since 1965–66. The very rapid changeover to HYVs took place as a result of organized programmes in the countries listed. (By programme we refer to a blueprint for a set of measures to facilitate and promote the correct use of the technology, and also the 'performance' or attempted realization of the norms of the blueprint.) The main components of such programmes were the following:

(1) A technological 'package' or recipe produced in scientific research centres and designed to fit the environmental conditions of the region in which it is to be applied.

(2) Arrangements whereby knowledge of this technology could be communicated to cultivators.

(3) Measures to ensure the availability of physical inputs such as HYV seeds, fertilizers, pesticides, machinery and fuel.

(4) Measures to favour the prospect of profitable sale sufficiently attractive to compensate for the greatly increased production costs and risks involved.

(5) Indispensably, some system of credit so that the payment for inputs and additional cultivation expenses could be financed, pending the receipt of income from the sale of the product after harvest.

In most cases all these components required intervention by the state in the functioning of the market economy. Sometimes these were provided by a co-ordinated set of services. In other cases the state provided a minimum of services but facilitated the expansion of the private sector to look after them or gave every encouragement to transnational corporations and their local affiliates. In a number of cases strong and effective organizations of cultivators were able to set up co-operative bodies to purchase and distribute inputs on terms favourable to themselves. In still other cases the state itself set up the organization for direct distribution.

Obviously one essential for launching such programmes was a genuine political will on the part of the dominant political élites, and this was born of the knowledge that external food dependence was likely to involve partial surrender of political independence and also to make heavy demands on foreign exchange, while periodic food shortages and high prices would threaten internal support, especially amongst sensitive town populations.

Another problem which has haunted programmes is the contradiction between their declared intention of operating according to the principles of equity and the harsh realities of competition between unequals which prevails in actual social and economic relations in the societies in question. The contradiction does not necessarily manifest itself at the 'pilot' stage of the project, where hand-picked staff (with a high level of professional dedication and consequently

Table 8.1. Estimated area planted to high-yielding varieties of rice (hectares)

	1965–66	1966–67	1967–68	1968–69	1969–70	1970–71	1971–72	1972–73 (prelim)
Bangladesh	–	200	67 200	152 200	263 900	460 100	623 600	1 069 600
Burma	–	–	3 400	166 900	143 000	190 900	185 100	199 200
Colombia	–	–	–	–	–	–	125 400	165 820
India	7 100	888 400	1 785 000	2 681 000	4 343 500	5 589 200	7 411 400	8 639 100
Indonesia	–	–	–	198 000	826 000	913 000	1 338 000	1 521 000
Korea (South)	–	–	–	–	–	–	2 700	187 000
Laos	–	360	1 200	2 000	2 000	53 600	30 000	50 000
Malaysia	42 300	62 700	90 700	96 100	132 400	164 600	196 900	217 300
Mexico	–	–	–	–	–	–	100 000	95 000
Nepal	–	–	–	42 500	49 800	67 800	81 600	177 300
Pakistan	–	80	4 000	308 000	501 400	550 400	728 500	643 500
Philippines	–	82 600	653 000	1 012 800*	1 354 000	1 565 000	1 827 000	1 752 000
Sri Lanka	–	–	–	7 000	26 300	29 500	29 600	17 600
Thailand*	–	–	–	–	5 000	115 000	315 000	350 000
Vietnam (South)	–	–	500	40 500	201 500	502 000	674 000	835 000
TOTAL (rounded)	49 400	1 034 300	2 605 000	4 706 000	7 848 800	10 201 100	13 668 800	15 919 420

*Unofficial estimate

Source: Dalrymple (1974a).

Table 8.2. Proportion of total wheat area planted to high-yielding varieties (per cent)

Country	1965–66	1966–67	1967–68	1968–69	1969–70	1970–71	1971–72	1972–73
Afghanistan	–	negl.	1.0	5.2	6.2	10.7	13.3	18.4
Algeria	–	–	–	–	2.2	6.7	14.5	27.9
Bangladesh	–	–	–	7.2	7.6	11.3	11.8	17.7
India	negl.	4.2	19.6	30.0	29.6	35.5	41.1	51.5
Iran	–	–	–	0.2	2.1	6.3	6.4	6.9
Iraq	–	–	0.3	2.0	9.6	9.0	45.2	22.9
Jordan	–	–	–	4.0	4.1	4.0	5.0	10.0
Lebanon	–	–	negl.	0.7	4.1	11.7	18.8	31.3
Morocco*	–	–	negl.	0.3	2.5	4.8	10.0	13.4
Nepal	1.2	5.2	12.9	25.9	33.5	43.0	50.6	65.8
Pakistan	0.1	1.9	16.0	38.0	43.0	52.3	56.7	55.9
Syria	–	–	–	–	–	4.3	6.8	21.2
Tunisia	–	–	0.1	1.8	7.1	10.7	6.0	10.4
Turkey	–	negl.	2.1	7.0	7.6	7.8	8.0	8.0†

*Based on unofficial estimates of HYV area.
†Based on 1971–72 HYV area.

Source: Dalrymple 1974a.

Table 8.3. Proportion of total rice area planted to high-yielding varieties (per cent)

Country	1965–66	1966–67	1967–68	1968–69	1969–70	1970–71	1971–72	1972–73
Bangladesh	–	negl.	0.7	1.6	2.6	4.6	6.7	11.1
Burma	–	–	negl.	3.3	2.9	3.6	3.6	4.2
India	negl.	2.5	4.9	7.3	11.5	14.9	19.9	24.7
Indonesia	–	–	–	2.4	10.3	11.2	15.9	18.0
Korea (South)	–	–	–	–	–	–	0.2	15.6
Laos	–	negl.	0.2	0.3	0.2	6.0	-3.3	5.5
Malaysia	10.0	14.7	20.6	20.1	26.4	30.9	35.7	38.0
Nepal	–	–	–	3.7	4.4	5.8	6.3	14.8
Pakistan	–	negl.	0.3	19.8	29.9	36.6	50.0	43.4
Philippines	–	2.7	19.8	30.4*	43.5	50.3	56.3	56.3*
Sri Lanka	–	–	–	1.0	3.9	4.4	4.2	2.5
Thailand*	–	–	–	–	0.1	1.5	4.0	4.9
Vietnam (South)	–	–	negl.	1.6	8.3	19.9	25.9	32.1

*Based on unofficial estimates of HYV area.

Source: Dalrymple 1974a.

Table 8.4. Total HYV area in developing countries (excluding countries with centrally planned economies)

Crop year	Wheat	Rice	Total
1965–66	9 300	49 400	58 700
1966–67	651 100	1 034 300	1 685 400
1967–68	4 123 400	2 605 000	6 728 400
1968–69	8 012 700	4 706 000	12 718 700
1969–70	8 845 100	7 848 800	16 693 900
1970–71	11 344 100	10 201 100	21 545 200
1971–72	14 083 600	13 443 400	27 537 000
1972–73 (prelim)	16 815 500*	15 658 600	32 474 100

*Includes Turkey at 1971–72 level

Sources: Dalrymple 1974a.

Table 8.5. Trends in per capita food production (1961–65 average = 100)

	Latin America	Far East[1]	Near East[2]	Africa[3]
1968	99	100	104	100
1969	102	102	104	102
1970	102	105	103	101
1971	100	102	101	102
1972 (prelim)	97	97	(106)	(101)

[1] Excluding China and Japan
[2] Excluding Israel
[3] Excluding South Africa

Source: FAO (1973), pp. 182–188.

an alternative motivation to that of class and individual interest) are able to administer fair shares of inputs which have been measured out carefully to cover global needs within the pilot area. However, when the programme is applied over wide areas with a diluted staff, and when inputs are in short supply, then competition is likely to penetrate the system and exclude the weak from participating. Indeed the very success of the technology is likely to force inputs into short supply and to raise their price or simply to create a black market. Prevailing business interests may tolerate controls and concessionary intervention in the protected area of the pilot programme but not in the national market place.

Some Agronomic Problems of the New Technology

Work on selective breeding and testing of cultivation practices and chemicals produced spectacular results in the yields of rice and wheat at the research stations. Under optimum conditions yields could be increased several-fold, and where this could be coupled with a shortening of the vegetative cycle, making possible a cropping intensity which permits two or three harvests in a single year, the scientists' achievements seemed to hold out dazzling prospects. Newspapers and politicians talked of 'miracle seeds' but overlooked the differences in cultivation conditions between the experimental stations and the very varied conditions to be found in the millions of farms in which the new technology was to be applied. But the research centres planted their seeds in conditions of expensively created artifice far beyond the scope and means of the average farmer. In contrast, the local varieties and even the locally improved varieties, although comparatively low yielders, could thrive within the range of variation of local physical conditions. The advantages of the experimental station for the high-yielding varieties was in respect of availabilities of the correct physical inputs, properly levelled fields, controlled irrigation, insulation from many forms of disease and pest, availability of scientific apparatus for the measurement of change in nature, an easy availability of technical advice to deal with problems as they emerged and an expert and constantly available labour force.

The new varieties in question were tailored to meet the needs of wet tropical countries either with irrigation or with reliable rainfall. Most Asian rice-growing areas were excluded from their use either because they were unirrigated 'upland' areas with uncertain rainfall or because they required special varieties of rice capable of adapting themselves to flood conditions or because of other climatic unsuitability. The success of wheat was based on the rapid development of cultivation in certain highly suitable areas such as North-West Mexico and the sub-Himalayan plains, in both of which irrigation networks had been built and in which the expansion of wheat production by means of the new technology was supported by equally rapid investment in tubewells, through which reliable and controlled use of water could be achieved. In attempting to assess the production effects of HYVs of rice, it is important to remember that the varieties developed so far are only suitable for a restricted proportion of Asian rice lands.

In the millions of farms to which the various packages or cultivation recipes for the new varieties of rice and wheat were proffered, conditions were extraordinarily varied. Even though deemed by national and international authorities to be favourable, in some areas soils were reasonably homogeneous over large areas while in others they were extremely varied. This was especially true in mountainous or hilly country and it means that any generally recommended combination of fertilizer is going to be correct only for a limited portion of the area. Losses from inappropriate fertilizer recommendations have had discouraging effects in some areas. Another important variation in soils is their moisture-retentive character, which affects yields drastically and requires appropriate differences in package. But the most important cause of variation in yields seems to be in water supply. In most areas so-called irrigation systems consist of confused and heterogenous mixtures of large-scale canal systems, open wells with primitive human or animal-powered pumping or lifting mechanisms, rain catchment networks and, more recently, tubewells. In the sub-Himalayan plains of India, canal seepage, waterlogging and alkalinity are frequent. Distribution from canal outlets by unlined ditches is extremely wasteful and in many rice areas, irrigation is carried out by a field-to-field method without water courses at all. Excessive fragmentation and the complex pattern of individual properties is accompanied by disorganization, lack of collective responsibility, and a ruthless struggle to obtain or to retain access in the face of the superior power of large landowners. The large canal systems themselves are seldom under rational management concerned with agricultural needs. A further important cause of variation in yields has to do with the quality and amount of inputs used, for instance, the quality of seeds is not always high. A major cause of lower yields is to be found in the use of inadequate amounts of fertilizer and untimely or delayed use of both fertilizer and plant protection chemicals due to poorly organized or overloaded delivery systems or local scarcity leading to a black market in supplies.

Further enquiry into problems of input supplies and delivery systems leads in two directions. On the one hand these problems are frequently inherent in a low level of infrastructure — unreliable transport, storage and distribution facilities, disorganized regulatory services, and other well-known insufficiencies. On the other hand, a poor demand for these inputs takes us into the factors determining the economic choices made by cultivators — whether or not to use some or all the recommended practices and materials and how to pay for them — but these are discussed in the section below.

There remains the thorny problem of the transfer of the technology *as an idea*. Quite apart from the economic constraints on adoption decisions, it is evident that cultivators who are accustomed to look to scientific centres for their agricultural knowhow and to industry for their inputs are likely to take the new technology in their stride, while those whose knowhow is passed down by older local cultivators and whose inputs are products of their own farms and villages face a difficult and complex transformation. The discontinuity implied by the 'jump' into this new and exogenous technology is commented upon by the economist Shigeru Ishikawa (1970), who questions the assumption that so radical a substitution of the science-based technology for the customary one can be easily achieved. He recommends the introduction of 'measures to accelerate the improvements which start from the existing state of technology' and he reports that in Japan the phase of agricultural development in which the growth rate was highest — the years immediately preceding 1910 — was that in which greatest emphasis was placed by the state experimental stations on 'varietal comparison and pure-line selection among native varieties'. In other words, Japanese cultivators made their fastest and most generalized advances in productivity as a result of the step-by-step improvement of their own local varieties and other improvements which set out from the locally existing state of technology. The same writer (Ishikawa, 1970, p. 6) also recalls reports published by the Asian Agricultural Survey of 1967 which served as a guideline for Asian Development Bank policy in the years immediately following and which stress the importance, for introducing new varieties of rice, 'of bringing about a definite quality improvement of the existing irrigation facilities all over the region . . . (with) focus on the construction of a terminal water and drainage system which is non-existent in most of the existing irrigated rice fields'.

The most serious estimates made of the overall production results of the introduction of the new technology in Asia are those of Dana Dalrymple, who has been associated with the US Department of Agriculture and USAID for several years with special responsibilities for monitoring the so-called 'green revolution' and who has undoubtedly had access to the most reliable data available in non-communist countries. In a recent publication (Dalrymple, 1974b) he refers to his working estimate, 'based on a combination of sources and hunches', that the HYV wheat package when applied on an extensive scale, might result in a relative yield ratio of 2.0, while for rice the ratio might be 1.25. He then infers from some recent survey data from the Philippines that these estimates may have been unduly high. The survey in question shows that the comparison between HYV and local lowland rice yields gave a ratio of 1.19 and if the area of comparison was reduced to eliminate areas of rain-fed rice from the lowland area, and simply to compare yields of local rice with yields of HYVs in lands considered suitable for HYVs, then the ratio dropped still further to 1.10, that is, an HYV yield of 110 against a local seed yield of 100. More recently he has reduced his estimate of the wheat ratio from 2.00 to 1.50 in view of the decline in aggregate HYV yields which he considers to reflect the extension of the technology in the Middle East (West Asia) to drier lands.

Without wishing to diminish the importance of grain yield per crop, the importance of modifications of photo-period sensitivity must be given full weight since this innovation made possible shorter growing periods and intensified land use, so that in certain conditions and with suitable cropping combinations it has been possible to use the same land for three or more crops in a single calendar year. However such an intensification involves radical modifications in infrastructure and in the organization of labour. It also requires experiments in cropping systems in the field and as a result calls for time before its potential can be exploited. But research facilitating greater cropping intensity can well have more positive effects on production than research increasing actual crop yields.

To sum up, the success achieved in wheat production technology is exceptional. However, wheat is the main food crop for rural populations in limited areas only of the tropical land-poor countries. Even in Mexico wheat is a prime source of urban food, while the prevailing rural subsistence crop is maize, in the field productivity of which little progress has been made.

The problem of adequate food for the Asian masses remains and it is a problem of rice production and distribution. It will not be solved by some new 'breakthrough' by the plant breeders but by a combination of approaches. The most important of these are the rational management of land and irrigation within land units determined not by proprietary interests but by geographical expediency, rationalized access of manpower to land, and the improvement of farming systems as a result of research whose point of departure is a full grasp of existing practice and conditions. Within such a framework the new technology can undoubtedly be elaborated so as to contribute to the necessary long-run productivity increases. The improvement of distribution is, however, another story, which belongs to the wider field of development strategy.

Socioeconomic Implications

Programmes to raise the production of foodgrain by means of the promotion of the new technology have had varied socioeconomic outcomes in the many countries into which they have been introduced. These differences are related to social, political and economic differences in the national societies themselves, and in the different regions of each country. In this respect the individuality of each situation depends on differences in agrarian structure, on the degree of industrial development and of infrastructural elaboration, on the capacity of governments to establish efficient services, on the style of development pursued by the government and the extent to which it enjoys or looks for political support from one or onother of the classes engaged in the productive process. Accounts have already been given of the main features of these programmes,[1] and no attempt will be made in this paper to summarize them. In discussing socioeconomic aspects, we shall confine ourselves mainly to what can be generalized from those non-industrialized countries with market economies which espoused the new technology as a major step in their development, that is, India, Pakistan, Sri Lanka, Bangladesh, Indonesia, Malaysia and the Philippines. We shall start with four such generalizations about elementary features of the technology and shall then outline the socioeconomic dynamics which they set in motion, yet whose outcomes may differ widely.

(1) The HYVs require a greater input of energy per unit of land — especially of nitrogen and of motive force — for a more complex, more controlled husbandry than is required in customary cultivation routines, in which local varieties are used which rely heavily upon their environment and are adapted to its idiosyncrasies. Amounts of nitrogen in the quantity required by the recommended packages are such that in most cases this input can only be supplied by manufactured artificial fertilizer. Irrigation requirements are best satisfied by canal systems or by ground water, and in practice controlled supplies of ground water, requiring oil-driven or electric pumps, have been the most effective suppliers of controlled moisture. In most of the areas under consideration, efficient irrigation is therefore also a consumer of energy.

(2) In practice, therefore, nitrogen supplies for fertilizer, and power and machinery for controlled irrigation (and often for traction) have to be purchased outside the agricultural sector. In addition, the heavy use of fertilizer and the absence of acquired immunities in the new plants frequently means that chemicals must be purchased in order to defend the growing plant against the profusion of pests and weeds which the technology fosters. Moreover, the new

seeds themselves must be bought on the market, so that adoption of the recommended practices greatly increases the *mercantility* of the unit of production (farm); that is to say, the new technology requires that the cultivator become a market operator for obtaining his inputs and for disposing of the product. Obviously very few cultivators produce or exchange quite outside the market, but adoption of the technology requires that market calculations play a central part in the organization of production, thus giving new importance to commercial skills and requiring to be reconciled to habitual reasoning and planning around predictable family needs and seasonal fluctuations.

(3) The necessary *mercantility* of the new technology elevates the creditworthiness of the producer into an asset of the highest importance, on a par with skill in husbandry. In practice this means that cultivators owning substantial property, particularly in land, can acquire credit at a reasonable price, whilst those whose hold on property is weak or who possess none at all and whose only attributes are their strength and their skill, are obliged to put their head into the noose of debt (informal credit) in order to obtain the necessary elements for the practice of the technology. Only in relatively few instances have institutional credit facilities been easily available for cultivators without property.

(4) In respect of the practice of the new technology, cultivators become dependent on centres of expert knowledge and supplies from outside their localities, and out of reach of the network of relations over which they can exert some influence.

To sum up, then, the new technology requires increases in the use of energy of various kinds, and of machinery and chemicals from the industrial sector. The producer is therefore more deeply involved in market relations and creditworthiness emerges as a prime attribute, while at the same time, in respect of knowhow and supplies, the cultivator's technological dependence is greatly increased.

The Expansion of Entrepreneurial or Capitalist Farming

These 'structural' trends arising from the introduction of the new technology, had the effect, in market economies. of favouring a surge forward of entrepreneurial or capitalist farming. Moreover two features of the strategy of most of these programmes have fitted them with a further bias towards polarization and uneven growth — namely, the concentration of programmes and inyestment in the best agricultural areas and the 'progressive farmer' approach. The first of these elements of policy has much to recommend it both from the point of view of those who wished to mark up rapid and early successes in adoption and yields, and who wished to build on the highest possible levels of existing investment in infrastructure and productive equipment. An alternative to this policy would involve a spreading of investment and the application of agricultural and social sciences to the problems· of cultivators, epecially small ones, working in indifferent and marginal lands as well as those enjoying optimal conditions. Just what it would take to obtain successes by such a policy, both in terms of overall production results and in terms of raising the farming and living standards of the poorer rural sectors remains a question for study and debate. But it would be hard to get such a policy accepted in political and administrative quarters in a society which relied on market forces for its driving impulse — the political will would be lacking.

The other element of policy common to most programmes and tending to accentuate polarization was the approach to the generality of cultivators by concentrating first on so-called 'progressive farmers'. It is of course true that enthusiasm for innovation varies amongst cultivators, and may be found amongst poor ones. But in practice the 'progressive farmer' commonly turned out to be the cultivator with relatively ample landholdings and access to capital as well as reasonably easy relations with the 'authorities' and an above-average education. Indeed it was seldom difficult to persuade such farmers to adopt the package recommendations since they had already made the critical leap into predominantly commercial farming and recognized the deal offered as a good one: inputs, credit and technical advice were assured and in some cases the product price was supported or at least subject to a guaranteed minimum. The tactic was widely successful and in most cases the first year's operation, carried out on the best lands of the 'progressive farmers', was rewarded with markedly higher yields. Where successful, the results encouraged other cultivators to experiment, many of them less well-endowed with land and capital and less well-connected. In optimum areas even poor cultivators strained themselves to obtain credit for inputs. But with the wider diffusion of the HYVs, average yields declined and yields varied greatly on account of the patchy quality of irrigation systems, irregular supplies, increased disease and improperly applied methods.

Where the 'progressives' were able to demonstrate the unusual profitability of the new technology organized in capitalist farms, cultivation itself as an enterprise began to appear attractive to those with some capital resources. Landlords who had formerly been content to receive share-rents in kind from meagre harvests were tempted to become direct producers, repossessing their rented land from their tenants to work it with hired labour, or to mechanize and to work with family labour. Other important consequences where the new profitability became an established fact, were an increased demand for land and consequently a sharp upward trend in land values, and a vigorous demand for commercial tenancies on a cash rental basis. Agricultural entrepreneurship also became an attractive option as a sideline for professionals and as a retirement occupation for civil servants, ex-officers of the armed forces and other middle-class groups who would not have considered it before. Larger surpluses, greater profitability and increased mercantility also attracted capital into transport, custom hire of equipment, machine maintenance, and in special cases into manufacture and various ancillary services. In this way, initial investment in programmes deployed in agriculturally developed areas to push the new technology have in a number of cases contributed to economic growth. But this is confined mainly to wheat-growing areas.

Another striking change which accompanied this advance in entrepreneurial farming was their improved productivity, noticed especially in India and Pakistan. Before the new technology established the profitability of cereal production, the yield level of larger farms compared unfavourably with small ones farmed directly by the owner or tenant and his family. Husbandry received more care and more labour time, and the smaller cultivator frequently spent more per hectare on production costs. But as entrepreneurial farming developed on the larger farms, it overtook the small family farm in intensity and in production costs as the entrepreneurial cultivator, his credit assured, calculated profits to be collected on each of the factors of production separately. The logical path he followed was to spend freely on fertilizer and plant-defence chemicals and to economize on labour by using tractors and by other forms of mechanization. It is this determination to cut costs per unit of production which engenders his expansionism and encourages him to extend his farm lands by purchase, or by cash-renting if he cannot find land to purchase, and thus to enjoy the full economies of scale on pumping equipment, tractors and harvesting equipment.

Pursuing the logic of the socioeconomic changes which accompany the widespread adoption of the new technology in areas in which locally adapted and customary technology has hitherto predominated, they can be summed up in the concept 'incorporation' used to mean the persistent outward expansion of the great industrial powers and their compulsion to incorporate peripheral human groups and resources in their communication and transport systems, their international market structure (including the manpower market) and their institutions and cultural forms (Pearse, 1975, chapter VII). Like many other programmes, both international and national, for rural development in Third World countries, programmes for the diffusion of the new technology are by their origin and nature agents of this incorporative process. So the question about the implications and outcomes of the large-scale introduction of the new technology must be answered within the framework of the larger question: what are to be the 'terms of incorporation' for individuals, entrepreneurs, proprietors, tribal communities, labourers without land, etc. In areas where such introduction takes place, who are the beneficiaries and do those with deficient diets eat better?

The Terms of Incorporation for the Poor Cultivator

The expansion of entrepreneurial agriculture following the pattern outlined, even where it contributed to the increase of overall cereal production, failed to make an extensive impression on the central problem of rural development. It did not perceptibly improve levels of livelihood, nor its quality, for the poorer sections of the rural populations, which may be considered as including between one-third and two-thirds of the national populations in the countries studied. Moreover, it has failed to prevent a further impoverishment of a considerable proportion of these poor. We shall now outline what were shown by the research to be the most important reasons for these relative failures.

The studies showed that cultivators who had no more land than an area capable of supporting a minimal family livelihood suffered handicaps in most cases which prevented them from benefiting from the higher production potential of the technology, in spite of the willingness of such cultivators to devote increased labour to production. These handicaps originated in a complex of factors associated with their socioeconomic situation, and for convenience they can be summed up under three headings:

(1) Minor diseconomies of scale, especially in relation to draught animals and pumping equipment, but also in relation to management — the travelling and bureaucratic operations which had to be performed to make use of special facilities were too greedy of time and money in relation to the amount of benefit to be received on a very small plot of land, and they interfered with other sources of income.

(2) The small farm in precapitalist agriculture is essentially self-provisioning, most of the labour requirements being met by family members, with material inputs coming from the farm itself or from the neighbourhood. The first call on the product is for feeding the family, but the seasonality and variability of harvests, and the reduced size of farms makes even this provisioning a precarious undertaking so that tolerable survival can only be assured by incurring debt in bad years and in sudden emergencies. This necessity while it may prevent destitution and starvation from overtaking the family, imposes a permanent state of dependence (and in some cases subjection) on the richer neighbour, on the relation, on a moneylender or village storekeeper, or on a landlord. Such a condition of indebtedness excludes the poor cultivator from the necessary state of creditworthiness referred to above as indispensable for moving into the new technology. It is not possible to establish the point in the size-scale below which this condition is likely to rule out the adoption of the technology, but if we use the idea of 'livelihood threshold' as roughly a farm size which makes possible the production of family needs in calories plus a further 50 per cent to be used or sold to purchase supplementary foods and other essentials, then the successful adoption is not likely to become general until farms surpass this threshold by several degrees.

Moreover the qualitative transition from self-provisioner to petty commercial farmer is a significant cultural leap.

(3) The problems involved in making it possible for the cultivator with an excessively small holding to increase production by adopting the new technology is obviously much more than an economic one. To make the best use of a certain productive technology as a small entrepreneur 'strength in the market place' is required, and this is what the small peasant producer most lacks. His economic weakness and usual negative capital situation (indebtedness) is complemented by a lack of social power resulting from occupying an inferior position in the ordering of classes in exceptionally differentiated and often hierarchical national societies. This situation weakens still further the bargaining position of the small peasant and potential entrepreneur when he is

obliged to compete for the elements of production, essential services and consumer goods, or to obtain a good price for his product. This social inferiority may be determined by his ascription to an ethnic group or caste or simply to a class recognized as enjoying restricted rights only; it is likely to be reinforced by exclusion from easy access to information systems through which legal, commercial and technical knowledge necessary for successful entrepreneurship could be obtained. Nor is it likely that his entrepreneurship can be aided by favoured personal access to system managers and nexus people such as the bank officials, extension officers, irrigation controllers etc., usually available through kinship and class-fellowship to better-off and 'progressive' farmers. In practice, as a result of this social inferiority, the common run of rural cultivators is likely to make poor bargains over the entrepreneurial activities which are essential for him to get expert advice on a new pest, ensure his turn for canal water, queue for scarce supplies of fertilizer, obtain timely services of a hired tractor and get together the necessary documents needed to secure institutional credit.

By way of illustration, two of the numerous case studies quoted in the UNRISD overview are given below, in resumé. One of these, a study of the effects of various programmes of rural development in four villages of the state of Uttar Pradesh in India (Hale, n.d.) shows how the class/caste hierarchy compartmentalizes relations in these villages and ensures the cornering by village élites not only of government facilities supposedly available on an equity basis, but also technical and other information diffused by radio and the printed word. The lower strata were found to have been excluded from places where public broadcasts were relayed, and also being illiterate were still ignorant of most of the essential data content of welfare and development programmes several years after their introduction, including that related to the new technology and the facilities available for obtaining inputs and credit. This was accounted for quite simply by the obvious conflict of interest in relation to the availability, docility and price of human labour. So long as an important section of the rural population was landless, the numbered élite whose extensive holdings required labour could obtain it at a low price. But official schemes to distribute state lands to the landless or to improve the entrepreneurial potential of the poorest cultivators were seen as damaging to élite interests, and successfully opposed by maintaining a close monopoly on incoming information, inputs and welfare measures.

A second study (Franke, 1972) is about a rice-growing area of Central Java. The whole region is characterized by skilled husbandry and high level of cropping intensity in excellent climatic conditions, but it suffers from excessive pressure on land and offers little by way of occupational alternatives to agriculture. As a result there is excessive land poverty and landlessness and a tight unremitting struggle for existence. An intensive study was made by Franke of the village of Lestari in 1972, when he found that of its 266 families, 168 had no arable land at all or simply garden plots, and the total area in paddy, the main food crop, was no more than 75 hectares, which, however, was cropped twice a year, and it was roughly calculated that normal harvests could produce sufficient food for 150 of the 266 families. As a result of conditions like these, in many parts of Central Java the institution of labour debt has become widespread. Variations in family income of the poorer majority, whether derived in kind from the family's farming activities or in cash from wages or gains on petty trading, created occasions when food for survival was lacking. If the needy family were that of a cultivator whose harvest was still many weeks off, he might raise a loan in cash or kind in return for a promise to sell the harvest or by recourse to a 'green sale', that is, by selling his crop while still growing in the fields at a reduced price to the lender-buyer. Or he might receive his loan in return for the pledging of his future labour to the lender at reduced wages. The effect of this institution, therefore, was to lower future production costs for the cultivators who disposed of surpluses, and this made it possible for them to accumulate further production capital. For the cultivator with lands which did not attain the livelihood threshold, some security against periodic hunger was provided, but at the cost of decreased income from labour sold and decreased freedom to choose how to dispose of his labour. It was found that 109 family heads had incurred labour-debt obligations, and these supplied cheap labour when required to seventeen surplus-producing cultivators. Franke shows that these arrangements provide some security for the poorer families, but in the pattern of general dependence which involves the submission of the borrower to the lender. Although the government programme introducing the new technology made credit available to cultivators, none of those who had incurred labour-debt took advantage of it. It is easy to see that this group, characterized by lack of reserves and vulnerability to seasonal fluctuations of income, would be dubious about substantial new debt-involvements even though the prospects of greater gains at harvest time had been demonstrated. From his overall knowledge of the order of social relations in the village, however, Franke considers that a move by one of the labour-debtors to use the new technology by participating in the institutional arrangements of the government would have amounted to 'an act of political resistance to the control exercised by the large capital-holders'. Indeed he considers that 'the entrepreneurial activity of the poor would be a threat to the entire structure of privilege and security built up not only for the poor themselves but also for the wealthy who receive most of the rewards'.

The 'Talents-Effect' and the Persistence of Poverty

Perhaps the most important aspect of the rural situation illustrated by these two case studies is the fact that rich and poor do not simply coexist. The accumulation of land by the rich creates a demand for labour which the poor are obliged to satisfy because of their land-poverty or landlessness; moreover, the entrepreneurial success of the rich is made possible by the hunger and importunacy of the poor cultivator who is obliged to surrender his bargaining freedom and even to pledge his future labour at a reduced price in order to sustain his family and meet current obligations. Excessive pressure on land for cultivation and a steadily growing population intensify and dramatize the operation of this principle. However, the descriptions make it clear that the economic peculiarities of land and labour are not alone in making exploitation possible: the advantage of the buyer of labour and the handicaps of the seller also rest on local class systems involving privilege and the consequent acquiescence by the majority (voluntarily or involuntarily) in the use of sanctions such as physical punishments, differential access to information about legal, administrative and financial systems by means of literacy and learning, the cornering of political influence and on other social factors. The interplay of the social and the economic which tends to strengthen the rich and enrich the powerful, as well as to weaken the poor and impoverish the weak, is so ubiquitous a phenomen and so fundamental in its operation that some simple phrase is required which goes beyond systematic economic concepts and is more widely human in its application. We are therefore adopting the phrase 'talents-effect'[2] to refer to situations in which this process of polarization is induced. At base we are using this phrase to connote the most elementary axiom of competitive behaviour, namely, that the more *talents* the player has at his disposal, the more he is able to pile up, using talents to mean *counters* in the universal game of seeking a livelihood. The greater the number and variety of counters, the better equipped is the player, while the holder of few counters has the greatest difficulty in retaining those few. While other societies, including many of the rich industrial ones, have developed mechanisms to control the momentum of this process, Third World rural societies undergoing further penetration by national and world market forces and 'modern' institutions are critically vulnerable. Economic growth or 'development by capitalist penetration of the prime zones of production and incorporation in the international economy appears to carry with it a dynamic poverty-generating principle unless the processes can be understood and the political will inspire governments to counteract economic polarization.

The Rural Crisis and the 'Employment' Approach

One approach to this manifestly dangerous situation which threatens growing loss of livelihood and marginalization of rural majorities consists of treating it as an employment problem and focusing research on the 'employment effects' of programmes and policies. The employment approach is supposed to lead to the allocation of public and private investment in such a way that where unemployment is increasing, production and other forms of economic activity deliberately promote labour-intensive technologies and forms of work. The employment effect of the new technology was reviewed in many of the UNRISD green revolution studies, and in the overview, and here we refer briefly to the gist of the conclusions.

More labour is required to perform the more complicated routines of husbandry called for by the new technology, and increased harvests also demand increased manpower and more transport per hectare cropped, but the net balance of labour required for the same global product will be less. However, since most of the new varieties have a shorter vegetative cycle and may be more flexibly fitted into the seasons of the year, double and even treble-cropping, when introduced, greatly increases both the amount of the product and labour requirements *per hectare per year*. This big jump represented by the successful intensification of cropping (that is, the introduction of double or treble-cropping) cannot in normal circumstances be achieved without considerable mechanization, especially as a means of introducing controlled irrigation and of accelerating harvesting and land preparation, so that the planting of the new crop can follow the harvesting of the old with appropriate despatch. It has been estimated that the tractor, used for land preparation, harvesting, threshing and transport, roughly reduces labour requirements per crop to the same extent that the new technology increased them. The mechanization of irrigation may displace labour used for more primitive systems thereof, but usually its net effect is to increase farming intensity and hence labour requirements. However, introduction of fuller mechanization such as tractor-powered dispersal of weedicide and fertilizer, aerial spraying and the use of combine-harvesters cuts back the labour force very radically. The combine-harvester has not yet become widespread in Asian wheat and rice cultivation, though it is drastically reducing employment opportunities in the more 'developed' areas of Latin America.

From this rough accountancy it can be inferred that government policy regulating the importation of machines and foreign exchange concessions, the subsidization of credit for mechanization and the control of the price and allocation of fuel and similar measures is capable of tipping the balance between more employment and less. However experience shows that governments are loath to intervene in this sense. For should the new technology be exploited profitably by entrepreneurial farmers, they are likely to increase their overall influence on policy accordingly, and if they can increase overall production, then the goal of maintaining levels of employment is likely to appear unimportant and at best the policy-makers are likely to opt for higher expenditure on public works for the hungry in place of food imports. Unemployment will be dismissed as a secondary ill which can be treated without affecting the whole balance of payments situation. Cases where governments have controlled mechanization in the interests of rural employment exist, but are not common, and the subvention (by means of foreign exchange and credit policy) of mechanization even though it is a cause of unemployment, has occurred. At the same time, we should not overlook the fact that the availability of employment does not guarantee that the remuneration and conditions of work will be such as to put an end to widespread malnutrition, ill-health and social tension. Labour may continue to be grossly underpaid.

Indeed there is some danger that by making the employment issue central, it comes to be too easily assumed that capitalist arrangements are a norm in rural life, with agricultural production already dichotomized between owners of the means of production and employed workers, and this certainly is not the case in respect of rural food production even though the trends point in that direction. In the rural Third World, most families still look to their own labour and their rustic tools, applied to whatever land they can obtain, to provide the bulk of the food component of their livelihoods. Cases where a substantial portion of the rural population belongs to landless families of a long-established landless social stratum are exceptional.

Finding the Correct Strategy

The general line of the strategy which has carried the new technology so far seems to be producing a steady slippage towards the further pauperization of a sector of the population the size of which varies from one country to another, and in some countries engulfs the majority of the population. This deterioration of conditions is not attributable to the new technology as such but it can be attributed to the joint operation of a type of economic growth which augments the talents-effect (expressed in economic polarization) coupled with a high rate of population increase. The strategy contributes to the increased profitability and the further capitalization of the initially well-endowed minority of cultivators and entrepreneurs of the agricultural sector in the already favoured farming areas in such a way as to put additional pressure on the undercapitalized majority. In relation to this group, the majority of cultivators with land slightly above or below the livelihood threshold are under pressure to maintain their economic viability, and are unable to improve their productive equipment and technology (tools, land and water). At the same time, there is downward pressure on real wages as the number of job-seekers moves beyond the level of population increase and no additional agricultural or urban jobs are created. But there are cases in which this slippage has been avoided and which are worth considering, namely Japan, China and Taiwan. Although the situation of each is unique, there are certain common features in the strategies adopted to deal with common problems of agricultural development.

Taiwan has made great progress in the productivity of agricultural land in food crops and yet has avoided the monopolization of profits by a class of entrepreneurial farmers with middle and large holdings and employing wage labour.[3] Holdings are extremely small but modernized, and though the family is the main source of labour, farmers are not concerned with self-provisioning: they want to do business. This peculiarity seems to be due to the fact that historically, Taiwan's rural population has for several generations been oriented to export cultivation, and as a result her farmers are entrepreneurs *par excellence*. Furthermore, for the whole of the present century the government of the country has been colonial or neo-colonial (occupation by Japan, followed by Chiang Kai-Shek and his mainlanders) and lacked an identity of interest with landed proprietors and large farmers who under other circumstances, and under an indigenous Taiwanese government might have become a powerful rural bourgeoisie. This unusual conjecture should be studied in relation to Taiwan's land reform and land-taxation policies, government investment in services aiding and facilitating small-scale agriculture and the formation and role of peasant organization as a political force and also as a basis for investment in infrastructure, land improvement, co-operative trading, processing industries and services supporting the small producer.

In Japan the level of agricultural technology has been raised steadily since the end of the last century by means of indigenous research on the basis of existing plant resources and systems of production. Moreover, while industrial development had absorbed a proportion of the increasing rural population, the avoidance of large-scale entrepreneurial agriculture has kept investment, credit and suitable technology flowing towards the small cultivator. Working farmers have also been able to represent their interests as a class through their organizations.

Like the other two, China excluded the large entrepreneurial farmer from the possibility of cornering resources and services. But unlike the other two she is committed politically to a society in which differences in material wealth are to be kept to a minimum while at the same time she must increase agricultural production in order to maintain her growing population and raise the productivity of labour in order to support an increasing non-agricultural sector (Stavis, 1974). Much could be learnt from the Chinese search for an adequate strategy by means of which to encompass her ends, but for the present paper it is the structure of productive organization in agriculture which is perhaps richest in lessons. Reference is made specifically to the hierarchical linking of *levels of capitalization* in such a way that, though inequalities may persist, especially between richer and poorer farms and regions, the talents-effect is kept from gathering economic and political momentum. Since 1962 the primary unit of agricultural production, known as the *workteam* has consisted of a group of families linked to one another by kinship and friendship and living together in the same village in which they enjoy possession of a defined segment of the village land. The economically active members of some twenty families might comprise such a workteam. Each family functions normally as a unit of consumption, and even as a unit of production and capitalization on a very small scale, in relation to backyard and household activities. The workteam is in fact a farm, run collectively by its participant families. This collective enjoys membership in a larger unit which may be a single large village or a grouping of smaller ones, known as a *brigade*, while a district of several villages corresponding to a network of brigades is linked to a market and transport centre and is known as a *commune*.

This system makes possible the insertion at the appropriate scale-level of the necessary specialized installations and functions required by economic life and of course of educational and social services. But each of these bodies is also capable of accumulating capital which can be invested in such a way as to benefit the sum of its constituents or else to benefit one or more of them. Thus a mechanism exists whereby serious inequalities within the different collective units can be compensated. While inequalities within the production team are likely to be transitory, responding to the cycle of family life and the age-grouping of its members, inequalities between production teams and villages within a commune, and — much more so — differences between communes across the whole vast country, are due to differences in the productivity of labour in different regions, on account of the differential distribution of fertility and of resources, of levels of investment in infrastructure and transport, of the availability of power, etc.

Burki (1969) in his study of the People's Communes, refers to 'state assistance to less developed regions of the country', and to 'massive financial and technical assistance to really poor production units'. He mentions also the diversification of the economies of poorer production units (presumably by external investment) and also by adopting a labour policy which ensures that recruitment for the non-agricultural labour force draws workers from poorer regions, thus raising resource availability *per capita* in that region's production teams. A further measure which has been reported is the regulation which obliges rich communes in areas suitable for the production of high quality commercial crops to continue to produce at least a portion of their own food needs in cereal staples rather than by maximizing profits with the commercial crop and purchasing food crops from outside. Others suggest that there has been some change of accent since the Cultural Revolution. While equality as a goal of policy has not been abandoned, less importance is given to the reallocation of resources and material aid from outside, and more to raising political consciousness and motivating renewed efforts at self-help and the achievement of self-sufficiency. More importance is also given to moral non-material motivations and numerous cases are reported of material gifts or the loan of experts and model workers from wealthier to poorer units.

Even though there are great differences between the social systems and institutional arrangements of the three countries quoted, yet there are certain features they share which we must associate with a picture of a generalized advance in the rural sector as regards both production and livelihood. Dichotomization between entrepreneur/owners and land-poor or landless workers has been avoided. An agricultural labour market is not the dominant provider of labour for production, and alternative occupation in wage-work is available in rural and urban manufacture and in the tertiary sector. The great majority of the working population has access to the means of agricultural production, either through small family properties or through larger collective farms in both of which they participate not only in labour but also in managerial decisions and gains from the sale of the product, and the level of their gains is influenced by the productivity of their labour. They also enjoy long-term benefits from the improvements of production technology by the accumulation and reinvestment of savings.

An important difference between these societies and those in which a bimodal scheme prevails is the position of the rural masses in relation to government policy measures and investment. In the case of the three countries quoted, the peasantry is central to the agricultural sector, and though they may be 'squeezed' their capacity to produce is essential to the policy. Moreover, in so far as agricultural producers have a voice in the formation of domestic and internal policy, this expresses the interests of the working cultivator rather than that of the non-labouring entrepreneur. In the bimodal agrarian structure (where capitalist and peasant agriculture coexist) this is not so, and the peasantry is liable to find itself pushed into limbo, with access to a diminishing family holding, and required to sell labour to rural or urban employers to make up the family livelihood. A number of facts conspire to produce this situation: the new entrepreneurial class, interested in cheap labour, speaks for the agricultural sector, though its interests are sharply opposed to those of the working cultivators and the landless over the price of labour. This class becomes the main agricultural pressure group in the tug-of-war over fiscal policy and the allocation of investment to rural infrastructure, and is able to corner the lion's share of the credit. Given the necessary capital, entrepreneurial agriculture finds it easy to equip itself with the tools and technologies which are the sophisticated creation of industrialized countries, and local research centres are under pressure to incorporate their activities in the international currents as poor and dependent relatives rather than applying their science to local situations and problems of peasant agriculture within the feasibilities of local factor endowments and existing or emergent skills. Without the benefit of research for appropriate technologies, without security, without credit and without a credible voice, the peasant sector stagnates and its increasing population ensures prospects of cheap labour for such other sectors of the economy which require it.

Concluding Note

In spite of the definition of the objectives of the study given at the beginning, there was ambiguity in UN circles over the assumptions underlying the study, especially in regard to its evaluative character and the nature of policy recommendations which should arise out of it. Certain voices could be heard urging that the general policy of the 'green revolution' should not be questioned but that research should identify any undesirably social consequences and, it was hoped, put forward some practical measures for countering these. Other voices favoured a less restricted approach. The propriety of making policy recommendations to the governments of member states was also held in question, and there was an understandable sentiment amongst the social scientists who were responsible for the research that a positive statement of recommendations would be out of place. At the last preparatory meeting it was agreed that the research should lead to a report to be presented to governments, accompanied by a text which might be paraphrased as follows:

Sirs, if you are about to embark on discussions about your agricultural development policy, and especially if you are interested in finding a land-saving cereal crop technology, we pray you to scan this report first, since it gives an account of what took place in a number of countries some of which bear a resemblance to your own. It should serve to advise you which issues require your special attention.

It was in this spirit that the study was carried out, but nevertheless by the time the fieldwork was completed two years later, it was assumed by the sponsors that policy recommendations, even if they were to be presented under the title 'Policy Alternatives', were an essential and required product of the research. And indeed by this time those who had set out on a task involving analysis and explanation had reached firmer convictions which they felt had acquired some authority.

A 50 page document finally emerged presenting a series of conclusions arising from the field research and the analysis of other studies and public statistics, and was published in Geneva in 1975, and at the same time it was circulated to member states by the UN Secretariat, with an introduction by the Administrator of the United Nations Development Programme. It consisted of three parts — the first dealt with conditions and constraints affecting the introduction of the new technology, the second with changes at the local level associated with its adoption, and the third with policy implications. Its contents and language goes rather beyond a sort of Highest Common Factor of the various interests involved, in the direction of an area of policy consensus of the researchers. Although it was circulated to all member states, probably to their Planning Offices and Ministries of Agriculture, the author is not aware of any feedback at the national level, and can make no comment on its impact. The main substantive reports are in manuscript and will appear shortly.

The whole problem about a discussion of 'policy implications' is of course that the range of feasible alternatives open to governments is limited by the interests of the sectors supporting them, and what may be feasible in one national situation can only be described as utopian in another. Nevertheless, utopian or not, the United Nations Organization is identified with a commitment to freedom from hunger,[4] and this fact establishes an obligation to propose a strategy which would ensure not only adequate production for overall needs, but a pattern of distribution which would ensure to all families a minimum of food necessary for health. In the light of the studies, therefore, and especially of the conditions prevailing in the three Asian countries in which the talents-effect did not seem to operate too sharply against the rural masses. Some guidelines for a new and adequate strategy can be proposed as a contribution to further discussion.

A new strategy must avoid a bimodal agrarian structure in which rapid advances in productivity are made mainly by the already well-capitalized, while the rural masses continue to stagnate and to rely upon the market place for food and on the labour market for money to buy it. Instead, the heart of the strategy has to be the creation of situations in which hitherto handicapped and exploited human beings can become more productive. This implies access to the means of agricultural production, and the summons to improve technology and raise productivity must promise tangible rewards in the steady amelioration of family livelihood and participation in joint efforts to abolish poverty, rather than to achieve distant production targets. Without such generalized access, attempts at the full mobilization of human skills and efforts are bound to shatter against the fierce conflict of interests between the entrepreneurs of food-business and the working producers over the price of labour, and achieve the further frustration of the poor by the play of the talents-effect in the market.

Of equal importance is the principle that the process of capitalization and investment in agriculture, infrastructure, food-processing, rural manufacturing and services should be participated in as fully as possible by working producers and their farms, whether these are individual family farms or some form of group farm. The essential precondition of this process is the existence of government measures and credit sources to prevent the appropriation of the culti-vator's surplus by petty commerical monopolies and moneylending. If excessive debt and the crude appropriation of surpluses by external capital can be avoided, then this process of local capital formation can proceed, provided that corporate firms can be created at local and district level on the basis of the invest-ments and active participation of member farms at the level determined by the appropriate scale of the new enterprises. Such corporate firms can also allocate investments with a view to providing employment in areas where population is dense in relation to available land, and take responsibility for land improvement and irrigation, field experimentation with new technology, environmental hygiene and other tasks fitting areas larger than that of farms.

A further principle which needs to be embodied in a strategy suitable for areas of general self-provisioning and prescientific technology is what may be described as a bias in favour of local self-reliance and full exploitation of the potentialities of local resources and knowledge in the improvement of agricul-tural production and livelihood. And complementary to this principle, great caution should be observed in placing too much dependence on technologies which rely on imports of seeds, chemicals and machines which are liable to sudden price changes and interruption of supplies, and which put too much decision-making power beyond the control of local agricultural organs and even of national ministries. In a word, use of external technological skill and equip-ment should be discriminating and non-habitforming.

This approach also has important implications for research. Instead of mounting programmes for the maximum diffusion of technologies based on the most sophisticated external research, it is suggested that local scientific resources, with selective use of suitable external elements, should make intensive studies of local conditions and locally received technology within those con-ditions, with a view to improving it in terms compatible with existing factor endowments and proportions and feasible for the typical existing unit of production and the type of unit which may evolve out of it.

Finally, it must be stated explicitly that there is little or no hope of seeing such a strategy adopted by a government unless the working agricultural population, by virtue of its own organized strength and its capacity to win and work with urban allies, can demonstrate a potential for maintaining that government in power. A far cry, perhaps, but circumstances may yet show it to be an attractive option.

Notes

1. Of the UNRISD Global Two studies the following have appeared so far:

No. 1 Notes sur les implications sociales de la 'revolution verte' en quelques pays d'Afrique (Report No. 71.5), by René Dumont.

No. 2 A selection of readings (Report No. 71.6), edited by Antonio Berreto.

No. 3 The green revolution: an economic analysis (Report No. 72.6), by Keith Griffin.

No. 4 Science and agricultural production (Report No. 72.8), by Ingrid Palmer.

No. 5 Food and the new agricultural technology (Report No. 72.9), by Ingrid Palmer.

No. 6 The social and economic implications of large-scale introduction of new varieties of foodgrain: summary of conclusions (Report No. 74.1).

No. 7 Growth with justice in Asian agriculture: an exercise in policy formulation (Report No. 74.2), by V. K. R. V. Rao.

No. 8 Le projet céréalier en Tunisie: Études aux niveaux national et local (Report No. 74.4), by Irene Hauri.

No. 9 Inégalités dans les milieux ruraux: possibilités et problèmes de la modernisation agricole au Maroc (Report No. 75.1), by Hendrik van der Kloet.

No. 10 The new rice in the Philippines (Report No. 75.2), by Ingrid Palmer.

The remaining seven reports have been circulated in draft and are now being prepared for publication in Geneva. They include country reports on Mexico, India, Sri Lanka and Indonesia, a village case-study from Malaysia, regional reports on South-East Asia and African south of the Sahara, and the overview report of the global study. Enquiries and orders should be sent to UNRISD, Palaid des Nations, Geneva, Switzerland.

2. On the 'talents-effect', see the parable of the talents in the Christian Bible, St Mark's Gospel, ending with the famous slogan, 'to him that hath shall be given and from him that hath not shall be taken even that which he hath'.

3. See Sung-Hsing and Apthorpe (1974). This study was initiated as a part of Global Two but published independently in consequence of political developments.

4. See the United Nations call for 'the elimination of hunger and malnutrition and the guarantee of the right to proper nutrition' in the Declaration on Social Progress adopted unanimously at the 24th Session of the General Assembly (1969).

References

Burki, Shahid Javed (1969), *A Study of Chinese Communes* (Cambridge, Mass.: Harvard University Press).

Dalrymple, Dana (1974a), *Development and Spread of High-Yielding Varieties of Wheat and Rice in the Less Developed Nations* (Washington: US Department of Agriculture).

Dalrymple, Dana (1974b), *The Green Revolution, Past and Prospects* (Washington: USAID).

Franke, Richard W. (1972), *The Green Revolution in A Javanese Village*, Ph.D. thesis (Harvard University).

Hale, Sylvia M. (n.d.), *Decision-Making as a Social Process; Individual and Collective Responses to Development Projects in India*, Ph.D. thesis (Vancouver: University of British Columbia). (Cited material by permission of the author).

Ishikawa, Shigeru (1970), *Agricultural Development Ştrategies in Asia*, (Japan: Asian Development Bank).

Pearse, Andrew (1975), *The Latin American Peasant* (London: Cass).

Stavis, Benedict (1974), Making Green Revolution: The Politics of Agricultural Development in China (Monograph Series, Cornell University).

Sung-Hsing, Wang, and Apthorpe, Raymond (1974), Rice Farming in Taiwan: Three Village Studies (Taipei: Institute of Ethnology, Academica Sinica).

Index

216

Horowitz, I., 96, 103
Horton, D., 176, 181
House of Commons Expenditure
    Committee, *see* Expenditure
    Committee (UK House of Commons)
Howarth, R., 48, 51, 52
Howes, R., 100, 103
Huizer, G., 142, 157
human ecology, 4
Hunt, A., 18, 28
Hunter, F., 58, 83
Hytton, H., 97, 103

industrialization
    and agriculture, 4, 13, 57–58
    and the state, 87–105
innovation, in agriculture, 11, 15–16, 17,
    150, 169–172, 183–211
Ipswich, 65, 70, 79–80
Ishikawa, I., 193–194, 211
Israel, R., 156

Jackson, D., 166, 181
Jay, R., 123, 127
Jayawardena, C., 22, 23, 28
Johnson, D. G., 16, 28, 51, 52
Johnson, G. D., 27
Johnson, J. H., 27
Jolly, R., 181
Jones, G., 5, 11, 28
Josling, T. E. 51, 52

de Kadt, E., 102
Kaldor, D., 97, 103
Karel, D., 178
Kantor, R. M., 56, 83
Kartodirdjo, H., 120, 127
Kautsky, K., 6–26 *passim*, 50
Kearl, B., 178
Kerblay, B., 115, 116, 127
Kerkvliet, B., 23, 29
Kerr, C., *et al.*, 3, 28
Kimball, S. T., 63, 82
King, A., 42, 52
van der Kloet, H., 210
Kroeber, A. L., 61, 83, 108, 127, 132, 157
Krishna, R., 178, 181
Kula, W., 109, 127
Kumar, K., 4, 28
Kuznets, S., 180, 182

labour relations, 21–25, 90–91
labour reproduction and the state, 95
Laclau, E., 135, 139, 142, 153, 156, 157

La Guardia, F., 41, 50
land
    and inheritance, 14
    as capital, 6–7, 8, 61–64 *passim*,
        143–145, 183–211 *passim*
landholding
    and class structure, 6–7, 61–64,
        110–124, 131–156, 172–177,
        183–211
    and social structure, 6–15, 110–118,
        172–177
landlord–tenant system, 8, 13, 14–15,
        61–64 *passim*, 110–118, 121–122,
        143–145, 171, 172–177
land reform, 166, 172–177
Landsberger, H., 22, 23, 28, 61, 64, 83,
        107, 109, 119, 120, 127
La Polambara, J., 39, 45, 52
Larson, O. A., 14, 16, 17, 28
Lasbarria-Cornhiel, S., 176, 182
Law, D., 100, 103
Lebas, E., 91, 92, 96, 101, 103
Lee, C. H., 89, 103
Lee, R. H., 125, 127
Lelyveld, J., 162, 182
Lemisch, J., 22, 28
Lenin, V. I., 119, 127, 132, 136, 139, 140,
        143, 157
Lenski, G., 6, 28
Le Roy Ladurie, E., 112–114, 125, 127
Lewis, O., 4, 28, 55, 64, 83
Linklater, P., 97, 103
Lipset, S. M., 6, 12, 28, 35, 36, 52, 104
Littlejohn, J., 55, 83
Lockwood, D., 60, 83
Lojkine, J., 95, 103
Loomis, C., 85
Lopez, P. M., *et al.*, 176, 182
Lowe, P., 71, 83
Lucey, D., 97, 103
Lukes, S., 62, 68, 72, 83
Luton, 60
Lyddon, D., 88, 90, 103
Lyons, 95

McCarthy, J., 36
McCrone, G., 16, 28
McCulloch, A., 56, 83
Mackay, G. A., 99, 103
McNamara, R., 162, 182
Macpherson, C. B., 12, 28
Madgwick, P., 59, 80–81, 83
mafia, 61
Malthus, T., 113–114